THE YEMEN
ARAB REPUBLIC

WESTVIEW PROFILES • NATIONS OF THE CONTEMPORARY MIDDLE EAST
Bernard Reich and David E. Long,
Series Editors

THE YEMEN ARAB REPUBLIC

Development and Change in an Ancient Land

Manfred W. Wenner

Westview Press

BOULDER • SAN FRANCISCO • OXFORD

Westview Profiles/Nations of the Contemporary Middle East

Published in 1991 in the United States of America by Westview Press, Inc., 5500 Central Avenue, Boulder, Colorado 80301, and in the United Kingdom by Westview Press, 36 Lonsdale Road, Summertown, Oxford OX2 7EW

Library of Congress Cataloging-in-Publication Data
Wenner, Manfred W.
   The Yemen Arab Republic : development and change in an ancient land / Manfred W. Wenner.
      p.   cm.—(Westview profiles. Nations of the contemporary Middle East)
   Includes bibliographical references and index.
   ISBN 0-89158-774-8
   1. Yemen.   I. Title.   II. Series: Profiles. Nations of the contemporary Middle East.
DS247.Y4W44   1991
953.32—dc20   90-24033
                                                                         CIP

Printed and bound in the United States of America

The paper used in this publication meets the requirements of the American National Standard for Permanence of Paper for Printed Library Materials Z39.48-1984.

10   9   8   7   6   5   4   3   2   1

Contents

Tables and Illustrations

vii

Preface

Modern Yemen 1918–1966 was published in 1967, and in that book I reviewed the modern political history of North Yemen and presented to contemporary students of the Middle East an overview of some aspects of the country. At the time, North Yemen was in the middle of a civil war, which had begun in 1962 and was to last until 1970, and although some correspondents had covered aspects of the conflict, the country was almost as little known then as it had been a decade, two decades, or even five decades earlier.

It is difficult to impress upon people who are not acquainted with this fascinating land the incredible changes that have taken place since that earlier book was written. Of course, the civil war has ended (in the hoped-for compromise), and now literally legions of tourists visit the country. An incredible variety of development programs have been completed or are in the process of being so, and one can obtain an array of modern goods and services in the major cities (while staying, if one chooses, in a modern Sheraton Hotel). In many ways, North Yemen has joined the modern community of nations, which its previous rulers had tried so hard to prevent.

In this present book, I hope to acquaint a larger audience with some of the characteristics of the country that account for its fascination. (Indeed, as I have discovered, no one who has been to North Yemen is not enchanted by it, for one reason or another.) This book is not a sequel to the earlier one, and in fact I doubt that such a sequel is even possible. The amount of research and scholarship concerning North Yemen that has been published in every conceivable discipline since the mid-1960s has reached the stage where no single individual could hope to synthesize and summarize it all in a coherent fashion. Instead, it is my hope, and my goal, to introduce people interested in the modern world to a unique country, to provide them with an adequate introduction to many of its facets, to have them understand (if not always appreciate) its characteristics, and finally, to make North Yemen and its people and their culture better known to, and perhaps better understood by, more people.

I would like to thank the writers of the various works I have read and consulted in order to try to keep up-to-date with Yemeni affairs and the rapidly changing characteristics of the country. Naturally, if I have made any errors of fact or interpretation, these should not be attributed to these scholars or to those individuals who have worked hard on various development projects in the country and various government officials with whom I have come into contact over the years.

Manfred W. Wenner

1
The Land

Terminology

The Yemen Arab Republic (YAR), which has become known in recent years as North Yemen, occupies only one part of the southwestern corner of the Arabian Peninsula that is referred to as Yemen (Fig. 1.1). Arab writers who have tried to explain the origin of the word "Yemen" have come up with two possible interpretations, both derived from the Arabic language. The first of these argues that it is related to the Arabic word *YaMiN*, meaning "right" or "on the right hand." According to this version, the area is called Yemen because it lies on the right (or south) of the Arabian Peninsula whereas Damascus (often referred to as al-Sham, meaning "north") lies on the left (or north). The second interpretation argues that the name was derived from the Arabic word *YuMaN*, meaning "prosperous" or "happy." According to this version, the name came from the fact that the area was obviously the most favored part of the peninsula (in climatic and agricultural terms). This particular interpretation accords favorably with the name given to Yemen by the ancient world: Arabia Felix (Happy Arabia), which distinguished it from Arabia Deserta.

In fact, neither of these explanations is correct. Like many other place-names in southwestern Arabia, the word "Yemen" is properly traced to the ancient South Arabian languages. Recent paleographic and archaeological studies have clearly shown that the majority of the area's place-names today are the ones used during the time of the ancient empires and city-states to describe possessions and conquests (although some were descriptive, most have no clear meaning that we are able to determine).[1]

Because the name Yemen is found in Arabic with an article, i.e., *al-Yaman*, it became the fashion among early European explorers and writers

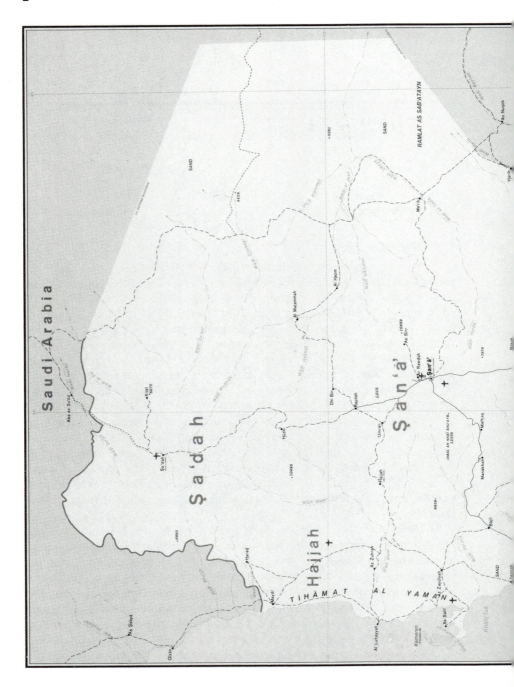

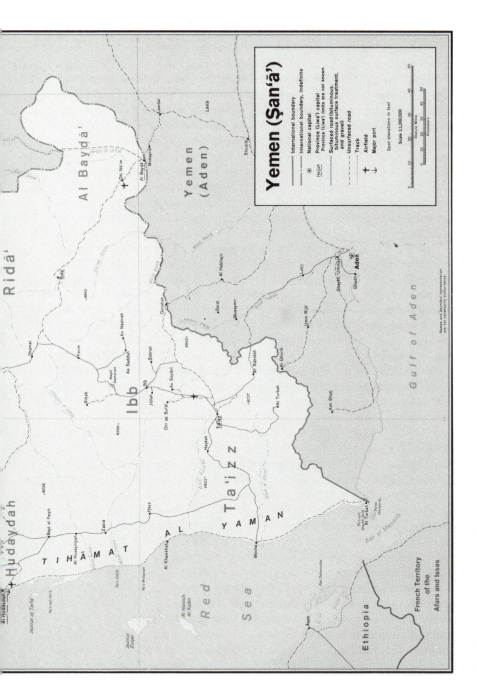

FIGURE 1.1   The Yemen Arab Republic

to refer to "the Yemen." However, this usage is no more logical than referring to "the France" because in French it is *la France.*

North Yemen was the only Arab state to become independent after World War I, though it had some difficulty in obtaining international recognition of that fact; in fact, it was not until nearly a decade after the war's end that some of the Western states began to accord the country diplomatic recognition. At the time, it was the only state with "Yemen" in its name, and therefore it was then not necessary to add any qualifiers or adjectives.

With the departure of the British from their possessions in southern Arabia in 1967, however, another political entity with the name "Yemen" appeared on the international scene. Originally calling itself the People's Republic of South Yemen, in order to draw attention to the facts that the border between the two Yemens was an artificial one (created by the British and the Ottomans many years earlier) and that unification was a mutually desirable goal, the name was changed in 1970 to the People's Democratic Republic of Yemen (PDRY). In popular parlance, however, the two states are generally referred to as North Yemen and South Yemen, if only because of the complexity/length of their official names. Since the two states have had rather different domestic policies, very different political histories in the nineteenth and twentieth centuries, and different foreign policies, it is usually necessary to distinguish clearly between them. In this work, such a distinction is made for the countries; "Yemeni" and "Yemenis" without further elaboration or qualification should be understood to refer to the country and people of North Yemen.

Unification

On 22 May 1990, North Yemen and the People's Democratic Republic of Yemen united to create the Republic of Yemen. Aware of the manifold difficulties involved in integrating the divergent political, economic, and social systems that had developed since the 1960s, the architects of unification established a transition period of thirty months to effect the merger.

Although the fact of unification produced widespread elation and enjoyed nearly universal support, there are elements in both countries who oppose the merger (for very disparate reasons). It is still possible that significant implementation problems could develop, especially when difficult decisions will be made on such controversial issues as the rights of women, the mechanisms and goals of political participation, the role of Islam in policymaking, and so on. The facts and traditions discussed in this book will continue to affect domestic and foreign policy for years to come.

Location

The location of the two Yemens—at the southern end of the Red Sea and Arabian Peninsula—has been the cause of conflicting claims and the subject of political disputes for many centuries. The politico-economic disputes of recent years have involved, to a greater or lesser degree, such countries as the United States, the Soviet Union, Saudi Arabia, Somalia, Oman, Ethiopia, Iran, France (which retains an interest in its former colony of Djibouti, formerly the French Territory of the Afars and Issas), and the Arab states of the Gulf, as well as a number of guerrilla movements (e.g., the Eritrean Liberation Front and the now-quiescent Front for the Liberation of the Occupied Arab Gulf). In fact, it is impossible to explain the current concern with developments in this region without reference to some traditional geopolitical concepts: control of sea and air access routes, energy resources, alliance patterns, and even the area's potential military advantage and possibilities for coercion because of communications patterns, terrain, and logistical requirements. The relevance and importance of these factors will be analyzed in greater detail later.

Although the relevance of geographic location has been slighted in recent years (in part because of a confidence in modern forms of communication), I believe that, at least in part, the influence of such smaller states as the two Yemens is indeed a function of their location. Furthermore, the interest of the major powers in these two states often results from the perception that they could disrupt or interfere with established patterns of trade and communications that are in or near their location (e.g., the Strait of Bab al-Mandab [Bab el Mandeb]).

Certain features of North Yemen provide a reminder that its location (on the Red Sea and on major fault lines that stretch up the Red Sea from Africa's Great Rift Valley) is not geologically peaceful. For example, plains to the north of Sana'a (the capital) are littered with the fossilized remains of various kinds of fish, including shellfish, while immediately west of the city one can find sizable geodes with little or no effort. Of more immediate concern, however, are events such as the great earthquake of December 1982, which destroyed dozens of villages and cost thousands of lives. More benignly, the foothills contain numerous hot springs and mineral baths, which the Yemenis (like Europeans) value for their curative properties.

Frontiers

North Yemen is one of the very few countries in the contemporary world without clearly demarcated frontiers to distinguish its territory from that of its neighbors. This situation is partly owing to the difficult terrain that characterizes this portion of the Arabian Peninsula, but it is also the result of some recent political events that have involved the two Yemens and of their relations with former and present political powers in the area.

In the north and east, the Yemen Arab Republic borders on Saudi Arabia; in the north, specifically with the Saudi province of Asir. A border was demarcated in this area between the two countries in 1934 after a short war, which Yemen lost. The most important consequence of this conflict was that Yemen had to renounce its claims to Asir in general and to the Najran Oasis in particular. Actual border markers were laid down only as far as the Najran Oasis; to the east of that location there are no internationally or locally recognized markers. In effect, there is a de facto "no man's land" between North Yemen and Saudi Arabia, the extent of which varies depending upon the ability of either state to exercise its authority. Today, this situation is primarily of economic rather than political significance, but it should be noted that most Yemenis have not given up hope of regaining Asir, a fact that has added to the many other frictions which have arisen between the two countries ever since the end of the Yemeni civil war in 1970.

To the south, North Yemen borders South Yemen (the PDRY). Here again, a frontier has been demarcated only to a specific point, which appeared to be an important position at the time. This frontier was originally platted in the early years of the twentieth century, when Great Britain was in control of the south and the Ottoman Empire controlled the north. In 1934, after numerous disputes between the imams of Yemen and the British authorities, a treaty was signed to minimize the possibilities of armed conflict; this treaty essentially confirmed the earlier frontier. It perpetuated the informality of the frontier past the original end point (at Qa'tabah), so disputes over territory in this region have continued. Until recently, the difficult terrain and the lack of any obvious resources over which more serious conflicts might arise muted the extent of such disagreements. However, the recent discovery of high-quality oil deposits in the Ma'rib region, and in the Hadhramawt region of the PDRY, has intensified the claims to these ambiguous territories which have, suddenly, become more important economically.

To the west of North Yemen is the Red Sea, which means the country has access to that body's resources, one of the world's major transportation routes. It also means involvement in a number of political disputes and strategic issues, however. Probably the most serious of these is over title to the Kamaran Islands, which were assigned to Great Britain when it was in control of the south and therefore passed to the PDRY upon that country's independence. Since North Yemen never recognized what it regarded as an illegitimate occupation, it occupied the islands in 1972 and has administered them since that time. The local population approved of the change, but North Yemen's occupation was never officially sanctioned. With the unification agreement of 1990, the issue of legal sovereignty became moot.

This lack of precision with respect to frontiers—including the fact that some areas are in dispute—and the lack of any cadastral survey make exact figures on North Yemen's land area impossible (or at least highly unreliable and open to manipulation for political advantage). It is, nevertheless, possible to make a rough estimate based on the following factors: (1) from east to west, the width of the country is between 300 and 400 kilometers (190–250 miles); (2) from north to south, the greatest distance is about 500 kilometers (310 miles), with most of the area between 400 and 500 kilometers (250–310 miles). Therefore, the land area covers about 135,200 square kilometers (52,200 square miles), about the size of Greece in the international arena and of Alabama in the United States.

PHYSICAL CHARACTERISTICS

Regions

Although there is no agreement among the various disciplines as how best to categorize the different areas of North Yemen, a few broad regional divisions are widely recognized. Unfortunately, the physical distinctions do not always coincide with distinctions along social, political, or economic lines, which means that often confusing and conflicting breakdowns are created by different scholars.[2] There are four basic categories (see Figure 1.2).

The Tihama. The coastal strip that lies along the Red Sea and separates the sea from the first low foothills of the mountain chain that runs down the western side of the Arabian Peninsula is known in both Saudi Arabia and North Yemen as the Tihama. It is characterized by very high temperatures (often above 45° C [113° F]) in the summer months and extremely high humidity (regularly above 85 percent). It varies in width from about 25 kilometers to as much as 65 kilometers (15–40 miles) and has very few visible geographic variations, rising slowly from sea level to about 500 meters (1,640 feet). The area receives very little rainfall, from 0 to less than 300 millimeters (12 inches) per year, and thus most of it can support only limited agriculture. There are, however, many alluvial and aeolian deposits of fertile soils, and in these areas major irrigation projects have been undertaken (using either fossil water supplies or water from replenishable aquifers near the mountains).

The Tihama makes up about 15 percent of the country's land area and contains a roughly equivalent portion of the total population. Most of its inhabitants are engaged in agriculture, fishing, or trade and com-

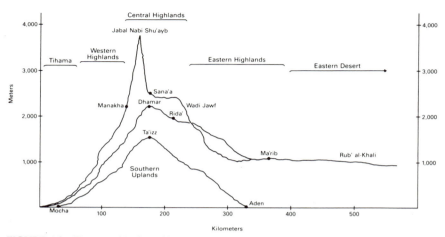

FIGURE 1.2   Topographical profile (east-west axis): Red Sea to Rub' al-Khali. Data from Hans Steffen et al., *Final Report of the Airphoto Interpretation Project* (Zurich: Swiss Technical Co-operation Service, 1978).

merce—the last because Hodeida (al-Hudaydah), the country's major port, and the smaller ports along the coast are significant links to the outside world.

Western Highlands. This transitional zone between the Tihama and the peaks of the central massif is characterized by formidable mountain chains interspersed by a few major river valleys, which descend from the central plateau to the Tihama (only three of which are suitable for use by motorized vehicles). This escarpment, generally thought to be the result of the rift between the African continent and the Arabian Peninsula, which also created the Red Sea, shows clear signs of volcanic activity as well as having outcroppings of granite and similar rocks. Although it supports a population roughly equivalent to its percentage of the total area, about 30 percent, there are no major population centers in this portion of the country. Rather, it contains thousands of small villages, most of which are perched on rocky crags and outcroppings, and the people use the alluvial and aeolian deposits as their agricultural base, usually on laboriously constructed and maintained terraces. Because of an incredible variety of microclimates and the availability of water, this region supports a wide variety of flora and fauna.

The ruggedness of the terrain and the dedicated independence of the inhabitants of this area have tended to make this zone a natural defensive barrier against inroads, whether of people or cultural traits, from the coastal zone and have also led to some demographic differences.

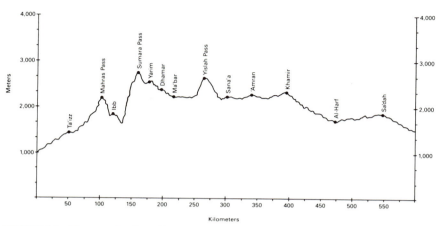

FIGURE 1.3   Topographical profile (north-south axis): Southern border with South Yemen to the northern border with Saudi Arabia. Data from Hans Steffen et al., *Final Report of the Airphoto Interpretation Project* (Zurich: Swiss Technical Co-operation Service, 1978).

Central Highlands. A large part of North Yemen consists of a plateau, running north and south, which is intersected by relatively low hills at an average height of about 2,500 meters (8,200 feet), although there are some ranges at the edge of this plateau that have peaks rising to almost 4,000 meters (13,120 feet)—the highest mountains in the country. It is on this plateau that most of the major cities are located, e.g., Sana'a in the approximate center and Ta'izz at its southern limits (see Figure 1.3). In fact, even prior to the construction of a major north-south artery, nearly all of the country's truly urban settlements were located along this central spine, especially in the fertile plains between Sana'a and Ta'izz, e.g., Ibb, Dhamar, and Yarim.

Although rainfall is high in the southern part of the plateau and rather sparse in the north, agriculture and animal husbandry have been the traditional economic activities on the plateau; at the same time, what little domestic trade and manufacturing exist in the country have also tended to be located in the major towns of this region. Despite these economic similarities, there are considerable social and political (as well as religious) differences between the northern and southern areas of this highland plateau.

Eastern Highlands and Eastern Desert. East of the last major piece of the central massif (known as the Sirat), one encounters what is probably the most striking contrast in North Yemen. There is an almost immediate drop in the amount of rainfall and therefore a quintessential desert environment: sandy soil, scrub growth, little agricultural development, grazing of animals the only major economic activity, and very few settle-

Village in the Central Highlands near Ibb. Photo copyright by Martin Lyons. Used by permission.

ments. Although there is evidence that this portion of the country had considerably more rainfall in ancient times, today it is almost completely dependent upon wells for its water supply as well as for the limited agricultural activity that does occur. Located at an altitude of between 1,000 and 2,000 meters (3,280–6,560 feet), the topography slowly descends to the Rub' al-Khali (Empty Quarter). Whereas previously the region showed little promise of any natural resources (besides salt, which has been mined in various locations since antiquity), this picture is changing, and the recent discovery of commercially exploitable petroleum deposits in the area around Ma'rib is likely to significantly change both the economy and the demography of this area.

Climate

The varieties of topography are reflected in the wide climatic variations to be found. In the Tihama, for example, the mean monthly temperature ranges between 33° and 42° C (91° and 108° F), with an associated humidity of 86–98 percent. Rarely does the temperature ever drop below 21°–26° C (70–79° F) even in the coldest winter. Because of this region's limited resources, inadequate rainfall, endemic malaria, and lack of defensive barriers, the people of the Tihama have developed a very different culture and life-style from those found in the mountainous highlands. Moreover, some of these same factors have contributed to a very different demographic mixture in the Tihama from that in the highland regions, and the extensive commercial and politico-military contacts that have affected the Red Sea littoral have also deeply affected the population of the Tihama.

On the other hand, the western and central highlands have a temperate climate. When one combines the variations in altitude with the variations in rainfall, as well as the variations in soil characteristics, one obtains an incredibly rich mosaic of microclimates.

Rainfall increases as one moves south from Sa'dah; by the time one reaches the plains of Dhamar and moves south to Ta'izz, there are many areas that receive up to 1,200 millimeters (47 inches) per year. These rains tend to fall in two relatively distinct periods: the "little rains" of March and April and the "big rains" of the summer months (July and August). These rains are the result of the southern monsoons (and the updrafts created by the mountains). Unfortunately for the highlands of North Yemen, the rains are not completely reliable, and when slight variations occur (as in the mid-1960s), the country can suffer droughts that can utterly destroy agriculture and have a significant adverse impact on the population and the long-term agricultural base.

Temperature varies with altitude: In the upland areas, winter temperatures often approach and dip below freezing, and frost and snow are not at all infrequent in the higher elevations (not to mention the occasional fierce spring hailstorms, which can cover the ground with a blanket of white in the space of a few minutes). The winter months make warm clothing a necessity, and the people are used to wearing sheepskins and wool garments during this season. In the summer months, the temperatures rise to 25° C and over (77° F plus) during the day, but the relative humidity remains consistently low. Because of this low humidity, the traditional stone buildings of this region have no provision for heat (and, of course, none for air-conditioning).

The eastern highlands and eastern desert, on the other hand, are a different story. As the land drops off to the Empty Quarter, one finds a typical desert environment: high temperatures, extremely low humidity, and a complete lack of surface water (except after the occasional cloudburst). The temperatures are regularly over 32° C (90° F) during the day and drop rapidly as soon as the sun sets.

These rather wide climatic variations have a number of effects: (1) they create conditions that permit everything from tropical to temperate zone plants to be raised; (2) they create a correspondingly wide variation in the fauna, which adapts to the various ecological niches; and (3) of great importance to any nation's development, they make nationwide agricultural planning and investment extremely difficult because of the large number of variations that need to be taken into account. The experiences of the various donor countries (i.e., the countries providing foreign assistance) have shown that, because of the incredibly complex variety of food plants within these different microclimates, overall (i.e., nationwide) programs of seed improvement, irrigation, fertilizing, and similar inputs cannot succeed. To put the problem in different terms, over the centuries the people of North Yemen have developed sufficiently different strains of the major crops to accommodate to these microclimates, and no single program of assistance can cope with the tremendous variations that exist and still be effective. The very expense of attempting such agricultural development precludes national effectiveness, and the result has been that some rural areas of the country have been disproportionately favored by development programs and schemes.

Soils, Flora, and Fauna

The combination of soils, temperature, rainfall, and altitude makes North Yemen by far the richest country, in agricultural terms, on the Arabian Peninsula. In the Tihama, a multitude of tropical plants and crops are raised for market, such as bananas, various citrus fruits, tomatoes, papayas, and other similar plants. Furthermore, the Tihama has been an important cotton-producing area, although production in this sector has fallen off in recent years because of depressed world prices. Plants that are found naturally are cacti, the tamarisk, and similar flowering tropical species. Although some surveys of flora and fauna have been undertaken, none is so complete as to make possible any definitive statement with regard to unique or endangered species in the Tihama that may be threatened by increasing agricultural development, urbanization, depletion of the aquifer, or infrastructural construction.

The entire landscape as well as the type of agriculture changes as soon as one moves through one of the openings in the escarpment and into the foothills. The first (rather scrub) trees make their appearance, but since the wood is unsuitable for timber, it is used primarily as fuel for the Yemeni stove, the *tannur*. The crops now consist of cereals (primarily millet and oats) and fruits (primarily nuts, figs, and various kinds of melons).

The richest agricultural land is found at the next level, that is, at about 1,500 meters (4,900 feet). Here the valleys have been carefully terraced, and an incredible variety of plants may be found. Economically, the most important of these is *qat*, a treelike shrub whose leaves are chewed in accordance with a uniquely Yemeni social custom, the socioeconomic and even political consequences of which will be discussed later. (Although *qat* is often labeled a narcotic, this claim is quite inaccurate.

The leaves do contain a mild alkaloid, but the operative chemical that is extracted from the leaves by chewing is not in the narcotic family.) At this level, the crops also include coffee, apples, pears, nuts, grapes, and the more prosaic but widespread cereal grains: sorghum, millet, corn, wheat, etc.

The highest elevations, around Sana'a and in the valleys north and south of the capital, produce the best varieties of *qat*, which is the dominant crop. However, the production of grapes and market vegetables has substantially increased, often bringing land into cultivation that has been unused for years.

Because of an unusual combination of economic and political factors, there has not been any extensive effort to increase the country's production of fruits and vegetables, though some signs of change are visible as a result of recent changes in government policy. Agricultural experts from donor countries have suggested that North Yemen is capable of producing far larger amounts of domestically consumed cereals, fruits, and vegetables than is currently the case and that commercial production (on local truck farms) of additional crops with a relatively high rate of cash return is possible. The major stumbling block for the past few years to such intensification and diversification is the set of problems associated with the emigration of a major portion of the country's labor force. The money that is returned in the form of remittances, which is generally outside the government's limited powers of taxation and enforcement, the people's long-suppressed desire for imported and luxury goods, their increased demand for a variety of foods they perceive as desirable, and the fact that most locally raised foodstuffs are more expensive than imported ones have all contributed to a decline in domestic agricultural production. These factors, and the many associated problems and controversies, are discussed in greater detail in Chapter 3.

Few studies have been undertaken for the specific purpose of collecting and cataloging the flora and fauna of North Yemen, and the works of some of the travelers of the past (e.g., Hugh Scott in the early 1940s) still contain some of the best information concerning those plants and animal species that are not raised for human or animal consumption.[3] Scott's work, as well as some later, more-specialized studies, describes an amazing variety of plant life in the various ecological niches. Unfortunately, population pressure, an eight-year civil war, and recent development programs have all played a role in sharply curtailing the number and variety of plant species that may still be found in abundance. One author has made a deliberate attempt to gather information on the uses to which many of the indigenous and imported plants have been put for pharmaceutical and cosmetic purposes,[4] and one hopes that such knowl-

edge will not be lost as far as uniquely North Yemen species are concerned—additional studies are in fact under way.

A similar situation exists with regard to fauna. A visitor to North
Yemen will probably notice the relative lack of animal species except
those raised for power, transport, or food. Again, it would appear that a
much greater diversity of species existed in the past, and the factors that
have led to a decrease in plant species have played the same role in
decreasing the number of animal species. There are numerous accounts
of such varied species as leopards, pumas, giraffes, rhinoceroses, and
other large mammals being prevalent in North Yemen as little as a hundred
years ago. Many of these reports are today dismissed as fanciful, especially
since no physical remains of such animals have yet been found.

Among the larger mammal species, especially those of interest to
tourists and wildlife enthusiasts, North Yemen offers little of the exotic.
The predator cats are probably extinct, as are the Arabian oryx and the
ibex, but a few hyenas may still be encountered in the warmer, lower
elevations of the south. Probably the only larger mammal that may be
encountered is the gelada baboon, which lives in the mountainous highlands, especially in the north and northwest (its favorite habitat is in
areas above 1,800 meters [5,900 feet]). These baboons are usually found
in rocky escarpments in the neighborhood of streams, and they travel in
groups. Travelers in motor vehicles in the remoter regions (e.g., in Mahwit
Province, northwest of Sana'a) have occasionally been the victims of a
rock-throwing attack by these primates.

In general, however, it must be said that the people of North Yemen,
and the other inhabitants of the Arabian Peninsula, have little or no
sympathy for any species of animal life that does not specifically benefit
humans. It was not until very recently that any Middle Eastern country
established a national park, and historically little effort has been devoted
to parks or even conservation. North Yemen is one of the few areas of
the Middle East with any stands of trees at all, but it is quite likely that
in the near future, all the trees will have been harvested for fuel and
North Yemen, like other areas of the peninsula, will have no forests left
at all. As little as a hundred years ago, extensive forests appear to have
existed throughout southwestern Arabia, but the demands for fuel and
construction supplies have resulted in far faster harvesting than natural
growth could sustain. The total estimated area under woodland and scrub
growth dwindles visibly every day, and the increasing mobility of the
population makes the rate at which such deforestation is taking place an
increasing rather than a decreasing problem. Although there have been
some relatively half-hearted efforts at reforestation, these have been
notoriously unsuccessful (for a variety of economic as well as social
reasons).

Perhaps most tragic of all, the quintessential symbol of North Yemen, the *jambiyya* ("dagger"), is really only highly valued if its handle has been made from the horn of the African rhinoceros. Although the price of such daggers is high (it is not unknown for a finer example to sell for more than $5,000), the domestic demand is still great. The result is that this symbol of North Yemen has been largely responsible for bringing one of the world's largest land animals to the brink of extinction (though the government has sought to ban the import of rhinoceros horn and encourage the use of water buffalo horn instead).

Water

As mentioned earlier, tremendous variations in rainfall characterize North Yemen: from essentially zero in areas of the Tihama to more than 1,200 millimeters (47 inches) in the southern uplands. One result has been the development of a rather sophisticated form of dry farming in certain areas; another has been substantial variations in crop yields from year to year in some of the marginal areas.

The most common way of coping with highly varying and inconsistent amounts of rain, however, is storage combined with irrigation. In the past, the area of North Yemen was perhaps most renowned for the irrigation and construction works of the Sabaean state several centuries before the birth of Christ. The most impressive of these structures was unquestionably the Ma'rib Dam (built in the sixth century BC, it lasted until AD 575), and its ruins are one of North Yemen's major tourist attractions today. Built to retain the seasonal and spring-fed flows of water from major mountains near Ma'rib, its construction was (and remains) a marvel of ancient engineering. It stretched nearly 1 kilometer (about two-thirds of a mile), and irrigation sluices and canals carried the water it stored for more than 1.5 kilometers (0.9 miles) into an incredibly large and complex system of fields and gardens. When this complex deteriorated (because of a lack of funds for maintenance and repairs (the result of a decline in revenues from the sale of frankincense and myrrh), the dam finally ruptured. The date of its final rupture is, in fact, uncertain; most scholars suggest that there were a number of breaches that, cumulatively, could no longer be effectively repaired, and that the most important one took place in 575. Others have given the date as the same one for the Persian conquest—an indirect indication of the perceived relationship between the control of water and political power in the eastern regions.

Today, irrigation projects are far greater in number and exist in more regions owing to two factors: the development of relatively cheap diesel pumps and the new-found ability of the people of North Yemen to afford

The great dam at Ma'rib: part of the southern section.

them. (The new wealth, as well as the interest of donors in irrigation projects, has also led to the construction of a new dam at Ma'rib, upstream of the historic one.) The result has been an alarming decrease in the groundwater supply. Wells are being sunk at a staggering rate in all areas of the country, and nearly all of the water so extracted is fossil water (in some cases literally thousands of years old). Studies made by some of the donor countries indicate that the water table in some of the upland plateau areas is being depleted at a rate which implies that some cities, notably Sana'a, will be facing critical shortages before the end of the century if not sooner. (It has been shown that in some areas the water table dropped from roughly 3 meters [9 feet] to in excess of 20 meters [66 feet] in less than five years; however, the lack of reliable time-series data makes it difficult to be completely accurate concerning the magnitude of the problem, much less its extent.)[5]

Mineral Resources

Although in the past North Yemen achieved some renown in industries that required the use of local mineral resources, e.g., the manufacture of blades using iron ore from the hills of the central plateau, there are no mineral resources today that are of commercial value. To the visitor, who can clearly see the copper in the mountains west of Sana'a (and other places), this fact seems as unlikely as it does to the average citizen of North Yemen, but although the ore lies close to the surface and its characteristic green color is clearly visible, it does not have a high enough concentration to make extraction economic.

The most important exception to this general lack of mineral resources is the discovery of oil in 1985. Geologists had suggested that there might be oil in North Yemen as early as the 1920s, but the search for it, undertaken by German, Japanese, and U.S. companies over the years, proved fruitless until the major area for exploratory drilling was moved from the Red Sea to the eastern highlands. A field discovered by the Hunt Oil Company, near Ma'rib, contains some of the highest-quality oil ever discovered, and a pipeline to take the oil to the sea, as well as a refinery complex, has already been completed. There is some debate as to how much oil will be available (some estimates have suggested upward of 500,000 barrels per day), but it is clear that this industry will have a significant impact on North Yemen's financial and foreign policies in the near future.

THE FUTURE

It is clear that some of the same problems that are afflicting the ecologies and lands of the developed states are beginning to appear in North Yemen as well. When an apparent decline in rainfall is combined with the overutilization of pastureland, the rapid rate of deforestation, the road-building and other infrastructural development programs, and the expansion of both rural and urban settlements (with the associated problems of sewage treatment and provision of sanitary water supplies), it comes as no great surprise that North Yemen is now experiencing such modern problems as air and water pollution, toxic contamination of land and water, and an overall serious degrading of the quality of life in many areas. The pall of copper-colored haze that is now quite visible over Sana'a a few hours after sunup shows what two decades or so of "progress" can do to what was close to a pristine environment. It can only be hoped that the people of North Yemen can still learn from the mistakes of others.

NOTES

1. Manfred Wenner, *Modern Yemen 1918–1966* (Baltimore, MD: Johns Hopkins Press, 1967), pp. 23–24 fn. 1.

2. The most complete survey and description of North Yemen's physical characteristics may be found in Horst Kopp, *Agrargeographie der Arabischen Republik Jemen* (Erlangen: Palm & Enke, 1981); see also Hans Steffen et al., *Final Report of the Airphoto Interpretation Project* (Zurich: Swiss Technical Co-operation Service, 1978), esp. Part One, "The Physical Setting," pp. 3–29.

3. Hugh Scott, *In the High Yemen,* 2d ed. (London: John Murray, 1947).

4. Armin Schopen, *Traditionelle Heilmittel in Jemen* (Wiesbaden: Franz Steiner Verlag, 1983).

5. Eckhardt Jungfer, "Das Wasserproblem im Becken von San'a'," in H. Kopp and G. Schweizer, eds. *Entwicklungsprozesse in der Arabischen Republic Jemen* (Wiesbaden: Ludwig Reichert, 1984), pp. 171–192.

2

People and Culture

POPULATION DATA

Until fairly recently, it was not possible to document the belief and assertion that North Yemen was more densely populated than other areas of the Arabian Peninsula; indeed, estimates of the country's population varied widely, from a low of about 3.5 million to around 5.5 million. In the 1970s, the government contracted with the Swiss Technical Cooperation Service to undertake the first full population and housing census in the country's history. Using sophisticated aerial reconnaissance techniques and supplementary personal validity checks, the Swiss team concluded that the population of Yemen on 1 February 1975 was 4,705,336 (see Table 2.1). This figure did not include any of the large number of Yemeni emigrants (i.e., the laborers temporarily working in the Gulf states and elsewhere, and it included only a small adjustment for potential underenumeration.[1]

As a result, the Swiss study has been the subject of fierce controversy. The Yemenis believed that the problem of underenumeration had been inadequately treated, and as a result of their displeasure with the numbers arrived at, they undertook their own census in 1981 (see Table 2.2). This census recorded a population of 7,146,341 physically in the country at the time of the census and an additional nearly 1.4 million citizens of North Yemen in other countries. (It should be noted that figures from the Swiss and Yemeni studies are not always reconcilable.)

Quite clearly, the two studies are in deep conflict. The Swiss study estimated the rate of population increase to be 1.9–2.2 percent (the result of one of the highest infant mortality rates anywhere in the world, owing to a low level of medical care and poor sanitation, including contaminated water supplies, etc.), but even taking that increase into account, the two counts are far apart in their totals. There is, of course, no objective method whereby the discrepancies between the two studies could be resolved, and these discrepancies make analysis and policymaking based upon such data open to even further debate. What the matter illustrates best of all

19

TABLE 2.1   Census of 1975

Type of Settlement	Number of Inhabitants	Number of Settlements	Percent	Inhabitants in Settlement Class (number)	(percent)
Grouping	Under 50	28,000	53.1	681,613	14.5
	50– 100	13,000	24.7	924,031	19.6
Small village	100– 250	9,000	17.1	1,393,041	29.6
Medium village	250– 500	2,000	3.8	669,120	14.3
Large village	500– 1,000	600	1.1	403,098	8.6
Small town	1,000– 2,000	83	0.2	110,026	2.3
Medium town	2,000– 5,000	34	0.1	99,723	2.1
	5,000–10,000	11	0.0	69,942	1.5
Large town	10,000–50,000	3	0.0	52,392	1.1
City	Over 50,000	3	0.0	302,350	6.4
		52,734	100.0	4,705,336	100.0

Percentage figures may not total 100 because of rounding.

Source: Based on data from Hans Steffen et al., Final Report of the Airphoto Interpretation Project (Zurich: Swiss Technical Co-operation Service, 1978).

is how seemingly innocuous data can become the subject of intense political interest, and census data in North Yemen are a particularly contentious issue (the Swiss study is not publicly available in the country).

In the mid-1980s, when many of the emigrants were returning home (owing to increasing resistance to their presence in Saudi Arabia and the general decline in the demand for their limited skills in the Gulf states as the price of oil declined and the economies of those countries began to change), most observers of North Yemen suggested a rough midpoint between the two studies. According to their thinking, North Yemen had a population of about 6.5 million, not including those emigrants still abroad, which were estimated by a number of foreign observers to have dropped to between 250,000 and 300,000.

The two census studies do agree on a number of points, however. First, the major population concentration is in the southern highlands; for example, the Ta'izz and Ibb governorates (provinces) account for about 40 percent of the population but only about 15 percent of the land area. In other words, and not too surprisingly, the population tends to be centered in the areas of highest rainfall and most fertile soils. Second, women outnumber men in all of the governorates except Hodeida (al-Hudaydah). This fact, too, is not particularly surprising, since it agrees with the widespread perception that a large percentage of the adult males are working abroad and sending remittances back to their families. Third, the censuses agree that the average household size is 5.2 persons, with families in the central and northern highlands tending to be a bit larger.

TABLE 2.2   Population Totals and Distribution, 1981 and 1986 Censuses

Province (Governorate)	1981 Population	Percent	1986 Population	Percent
Sana'a	1,744,744	20.4	1,856,876	20.0
Ta'izz	1,553,520	18.2	1,643,901	17.7
Hodeida	1,085,376	12.7	1,294,359	14.0
Ibb	1,347,987	15.8	1,511,879	16.3
Dhamar	787,109	9.2	812,981	8.8
Hajjah	880,619	10.3	897,814	9.7
Sa'dah	332,364	3.9	344,152	3.7
Mahwit	292,973	3.4	322,226	3.5
Bayda	327,539	3.8	381,249	4.1
Ma'rib	108,814	1.3	121,437	1.3
Al-Jawf	83,074	1.0	87,299	0.9
Totals	8,540,119		9,274,173	

The above totals include what the North Yemenis term "unenumerated population for technical reasons" (i.e., the difficulty in actually reaching certain areas of the country) as well as the number of migrants outside North Yemen, who are still considered North Yemenis for nationality purposes. (In the 1981 census, the number of migrants outside North Yemen was given as 1,394,778; in 1986, this figure was given as 1,168,199.)

Source: Yemen Arab Republic, Statistical Year Book 1986 (Sana'a: Central Planning Organization, 1987).

Last, but definitely not least, the two censuses as well as smaller studies by individual researchers provide evidence of the extremely decentralized pattern of population distribution in the country. Within its land area (about 135,000 square kilometers [52,000 square miles]), the country has a total of more than 50,000 distinct settlements, i.e., towns and villages, which means that, despite current urbanization trends, North Yemen is characterized by decentralization on a scale unmatched anywhere else in the modern world. Further, more than 86 percent of the population lives in villages of less than 1,000 inhabitants; correspondingly, only about 11 percent lives in settlements of over 2,000 inhabitants. On the other hand, urbanization and population concentration in urban areas have been increasing since these censuses were conducted. At the time of the 1975 census, there were only three cities with a population of over 50,000, together making up about 6.5 percent of the total (Sana'a, Ta'izz, and Hodeida). By the mid-1980s, most observers agreed that the three major urban centers had doubled their population by as early as 1980 and had increased by perhaps as much as another 20 percent by 1985, increasing their percentage of the total to as much as 10–12 percent; Sana'a alone was believed to have more than 200,000 inhabitants.

In March 1986, the country undertook another census, and according to its results, the total population of North Yemen had risen to 9,274,173 (see Table 2.2). If these results are to be believed, the country's total population placed it in the first rank among the Arab states. Perhaps of greater significance is the fact that the population of the capital city was now said to be 427,185, which meant a growth rate of roughly 100 percent since the last census (of 1981).[2]

ETHNOGRAPHIC DIVISIONS

Although ethnographic differences among even relatively small populations are quite common, the range of distinctions and categories that are socially meaningful in North Yemen must surely represent one of the more startling instances in the modern world. These distinctions include those with a historic origin; those based upon religion and similar cultural phenomena; and those based upon life-style, particular events, circumstances, or professions (occupations).

Historical Divisions

Genetically and linguistically related, the Arabs of the Arabian Peninsula have been divided into two major groupings since the beginning of their recorded history: this distinction is generally between the 'Adnani (northern) and the Qahtani (southern) Arabs. Although this distinction is now largely irrelevant elsewhere in the Arab world, such is not always the case on the peninsula in general or in North Yemen in particular. Some of the existing feuds and differences can be traced back to this pre-Islamic distinction; what is of greater importance, however, are the facts that the differences affect contemporary events and that they can move people to political action. The best instance of this importance is the reinvigoration of the distinction in the last days of the Hamid al-Din family's rule and occasionally during the ensuing civil war of the 1960s.

Nevertheless, it is difficult to determine whether the distinction is being applied after the fact, that is, applied because it overlaps some other distinction and therefore helps to draw the lines of conflict more clearly, or if it is being applied because it is the ultimate cause of an even older conflict that has been revitalized by some other (and newer) disagreement.

In North Yemen, all the imams since the late ninth century AD have belonged to the Rassid dynasty, which claimed descent from the Prophet Muhammad, thus making them 'Adnanis. The last imams of North Yemen were, more precisely, members of the Hamid al-Din family, and when they encountered various political problems in the later years of their reign, they claimed Qahtani ancestry in the hope and expectation that it would legitimize their rule among the tribespeople of the central and northern highlands—all of whom proudly and knowledgeably trace their Qahtani heritage. Although the imams claimed to have inherited the mantle of the ancient Himyarite civilization as well (symbolized by such actions as always using red ink [Himyar = red] in official documents), there is no way of knowing whether or not these claims and actions bolstered their prestige and/or pacified their opponents to any significant degree.[3]

Religious Divisions

The variety and number of religious belief systems that have had (and still have) adherents in southwestern Arabia is surprisingly large.[4] In the pre-Islamic period, archaeological and paleographic evidence indicate that a number of gods were important, including ones associated with the moon, the sun, Venus, and perhaps others. Some contemporary anthropologists and ethnologists claim to be able to see remnants of these pre-Islamic belief systems in some of the more traditional legal systems as well as in some behavioral patterns in the more remote rural areas.

At about the time of the second Jewish Diaspora (first century AD), a sizable group of Jews lived in the central mountains of North Yemen. At roughly the same time, a large Christian colony also appeared, centered on a bishopric at Najran but with another important grouping located in Sana'a (where the Grand Mosque appears to have been built with stones from that group's cathedral and may contain pillars from an ancient Jewish house of worship as well). Available evidence indicates that these two groups did not treat each other very well: the Jewish state actively persecuted the Christians, thereby helping to bring about an invasion by the Christian Ethiopians, who in their turn then persecuted the Jews when they came to power. This particular conflict was brought to a close by the rule of the Persians in the last quarter of the sixth century AD. A small colony of Zoroastrians, which existed in Aden until recently may at least in part have originated as a result of this particular invasion and occupation (though it was composed mostly of Indian Parsee/Zoroastrians in its last years).

Shortly after the Persian conquest, Islam appeared on the scene and the religious and religio-political conflicts seem to have made submission to the new faith a particularly easy and rapid one (as it probably offered relief from the excesses of both Christians and Jews). In turn, North Yemen's early conversion to the new faith gave it a favored position within Islam, especially in the eyes of Muhammad. In fact, two of North Yemen's most famous mosques—the one in Sana'a known as the Grand Mosque and the one in Janad, near Ta'izz—are widely believed to be two of Islam's earliest structures.

Islam, however, was no different from other major faiths in that it underwent various divisions and factionalization, which led to the next most important distinction among the Yemeni people today. Indeed, the split between Sunni and Shi'a Islam is probably the most important one—politically, socially, and even in some respects, economically—in modern North Yemen.

The overwhelming majority of Muslims are Sunnis, but early in the Islamic period, the highland people of North Yemen chose to sympathize with the cause of Ali, the son-in-law and cousin of the Prophet; that is to say, these people adopted the Shi'a belief that only the descendants of Ali should succeed to the Muslim office of khalifa ("caliph," or "successor" [to Muhammad as leader of the Muslim community]). As has happened time and again in the history of the Middle East, it was the people of the mountainous regions, which were difficult to reach and administer, who adopted this minority view. In North Yemen, two Shi'a sects were established, and they have maintained their distinctiveness into the twentieth century. The first of these are the Zaydis—the most numerous and the most politically influential; the second are the Isma'ilis—occasionally influential in the past, but today this sect has no more than roughly 50,000 adherents, only a remnant of its former numbers, and it has lost much of its power.

The Zaydis. Even today it may be argued that the rise of the Zaydi state in the ninth century AD was the single most important event in North Yemen after the coming of Islam, primarily because many of the social and political characteristics of the country today are utterly inexplicable without knowledge of, and reference to, this Zaydi inheritance and influence. The social structure, the economic relationships, the attitudes toward the state and its functionaries—the whole life-style of the highland population—have been indelibly marked by the Zaydi imamate, despite the exile of the imam and the uncertain status of the imamate as an institution since the revolution of 1962.

The name of the sect is derived from Zayd, who was one of the two grandsons of Husayn, who in turn was one of Ali's two sons (by his wife Fatima, who was Muhammad's daughter). As is the case with other Shi'as, the Zaydis will recognize as their spiritual leader (known as an imam) only descendants of the Prophet through his daughter and son-in-law (Ali). Unlike other Shi'as, however, the Zaydis recognize Zayd as the fifth imam in the line of succession after Muhammad (other Shi'as recognize collateral lines, which leads to some of the divisions within Shi'a Islam).

The first of the Zaydi imams was al-Hadi ila al-Haqq Yahya ibn al-Husayn (died 911 AD) but he was not from this branch of the Prophet's family. He, and nearly all of his successors as imams of North Yemen, were from the Rassi House, descendants of Hasan (the brother of Husayn) through his two sons. This seemingly minor point illustrates a crucial issue on which the Zaydis differ from their Shi'a coreligionists: in the view of the Zaydis, Ali's succession to leadership of the Islamic community was owing to his special merits. As a result, the Zaydis have never accepted, at least in principle, familial rule (i.e., primogeniture). In fact, the office of imam was a highly selective one, and any candidate for the position had to fulfill a number of specific conditions set by Zaydi law and custom.

The major criterion that eliminated most of the population from being a candidate for the imamate was the requirement that one be descended from Muhammad through his daughter Fatima. An important corollary, which has profoundly influenced Yemeni history and politics, is that a candidate must publicly seek the office and claim recognition. In other words, the concept of the "hidden imam," which characterizes other Shi'a sects, is specifically disavowed in Zaydi law and tradition.

Although there is some dispute among Zaydi scholars as to exactly how many conditions a candidate for the imamate must fulfill, the most commonly recognized number is fourteen: (1) male; (2) freeborn; (3) a taxpayer; (4) mentally sound; (5) possess all five senses; (6) possess all hands and feet (designed to exclude individuals who have suffered the traditional punishments for crimes); (7) just; (8) pious; (9) generous; (10) endowed with administrative ability; (11) Fatimi (i.e., descended from Fatima; this condition eliminates the Isma'ilis from candidacy); (12) Alawi (i.e., descended from Ali); (13) brave (a prescription designed to eliminate children and concealed "mahdis" from candidacy—a mahdi, or rightly guided one, is the expected messiah of Muslim tradition); and, (14) a *mujtahid* (i.e., one learned in Muslim law and theology and thus capable of interpreting the Quran and other relevant Islamic materials).

The imam is considered to be imbued with "the guiding light of God," and his decisions on matters of faith, morals, law, economics, and even the personal lives of the members of the community of believers of which he is both spiritual and temporal head are infallible. (The rule of the Ayatullah Ruhollah Khomeini in Iran has, perhaps, given the average Westerner some conception of the kinds of authority it is possible for a Shi'a leader to possess and wield.)

Nevertheless, the imam is not without restrictions on his power(s). He is, first and foremost, limited by the strictures of the Quran (Koran, the Muslim scriptures), the Sunna (body of Islamic custom and practice), and by Islamic law as it is understood and propagated by Zaydi theoreticians and theologians (the *ulama*). He is not, technically, required to consider even a unanimous decision of the council of religious elders and scholars as binding, but in practice the freedom of action of all imams has been restricted by the views of this body.

The Zaydi imam is considered *amir al-mu'minin*, i.e., commander of the faithful, and the successor to the Prophet as the leader of the true

Islamic community. These titles serve to emphasize the claims of the Zaydi imams to this role, and the Zaydi belief that others have strayed from the true path has led to an occasional outbreak of fierce intolerance in their treatment of other Muslims. The converse of this situation has been the long-term inclination to be quite lenient in the treatment of non-Muslims (in accordance with the Muslim guidelines concerning *dhimmis*, i.e., protected peoples), most especially the Jews (the Christian community appears to have disappeared rather early except in such places as Najran).

During the centuries when the imams were both temporal and spiritual rulers of the Yemeni highlands, all people who, according to Zaydi theory, could be candidates for the imamate made up a privileged class and were known as sayyids. Their claim to descent from the Prophet assured them of special perquisites and status, and it has been argued, with considerable merit, that the Zaydi state was administered largely in the interests of this class, variously estimated to have numbered between 5,000 and 50,000. The imam, who in theory was elected by his fellow sayyids, took the interests and wishes of this group into consideration in the making of public policy, and in order to pacify this interest group, the imams dispensed patronage in various forms, the most common one being a government position. As a result, most of the local affairs of the state were in the hands of the sayyids: they administered justice (as government judges in towns), they assessed and collected the taxes, and they performed the myriad other functions of even the most rudimentary government administration. Although not originally an independently wealthy aristocracy (based upon, say, land or commerce), the sayyids used the available opportunities to amass wealth, though only rarely in gross disproportion to the society at large. Eventually, this wealth provided them with sufficient resources to become landowners or controllers of equally important resources (e.g., water). On the whole, however, very few of them were able to amass fortunes that would be considered large by Western standards.

The imams were largely separated from the general population by this intervening oligarchy, and as a result, resentment against the government and its activities was largely directed against the sayyids; the imams often continued to enjoy a considerable measure of public respect and loyalty. (Although it is considered rather heretical or subversive to say so, it is not all that uncommon for people in North Yemen today to be heard remembering the imamate with a certain amount of nostalgia, though only in very limited terms. The most common instance, perhaps, is praise for the imamate's ability to make North Yemen self-sufficient in foodstuffs.)

Probably the single most important accomplishment of the revolution of 1962, then, was the radical decrease in the numbers and power of the sayyid class, at least as far as the average citizen of North Yemen is concerned. Nonetheless, almost 30 years after the revolution, the sayyid class still exists, and its members may still be seen, clothed in their traditional garb, in villages, towns, and even the major cities. In fact, in some respects, their traditionally important role in public administration has only barely diminished because after the Compromise of 1970, which ended the civil war, the new government needed literate civil servants in large numbers in order to implement the many reform programs that had been promised or launched in the effort to obtain popular support and in practical terms, it was largely the sayyids who could fulfill this function. Many of them, seeing the important changes that were in the offing, managed to convert their previous positions and perquisites into more modern measures of wealth and status. As a class, then, their influence has greatly diminished; as a group of educated, relatively wealthy, and even privileged individuals, they continue as an elite group in a somewhat altered form.

In theory and practice, of course, the revolution of 1962 eliminated the imamate. Why then review the theory and practice of the Zaydi imamate and its functions? First, although the last reigning imam (Muhammad al-Badr) *was* deposed, he was not killed; he remains a shadowy background figure in retirement and seclusion in a village on the outskirts of London. Second, the theoretical justifications for an imam and the imamate were not eliminated as a result of the revolution or by the Compromise. Third, and probably most important, the eight years of civil war after the imam's deposition as well as the years of secular rule that have followed have had surprisingly little impact upon Zaydi theory and practice. Despite the radically altered political conditions, it would appear that the essential social fabric, which is based upon Zaydi theory and practice, has not been seriously disturbed or altered by the events since 1962. In fact, it is quite conceivable, considering the fluidity and temporary nature of most of the political regimes that have ruled since 1962, that the imamate could once again be restored, at least in the Zaydi areas of the north.

To believe that the patterns and traditions of the past will so quickly disappear, and without a ripple, in the contemporary Islamic world is, I believe, to seriously misread the situation. If nothing else, one should not forget that movements exist throughout the Islamic world which have as their goal the restoration of a political and religious pattern that is perceived to be more attuned to the Islamic mode of living. Although, for the moment, North Yemen could be considered a counterexample to the common perception in the West that Islam is now the primary political ideology among all Muslims (because the Yemenis agreed to the abolition of the imamate), this view is too simplistic. First, there are many devout Yemenis who believe that the current system, for all its flaws, is more Islamic than the previous one because it more effectively provides Muslims

with the goods and services to which they are entitled; second, there are
other devout Yemeni Muslims who wish to see a non-imamic Muslim
state established, which would be based more clearly on the Shari'a (as
understood by either of the two major communities); and third, there are
others who would create a completely different system based upon a
different set of domestic and foreign policies. In other words, in North
Yemen, as elsewhere in the Islamic world, there are multiple definitions
and interpretations of what constitutes an "Islamic system" of governance
and administration.

Isma'ilis. The other group of Shi'as associated with North Yemen
are the Isma'ilis. Like other Islamic sects, this one has also had its doctrinal
and leadership disputes, and these have resulted in the formation of two
distinct Isma'ili groups.

First, one should note that the Isma'ilis of North Yemen belong to
the Musta'lian, or western, branch of the faith; they are not, therefore,
followers of the well-known Isma'ili leader, the Agha Khan (who is the
recognized head of the Nizari, or eastern branch). Second, the most
important split to affect the Isma'ilis of North Yemen took place in the
seventeenth century, and it resulted in a majority group known as the
Sulaymanis and a minority one known as the Dawudis. The Sulaymanis
are known (in North Yemen) as the Makarima, because the leadership of
the sect became hereditary in the al-Makrami family. Because of conflicts
with the Zaydis, with whom relations have never been particularly good,
the home of the reigning community head (known as the *da'i* ["leader"])
has been in Najran throughout the twentieth century. It is in this general
area that an Isma'ili tribe—the Yam—is dominant, and it is likely that
Isma'ili-Zaydi relations in the past were an important part of the disputes
over the Najran Oasis. (Since the revolution, these conflicts have greatly
abated.)

The Dawudis, although a distinct minority, are related to the Bohor
Dawudis, a branch of the faith with many adherents in East Africa and
India. They are, as a result, more closely linked with the outside world,
and indeed, they administer two holy sites in North Yemen to which a
small trickle of pilgrims from other countries occasionally come.

Ever since their appearance in North Yemen, the Isma'ilis have been
associated with two distinct geographical areas. The first of these is the
Jabal Haraz region, west of Sana'a, around the city of Manakhah; the
second is around Najran. Estimates of the number of Isma'ilis in North
Yemen are not reliable; it is doubtful that they exceed 50,000. It is therefore
remarkable that all of the cabinets for the first two decades after the
revolution included at least one Isma'ili in a clear effort to bring about a
reconciliation between the communities after the antagonistic policies of
the Zaydi imams toward the Isma'ilis.

Shafi'is. Sunni, or "orthodox," Islam is, like Shi'a Islam, divided. In Sunni Islam, the divisions are known as "schools" because each is based upon the work of a specific legal scholar of Islamic law. Four such scholars developed a following sufficient to warrant having a specific orientation toward Islamic law named after them—Ibn Hanbal, al-Shafi'i, Maliki, and Hanafi—and it is the Shafi'i school that predominates in southwestern Arabia. More specifically, the Shafi'i school is the dominant one in South Yemen, the Tihama of North Yemen, and the southern uplands of North Yemen, i.e., from around Ta'izz to the south.

The Shafi'is never recognized any religious right of the imam of the Zaydis to interpret or create new law with respect to their own activities or their community. On the other hand, they did acknowledge—more or less—the Zaydi imam as the temporal ruler of North Yemen after World War I. There developed, as a result, a community of interest between the imam, who was responsible for the administration of justice and the appointment of judges, and the Shafi'i *ulama*, who proposed candidates for judicial posts in the Shafi'i areas.

In reality, the differences between the Zaydis and the Shafi'is are quite minimal; indeed, the Sunnis of southern Arabia have been known to refer to the Zaydis as the "fifth school" of law. For example, the Zaydis do not promote the major celebrations associated with the death of Husayn (the most important of all Shi'a martyrs) on the tenth of Muharram, generally considered the most holy of Shi'a holidays; they do not practice *taqiyyah*, i.e., dissimulation, about one's religious faith in order to avoid feared persecution; they do not accept or condone *muta'* (temporary) marriage; they essentially ignore and do not accept the kinds of mysticism and secret knowledge that are prevalent in other forms of Shi'ism; and they have been notoriously lax about eliminating saint worship and animism in its various forms—both of which are quite prevalent and visible in rural North Yemen. There are, to be sure, outward manifestations—particularly in the call to prayer—that may be used to distinguish between members of the two communities. But the average Yemeni, whether Zaydi or Shafi'i, understands little of the doctrinal differences, especially the esoteric points of law and theology that are sometimes involved. For the average person, the most important difference is likely to be in the different oral traditions the two groups have about each other.

In the political world, the crucial difference between them grew out of their very different experiences during the two periods of Ottoman domination. During the second Ottoman period, beginning in the nineteenth century, the Shafi'is became the commercial, trading, and merchant class of the country, even in such quintessentially Zaydi cities of the highlands as Sana'a. Deeply suspicious of their closer relations with the Turks and their commercial activities (which gave them continuing contact with the outside world), the Zaydi imams gradually heightened the existing differences and began to seriously restrict Shafi'i commercial and trading opportunities and activities. These restrictions naturally contributed to Shafi'i resentment of the overlordship of the Zaydis, and eventually, this resentment led to political activity that was directed at altering the very form and substance of the political system. Inevitably, the strongest support for the revolution of 1962 came from the population of the Shafi'i districts. It is of some interest, therefore, that the proportion and influence of Shafi'i ministers in the government cabinets and political activities have undergone a pronounced decline since the end of the civil war, but it is difficult to tell whether this decline in influence is a portent of problems in the future or an indication that the relevance of religious affiliation in domestic politics may be waning. It is, however, important to remember that the oft-cited split between the Zaydi and Shafi'i communities is more of a socioeconomic and political cleavage than a religious one.

Jews. For centuries, the Jews were the largest non-Muslim group in the area; indeed, they were the *only* non-Muslim group to permanently reside in North Yemen and have a recognized status. The origins of these Jews are somewhat obscure. Some authorities have suggested that because of their physical characteristics, which make them indistinguishable from the Muslim Yemeni highlander, they are at least in part the descendants of indigenous peoples (tribes) who adopted Judaism in pre-Islamic times. Others have suggested that their origins may be traced to the second Diaspora (first century AD), when Jews emigrated southward from Palestine and started colonies in all of the major west Arabian cities, from Gaza southward to Aden. (In Aden at the time of the British takeover in 1839, for example, they made up about 45 percent of the population.) According to this explanation, the physical resemblance between the Jews and Muslims in North Yemen is accounted for by nearly two millennia of intermarriage.

Under the Zaydi imams, the Jews were considered a protected group under the terms of the Shari'a (the sacred law of Islam). Although subject to a number of restrictions—affecting residence, transportation, clothing, and a few other more trivial matters—Jews were permitted to engage in industry, trade, and own land, and they were generally an accepted part of the social order (though, of course, not equivalent to Muslims). In fact, the Jews were overwhelmingly engaged in craft occupations, i.e., smithing, metalwork, glass, textiles, and so forth. Certainly all the evidence indicates that the Yemeni Jews were far better off than their European counterparts, and apparently the imams were, by and large, scrupulously fair in their treatment of them. It cannot be, for example, a coincidence that all the wholly Jewish settlements in North Yemen were (and are) located in Zaydi districts, not Shafi'i ones.

The number of Jews in North Yemen in the past is difficult to ascertain; most estimates suggest that there were no more than 75,000 at the time of World War II. Shortly after the establishment of the state of Israel in 1948, the vast majority of the Jews in North Yemen left for the new state in an airlift which the United States helped to organize. As a result, a large section of Sana'a known as the Qa' al-Yahud (the Jewish Quarter) was, for the first time in more than a millennium, empty of Jews, and whole villages in the north were abandoned. The number of Jews in the country in the early 1980s was probably around 2,000, and they were concentrated overwhelmingly in a few rather isolated villages in Sa'dah Province. Most interesting, in the light of their well-known problems in finding full acceptance in Israeli society, were persistent rumors that a few of the earlier emigrés had returned to these villages. Some of the Westerners who visited there in the 1980s found that many of the customs, views, and behavior in these villages continued to be unique but that some of the Jews had been influenced by the republic, a new-found prosperity, and their perceptions of the state of Israel.

Tribal-Urban Divisions

Probably most important for an understanding of the social, political, and economic characteristics of North Yemen—both past and present— is the division of the country between those people who are essentially tribally oriented and those whose life-style is oriented toward the few urban centers and larger towns.[5] It is important to note that "tribal" in this context refers only to a method of social and political organization; it should not be understood to mean the stereotypical image of the nomad who ekes out a meager existence tending animals in the desert, nor does it refer to people who have no interests or understanding of any issues outside the limits of very restricted kinship groupings. The key difference between the two groupings is an orientation in attitudes and life-style.

Although most tribespeople are settled cultivators, that is, they own agricultural land which is the basis of their participation in the economy, they have a long tradition of independence from government regulation and therefore feel contempt for the city dweller who engages in commerce, trade, or manufacturing. They cherish the ideal of autarky and consequently denigrate the town dweller's acceptance of government administration, which acts to protect lives and property and makes decisions concerning life-style. Traditionally, the distinction between the two groups has been based on the public carrying of arms: the tribesman is usually decked out with the Yemeni dagger (*jambiyya*, more properly *janbiyya*), worn front and center on a decorated belt, as well as a rifle; the average city dweller is unarmed, though the practice of carrying a *jambiyya* has become rather widespread (as an indication of social and political status).

Shafi'i tribes, located primarily in the Tihama and the foothills, make up about one-fifth of the recognized tribal units in North Yemen; the remaining four-fifths are Zaydi, and they predominantly live in the central and northern highlands as well as the eastern desert regions. Since the two major Muslim groupings each constitute about one-half of the population, it is clear that tribal affiliation is far more prevalent and important among the Zaydis. Furthermore, it means that the religious cleavage tends to be reinforced by this difference in residence.

The differences between the tribal and urban groups can be best summarized by briefly listing the two major characteristics of the *qabili* ("tribesman," from the Arabic for tribe, *qabil*). First, the tribe is the focal point of individual loyalty, and each tribe (which is essentially a nation) has its own territory, recognized grazing grounds, wells, market towns where it carries out its business activities, allegiances, friends and enemies, history, leadership traditions, elite families, and so forth. Needing, and in the past obtaining, little or nothing from any government, the tribes and their members made a virtue out of necessity and argued that they were completely independent. Conditions have clearly changed since the end of the civil war (especially with respect to obtaining services from the central government), but tribal values have not changed as rapidly. Second, the tribe as an institution is a very conservative organization, and nearly all attempts to introduce administrative, legal, or social changes tend to be met with intense and prolonged resistance. As a result, the traditional modes of conflict resolution and the bases for sociopolitical action have changed very little. On the other hand, even though the value system has remained relatively constant, the economic role of the tribe, and its relationship with the government, have undergone some significant change, as the government has been able to provide goods and services that the tribes could not (new roads, potable water supplies, clinics, and schools).

SOCIAL STRATIFICATION

Descriptions and analyses of the social system in North Yemen have been the subjects of considerable controversy.[6] In no small measure this problem has been the result of using descriptive terms whose origins lie in other cultures and times; the most obvious examples are the terms *caste* and *class*. Early European travelers tended to use the former term; under the influence of nineteenth-century ideologies and analyses, the latter term came to enjoy greater vogue. In both instances, however, the descriptions and analyses were colored by the ideological orientation and previous experiences of the writer.

In part, however, it is the very complexity of North Yemen's geography and population that has made unambiguous descriptions of the country's social system difficult. Indeed, it may be argued that no single analytical concept is adequate to either a description or an analysis of Yemeni society. On the other hand, that statement does not mean that general observations are impossible, nor does it mean that comparisons between North Yemen and other societies are not possible. In the most recent attempts to describe North Yemen's social system, scholars have used four major criteria in striving for completeness and accuracy: genealogy, occupation, location, and wealth.

The Tribespeople (qabili)

The tribespeople perceive themselves to be, and are generally so regarded by others, the most important and most elevated element in the social structure. This perception stems from four factors. The first is their ability to trace their genealogies back into pre-Islamic times (and the major families and states of that time). This Qahtani ancestry places them in North Yemen earlier than the various other groupings with whom they live and compete. Second, although their traditional independence is in many respects illusory and the result of a complex system of intermediaries and subsidiary groups with whom the tribespeople work to market their agricultural and animal goods, it enables them to enter the marketplace as independent actors. Third, since they have on occasion resorted to armed conflict to settle disputes (of all kinds), and the governments in the past have been unable to resist the might of the tribes, their claims to political independence are widely accepted. And, fourth, though not wealthy by Western standards and indeed often considerably less well-off than the urban population in terms of the goods and services to which they have access, the ownership of land brings most *qabili* at least a comfortable income in years of adequate rainfall.

The Sayyids (sada)

Until the revolution of 1962, the sayyids stood at the apex of the social pyramid. This position was the result of, first, their genealogy, although in their case the prestige accrued because of their descent from Muhammad. Second, their importance was enhanced by their usual role as arbiters and peacemakers, a crucial function in a society where tribal values and the concept of collective punishment were the norm. Third, in the rural areas, they ministered to the sick (with the assistance of the Quran) and carried out the kind of interpersonal assistance that psychologists and psychiatrists perform in the West. Fourth, their education and literacy enabled them to perform secretarial, notarial, and recording functions. This ability placed them in the position of being the visible intermediary between the population and the government for all functions requiring paperwork—and thus earned them a good deal of enmity that would have otherwise been directed against the imams personally. And, fifth, as a result of the functions they performed, they became the major public support of the traditional government and thus also the major beneficiary of the perquisites the traditional system had to offer.

People Engaged in Trade and Commerce (nuqqas or awlad al-suq)

Perhaps easiest categorized as "those without ancestry," i.e., people who have no genealogy to be proud of, this group consists overwhelmingly of detribalized families and individuals whose livelihood is based upon trading, manufacturing, and various other commercial and service activities, and they usually live in a trading center or larger town. Nevertheless, distinctions may be (and are) made among such people. The traditional breakdown had four major categories: (1) the *khadama*, that is, people who perform services for others and whose actual employment would be a part of the service sector in a modern economy (even though specific jobs may no longer exist, e.g., bloodletting); (2) the *abid*, the descendants of slaves and the personal retainers and retinue of those who can afford to keep servants; (3) the *yahud* (Jews), who played an important role in the traditional economy through the specific trades they tended to engage in, e.g., jewelry making, brewing, etc.; and (4) the *akhdam*, in many respects, the most unusual group in North Yemen and the closest one to a caste. The *akhdam* are detribalized and distinguished from the remainder of the population by their darker skin color as well as by their social roles and place of residence (usually slums on the edge of a larger town or city). Most Western scholars consider these people to be the descendants of Nubians and Somalis who were imported in the past as slaves. They appear to have retained many African traditions (including in their social relations), and they continue to be almost totally separate—socially and genetically—from the highland populace and people in higher social positions and ranks.

In the view of the tribespeople and the sayyids, the idea of providing a service to others is demeaning; it reflects badly upon one's economic, social, and political independence. Even so, the society as a whole makes distinctions among the different kinds of services that are offered.

At the lowest rank are those people whose jobs are associated with the human body and its characteristics, i.e., blood, hair, excretions. There-

fore, the bloodletter, the barber, the cleaner of public facilities, the collec-
tors of wastes, etc., are the lowest of all. An important fact is that even
with the immense socioeconomic changes wrought by the revolution and
its aftermath, it remains nearly impossible to move out of this category.
Next come the people who provide more "genteel" services: the hotel
proprietor, the restaurant owner, the greengrocer, etc. With newly accu-
mulated wealth, it has become possible to move out of this category.

The next level defies logical explanation. In North Yemen, both the
blacksmith and the weaver are considered to be of low status; indeed, in
some areas, they barely rank above the very lowest ranks. Marginally
above the proprietors are the skilled artisans, i.e., individuals who carry
out many of the functions the Jews tended to perform: silver- and gold-
smithing, glassmaking, the making of jewelry, plastering, stonework, etc.

In the middle group are the traders, the wholesalers, and the men
of commerce. Although their existence and roles are barely recognized (at
least publicly), they perform the essential function of purchasing the
produce and animals of the tribes for eventual resale in the market towns,
thus preserving for the tribespeople the image of economic as well as
political independence. Traditionally, this middleman group has also had
the greatest contact with the outside world—because many of them are
exporters and importers. Thus, in the past, they were supportive of
movements and efforts to modernize the imamic system, and they have
consistently supported the republic in its efforts and programs.

New Social Categories

The revolution and its aftermath have led to the formation of at least
two new categories within the Yemeni social system. The first of these is
the military; the second is what has been variously called "the new middle
class," "the new professionals," etc. In more recent years, another new
grouping has appeared as well, the so-called youth, whose characteristics
are difficult to summarize.

The Military. Under the imams, the military was almost indistinguishable from an armed personal retinue; the new military, on the other
hand, exists as a real social force outside (or in addition to) the traditional
social categories. I do not suggest that everyone accepts its current role
and status; it is, nevertheless, an organization largely separate from the
traditional groupings and one that has its own distinct interests to protect.
Still, traditional loyalties (regional, tribal, etc.) and social distinctions have
not disappeared within the military. In fact, the government takes tribal
origins, religious affiliation, regional origin, and other such matters into
account in the military's organizational structure and chain of command.
Recruitment, for example, is still largely based on similar tribal or regional

Local merchant in the Sa'adah Suq (the "Gun Suq"). Photo copyright by Martin Lyons. Used by permission.

origins, and the government cannot afford to end the present system, even though it does tend to perpetuate regional and tribal loyalties.

It should be noted that the majority of the army is recruited from among the *qabili*, partly because of the slow reduction in tribal subsidies undertaken by the government in the mid-1970s and partly because all previous governments recruited from among the tribes—a natural development in view of their traditions and training. As a result, the North Yemen army does not recruit from many other segments of the population, and the army is not viewed—either by the population at large or by specific segments within it (e.g., the *akhdam*)—as a mechanism for social advancement. On the other hand, people who do enter the army and wind up in one of the technical or officer schools can expect to improve their social position as a result. The perquisites associated with a military career have substantially improved in recent years, and the population at large generally now accepts the military as having a recognized position within the society.

The New Professionals. The term essentially refers to "intellectuals," i.e., individuals who have obtained an education (usually abroad) in some specialized skill or discipline and have parlayed that education into respected administrative careers within the government. This grouping also includes journalists, teachers, scientists, higher-ranking and more-educated officers, specialized administrators, and individuals with similar kinds of positions in such bodies as the Confederation of Yemeni Development Associations.

Although these individuals generally occupy specific positions because of their technical expertise and skills, it is necessary to add that the individual's origins (regional, tribal, religion, etc.) are rarely forgotten or considered irrelevant. Even foreign personnel (seconded to North Yemen by the United Nations, for example) soon become aware of whether or not the individuals with whom they must deal are Zaydi, belong to one of the traditional elite families, are members of a particularly important tribe or tribal confederation, etc. Even in such modern institutions as the National Institute for Public Administration—staffed by both Yemenis and foreigners—it is clear that some lines of command bear no relationship to those found on the organization chart; rather, they depend on traditional links among the relevant individuals.

The Shubab. Strictly speaking, *shubab* is the plural of "youth," and the word was used to describe a particular age category (late teens, early twenties) and that group's general behavior pattern when it first appeared in common usage. In more recent years, *shubab* has become a generic term for people who are quite candid in their resentment of, and opposition to, the role of foreigners (both Arab and non-Arab); who are ambiguous about the functions and role of the secular government; who are impatient with the slow rate of change in certain fields (as well as their inability to participate in the decision making concerning the changes); and who are often prone to decisive (if not always effective) and rash action in order to demonstrate their dissatisfaction with and putative power in contemporary society. This group has become, particularly as far as donor programs are concerned, a social element planners and administrators must effectively cope with if they are to succeed.

The Qadis *(qudat)*

In other Islamic countries, the term *qadi* refers to an individual trained in Islamic law and principles, i.e., an Islamic judge. In North Yemen, such an individual is called a *hakim*, and *qadi* refers to individuals who are not sayyid by origin, but who have obtained an extensive traditional Islamic education. It is, in other words, a title one receives in recognition of significant educational achievement in the traditional Islamic sciences. Since such an achievement involves a considerable investment in time and money (to attend the requisite educational institutions), the ability to become a *qadi* is effectively limited to people with above average means. In North Yemen today the term is also used for people who have gained educational achievement in disciplines that are not strictly Islamic. It should be noted that an extraordinarily high percentage of North Yemen's political elite, both before and after the revolution, has been drawn from the ranks of the *qudat*.

SOCIETY AND CULTURE IN THE 1980s

Although delimiting the culture of any single Arab state from that of any other presents real difficulties, there is little doubt that such differences do indeed exist, and perhaps the best place to begin is with the interest in the past. In other Arab states, the overwhelming majority of the (Muslim) population sincerely believes in the low value that Islam places on the achievements of the Jahiliyya—the Age of Ignorance that preceded Islam. Although highly educated Muslims in these countries (e.g., Egypt or Iraq) are aware of and take pride in the accomplishments of their pre-Islamic eras, there is little doubt that where the commitment to Islam is highest and educational achievement is lowest (in the rural areas especially), the population knows little and cares less about the pre-Islamic period.

In North Yemen, on the other hand, the level of pride in the pre-Islamic past is high. In the most inaccessible parts of the country, essentially illiterate and "unsophisticated" villagers will refer with pride to the pre-Islamic period; they are delighted to show the visitor buildings, inscriptions, monuments, and other remnants of that time, and they will extol the virtues and accomplishments of that period. Furthermore, there are deliberate efforts to demonstrate genealogical as well as historical connections between the present and the great civilizations of the past (usually simplified into Qahtani descent in the first instance and to the Himyarite period in the second).

This unusual pride in the pre-Islamic past does not mean that the Yemenis ignore or denigrate the Islamic period. In fact, this area was one of the first to come under the influence of the new faith, and most observers of contemporary North Yemen would argue that the central fact of the country's history in the last 1,500 years or so was the formation of the Zaydi imamate. Therefore, no real understanding of contemporary North Yemen is possible without reference to Islam and its characteristics, but without a brief introduction to the country's political history in the past two centuries, much of the role of Islam is also likely to be meaningless.

In that political history, it is the last occupation of the area by the Ottoman Empire (from 1872 to 1918) that is of most immediate relevance. Seen by the Yemenis as incompetent, hopelessly corrupt, and essentially uncaring if not downright hostile to Yemeni religious sensibilities (especially among the highland Zaydis), it was probably inevitable that opposition to the Ottoman/Turkish authorities would have its roots in the religious community. As was to be the case in Iran in the 1970s, the mosque was the only place where people could meet in relative freedom, and the only place where the people could congregate freely to discuss current events. As a result, the mosque inevitably became the place where people could plot political action.

It is, therefore, not surprising that after independence, the imams incorporated their religious orientation into every aspect of their rule, thus creating a thorough intermixing of religious and political supports. No doubt the imams believed that such a mixture would be less open to exploitation by any opposition (domestic or foreign). In this effort the imams succeeded far better than they or anyone else realized: for the Zaydis, North Yemen is *their* state, and they continue to play the dominant role in its political, economic, and social life and mores. Nowhere is this influence more clearly found than in the legal system.

Law and the Legal System

Perhaps the most dogged effort by the imams to assert their rule and power over all of North Yemen was in the attempt to impose the Shari'a (the Islamic code of law, as interpreted and understood by the Zaydis) on areas where alternative legal systems had long been dominant.[7] The legal system most affected by this campaign was the traditional system of tribal law, known as '*urf*, which had been more widely accepted and implemented in the rural areas than the Shar'ia.[8] The revolution of 1962 changed very little with regard to the legal system. There was a certain secularization of the law in the urban centers under the control of the republicans and/or the Egyptians, but in the country as a whole, the main difference was a more relaxed and even liberal interpretation of those elements of Zaydi law that the imams had so stringently enforced. In fact, this increased liberality has become a major issue in the relations between Saudi Arabia and North Yemen: the former, which covers the deficit in the Yemeni government's operating budget, has often asked for, and sometimes obtained, changes in the government's policy with respect to certain elements of the Shari'a as a quid pro quo for continued support.

Since the end of the civil war in 1970, the government has been making efforts to introduce more modern codes in those areas of public life where their effect will be least disruptive to the sensibilities and life-style of a population that is still more used to traditional principles. Transitional codes are being introduced with the assistance of legal experts, notably from the Sudan (which is in itself a commentary on North Yemen's relationships with its more immediate neighbors on the Arabian Penin-sula). In general, these newer codes are being introduced first in such fields as commerce, trade, banking, and credit. At the same time, however, there are subtle but pronounced pressures to have the judiciary employ more "modern" concepts of equity as well as other secular principles in both civil and criminal cases being adjudicated. As one might expect, in view of the country's past as well as events elsewhere in the Islamic world, there has arisen a current of opposition to these changes, which has manifested itself in the existence of a variety of Muslim organizations.

The average visitor to Yemen, however, is not likely to be aware of legal issues or problems; he or she is more likely to see various aspects of the physical and human landscape as distinctive features of contem-porary life and culture in North Yemen.

The Physical Landscape

Probably the two features of North Yemen that most clearly strike the eye of the visitor are the terraced mountains and the architecture.[9] Over the millennia, the Yemenis developed the technique of terracing their mountainous terrain in order to preserve the precious topsoil, as well as various mechanisms to conserve the available rainfall. Although the technique of terracing mountainous slopes for agricultural purposes is not unique to North Yemen (indeed, it is found on nearly all continents), there are few places where the technique is so widespread, so sophisti-cated, and so immense in its extent. For example, there are terraced

Terrace agriculture in the region around Kohlan.

mountainsides south of Sana'a on the road to Dhamar where, measured from the depth of the valley floor to the uppermost reaches of the mountains, the vertical drop is more than a kilometer (about two-thirds of a mile), and every terrace carefully feeds its excess water onto the next lower one.

On the least fertile surfaces, usually on rocky crags and outcroppings, one finds the archetypical Yemeni village: a small cluster of multistoried buildings whose inhabitants (usually fewer than 200) raise their crops and animals on the terraces that are to be found on all sides. The nearly inaccessible location of these villages serves a dual purpose: it uses no land that could be used for raising either crops or animals, and it provides for easy defense. This latter characteristic, of great importance during the many centuries of civil war and incompetent governments, also contributed significantly to the rural tradition of local independence, suspicion of outsiders, and resistance to any efforts for effective administration. Of course, at the same time, such a location has kept these small villages utterly isolated and unable to provide the kinds of services that are increasingly being demanded of the government (schools, clinics, roads, and piped water supplies).

Some of the same factors no doubt contributed to the development of the architectural style in the foothills and highlands: a house of at least four stories, with external decorations and features designed to make it appear to have even more. Built upon a base of massive stone blocks are walls of stone, brick, or adobe (depending upon the area of the country), which tend to be very thick—both to support the great height (upward of 18 meters [60 feet]) and to provide insulation, which enables the average Yemeni highlander to do without heat or air-conditioning. The windows and stonework are often outlined with whitewash (which is actually ground alabaster in a water base), and there are also tinted-glass archways and similar decorative touches over the windows.

Yemeni tradition speaks of such multistoried buildings long before Christ; to the Yemenis, this is *the* style, and it is valued for precisely that reason. Both the government and the population support the continued use of this traditional style, even though some new buildings are in the "international style" (i.e., steel, concrete, and glass), often very expensive in terms of heating and air-conditioning requirements.

Shortly after the revolution, there was an immediate demand for new buildings to house new offices and agencies, as well as to accommodate new businesses and other activities, and a rash of two- and three-storied buildings in plain concrete resulted. Many of these are found along major arterials in Sana'a and in the major towns along the main north-south road. They are as uniform and uninteresting as quick construction anywhere in the world, and they have markedly contributed to the perception—among Yemenis as well as visitors—that one of the country's most appealing characteristics and inheritances is being diminished for reasons of expediency, cost, and speed of construction. Furthermore, a few high-rise glass towers (in the neo-Egyptian style) have also been put up (most notably the tower of Yemen Airways). There has been considerable public dismay concerning this trend, and the result has been an insistence that the traditional style be retained for public buildings—the new Bank for Reconstruction and Development, on Tahrir Square in Sana'a, is perhaps the best illustration of this policy.

The traditional houses contain a variety of rooms. The lower floor is generally used to stable animals, whose heat radiates upward to provide whatever heat is needed. Upper floors are generally undifferentiated—with rearrangement both quick and easy if desired—though the highest rooms are usually reserved for sleeping because of their distance from rooms where odors are generated—i.e., kitchen, laundry, and toilet—as well as their greater access to light and air.

The best room in a Yemeni house, the *mafraj*, is the highest, and it is used for socializing, entertaining, and other leisure activities. Nearly always whitewashed and delicately decorated with calligraphic or geometric patterns (some of which are quite Hellenic in appearance), this room contains the best carpets and many cushions as well as a divan or two.

Traditional highland architecture.

Retaining traditional architectural motifs in contemporary buildings: the Yemen Bank for Reconstruction and Development in Sana'a.

Mosque and tomb of Queen Arwa (d. 1138), Jibla.

In the Tihama, most houses are in the African style—often conical in shape and made of local vegetable materials (i.e., stalks, branches and reeds)—and each house is surrounded by a wall that encloses the family's garden and animals. In the major city of the Tihama, Hodeida, vaguely European concrete buildings now predominate. Often tinted or painted in pastel shades, they are reminiscent of the decaying harbor cities on tropical seacoasts throughout the world. The older style of building, with its wooden latticework over the windows to provide privacy while allowing the sea breezes to waft through the rooms, has almost disappeared. The buildings in some of the other Tihama cities—e.g., Zabid, Bayt al-Faqih, and Mocha (al-Mukha)—are constructed almost entirely of baked brick or adobe, since the sources of stone are too far away and the expense of transporting it, with rare exceptions, too great to warrant its use.

Although the country was an early convert to Islam, there is no distinctive Yemeni building style for mosques—that quintessentially Muslim building. The best known of the country's mosques, the Great Mosque in Sana'a, appears to have been built on (or next to) the site of a large and well-known pre-Islamic building (the Ghumdan Palace), and it contains pillars, stonework, and other signs of borrowings and re-use from its major predecessors (including Jewish and Christian houses of worship). In various towns throughout North Yemen, one may find mosques built in practically every conceivable architectural style, with obvious borrow-ings from the Indian subcontinent and elsewhere.

The Human Landscape

Clothing is usually the most obvious characteristic of a people to make an initial impression, and highland Yemeni clothing is indeed unusual.[10] The traditional male attire is a kind of front-pleated wraparound skirt (known as a *futa*), which extends roughly halfway between the knees and the ankles. Shirts, in every variety, color, and cut, are usually tucked into the skirt and kept there by means of a broad belt, the major purpose of which is to carry the *jambiyya*.

The average male wears this dagger front and center; its size, which indicates that it is no longer widely used either as a cutting instrument or as an effective fighting weapon (though fights that involve their use are not unknown), and the characteristic shape of the hilt have led many observers to suggest that the *jambiyya* is a phallic symbol. Considering its previous uses and the limited number of designs possible for a blade and hilt, it is possible that this factor was involved in its early development, but it is certainly not so perceived by anyone in the country today.

The dagger's symbolic significance is far greater now than its use-fulness; in fact, many Yemenis carry a small Swiss Army knife behind it for practical purposes. The *jambiyya* is first worn by boys as a sign of their transition to adulthood and citizenship, and men who have been charged with a crime must forfeit the right to wear it (a man's *jambiyya* is commonly accepted as sufficient bond for his release until the actual trial). Sayyids and *qadis* are distinguished from the average citizen by their all-white garb, the more precise cut and fit of their clothing, their headgear, and by the position of their *jambiyya*, which in their case is worn at an angle on the right side, almost on the hip. In other words, how and where the dagger is worn is a sign of social status.

Perhaps the *jambiyya*'s greatest notoriety in recent years concerns the fact that one of the traditional materials for its handle has been rhinoceros horn. Besides producing a hilt of a luminescent, pearly green color, hilts made of this horn have been attractive for people with the money to buy them precisely because of the high cost. Efforts by the government, as well as international wildlife bodies and citizen groups, have resulted in a decline in the use of rhinoceros horn (and replacement by water buffalo horn), but daggers made with it continue to be available for those with the means to afford the now even higher price.

In recent years, men's clothing has undergone some alteration, and the shirts now tend to be covered with a vest of some type and then a Western-style jacket (which is commonly replaced in the winter months

Highland Yemenis ('Amran).

with a sheepskin jacket). Atop the head there is a turban, usually a
nondescript length of cloth, but members of the elites (e.g., *qadis*) wear
better quality and more specialized turbans to indicate their status, rank,
and wealth. Moreover, certain colors and types of cloth have tended to
become associated with particular regions, tribes, and social groupings,
though the visitor is not likely to notice these differences at first. Furthermore, finely crocheted caps of various kinds are also worn in certain
areas and by certain groups.

It is, however, the dress of women that has undergone the greatest
change in recent years. In the Tihama and in the rural highlands, women
did not (and still do not) wear the veil. They wear a long-sleeved, full-
skirted dress, which reaches well below the knees; beneath this is usually
a pair of cotton trousers (or opaque cotton stockings). In the cities, on
the other hand, most women wear a long, black, dresslike covering over
their outfit. Resembling the Iranian *chador*, this covering has, in recent
years, increasingly replaced the more colorful versions of the past, when
certain designs tended to be associated with particular cities or even
social classes. The most important change has been the increase in the
wearing of a veil, which appears to be owing to two major causes: (1)
the influence of the Saudis and their more conservative ethic with respect
to women, especially women in public, and (2) the belief that the veil
indicates a certain income and status level, probably also a result of
foreign influences.

Despite this apparent increase in conservative dress, Yemeni women
are considerably more liberated than their colleagues in other peninsula
states (with the exception of Marxist South Yemen). It is not unusual to
have women in service positions, i.e., as bank tellers, salespersons, etc.;
women are free to drive motorized vehicles (including trucks and mo-
torcycles); and they have always been sexually more liberal than other
women on the peninsula (and perhaps even in the Arab world as a whole).
This liberation, however, does not mean that the position of women in
North Yemen is enviable; the kinds of chores they must perform, their
lack of educational opportunity, and the subservient position that generally
characterizes women in North Yemen mean that being female in that
country is difficult, to say the least.[11]

It is only recently that the nuclear family has become a part of the
social scene, i.e., a man and wife establishing their own household rather
than becoming a part of a larger household, which might include as many
as three generations. An important concomitant of this development has
been a radical escalation in the bride-price, which is not the same thing
as a dowry (an accepted part of the Muslim law and practice relating to
marriage). In rural areas, the bride-price has often been in the area of
50,000–75,000 riyals (at a time when $1 was equal to roughly 5 riyals;

Husband and wife winnowing. Photo courtesy of Tom Stevenson.

such exorbitant prices are only possible as a result of remittance wealth and have come to be regarded as an indicator of the honor of the bride).

After marriage, which is still usually arranged, the woman becomes a part of the husband's household but retains important links with her own family, to which she may return in the event of difficulties, divorce, etc. (If these kinds of problems arise early in the marriage, the bride-price must be returned.) One important feature of Yemeni society, however, is that the woman is entitled to her own inheritance and may have, and dispose of, her own wealth. The husband is required to provide for the expenses needed to maintain the household, and if the woman wishes to have extra spending money, she is permitted to earn it by raising produce, selling handicrafts, etc.

One important change in the role of women in rural Yemen is a by-product of the high rate of emigration by adult males. Women have taken over more of the actual day-to-day operations of agricultural production, and often they now have primary responsibility for water, food processing and preparation, domestic animals, fuel, fieldwork, and the marketing of some items. (There are some tribes in which the women have the sole responsibility for the marketing of all surplus goods and produce, but this situation is rather rare.) Men, on the other hand, continue to take primary responsibility for such things as the construction and maintenance of buildings, walls, terraces, etc.; long-distance transport (largely via four-wheel-drive trucks of immense size); public roles (such as participating in the making of community decisions); and decisions concerning household expenditures (though in some families where most of the adult males are gone, this role has also fallen to women in recent years).

Arguably the most important development of recent years to affect gender roles and nearly all aspects of life in North Yemen is the radical increase in personal mobility that has resulted from the construction of roads and the introduction of motorized vehicles (of all sizes and descriptions). Rural women can now travel to larger towns to shop, meet cohorts, obtain medical services, and even attend classes. At the same time, the exposure to mass media has sharply altered expectations, desires, and perceptions concerning present and future roles.

Changes have also taken place in the Yemeni diet.[12] The traditional diet was both unimaginative and not particularly nourishing—in fact, the two major contributions North Yemen has made to the diet of humankind, coffee and qat, are both alkaloids rather than nourishing foodstuffs. Under- and malnutrition are major problems, since the diet is low in calories and protein. As a result, and because of the Yemeni genetic inheritance, the average Yemeni is both very slender and relatively short (by Western standards). Despite the facts that North Yemen is comparatively rich in agricultural resources and that a large variety of foodstuffs can be grown, diversity has not been evident in the traditional diet.

Until an import distribution network was developed after the end of the civil war, the average Yemeni had a diet that consisted largely of bread dipped into a variety of gruel-like dishes for additional nutrients. Although a bit misleading, it is possible to characterize the national dish, hulbah, as essentially a dip made from fenugreek, chilis, and when possible, eggs and an occasional piece of (chicken) meat. Although relatively good breads made from locally produced and milled grain used to be widely available and occasionally still are (for example, the excellent kudam, baked from whole wheat and sorghum flour for the army and the prisons), the newer style breads and other foodstuffs that are now widely available are not nearly as nutritious as the older foods. Indeed, with the increasing preference for white bread and canned "juices" (with less than 20 percent juice, the rest sugared water), the under- and malnutrition problems that affect most of the population have in many instances gotten worse. On the other hand, there has been some improvement in the diet, especially in comparison to the imamic period, because of the number and variety of vegetables and fruits that have become widely available (usually from local truck farms).

Dishes the traveler is likely to encounter outside the major Western-oriented hotel chains and restaurants are fish, especially on the coastal plain; *ful,* a bean dish; *madid,* a grain gruel with yogurt and chilis; *asid,* a porridge of sorghum and wheat usually served with a hot sauce for dipping; and a variety of local dishes, which will include rice, tomatoes, chilis, garlic and leeks, and pasta. As income levels rise, eggs and chicken are added to the fare.

One interesting side effect of the increasing numbers of both Arab and Western tourists, businesspeople, and consultants has been the development of a rather fierce local pride in domestically produced foodstuffs. Such products are known as *baladi* (i.e., of the country), and, ironically, they are often inferior in quality and appearance to food imported from abroad, as well as considerably more expensive. Nevertheless, the Yemeni who can afford to do so will purchase such locally produced items—e.g., honey, flour, even canned goods and similar items—whenever they are available. This preference guarantees a domestic market for these domestically produced goods, which may be of substantial importance to the economy in the near term as well as the future.

Qat

Not least among the characteristics of culture in North Yemen is *qat* chewing.[13] Although the *qat* shrub grows in Ethiopia, Kenya, and South Yemen, it is in North Yemen that its cultivation and consumption are most highly developed. *Qat* (*Catha edulis*) is a woody, almost treelike shrub, which grows more than 3.5 meters (12 feet) tall, and it grows best at higher elevations (760 meters [2,500 feet] and higher), in the same kind of soil and with the same sort of water conditions that are conducive to growing the coffee tree.

Using *qat* means harvesting the smaller, newer leaves and slowly chewing them, with the addition of water or some mildly flavored beverage (in recent years, Western soda pop). The leaves remain in the mouth for long periods of time (hours), and the leaves slowly give up their volatile oils, that is, the alkaloids that give the chewer a mild "high." *Qat* is not a narcotic. Although its use may lead to a certain social and/or psychological dependence, it cannot be considered addictive in the way heroin or cocaine are. Furthermore, giving up *qat* chewing produces none of the side effects associated with withdrawal from the drugs more widely used in the West (including nicotine).

Qat chewing in North Yemen is quite widespread, probably more so now than before the revolution. A high percentage of the urban population engages in *qat* chewing on most afternoons, with sessions (in the *mafraj*) usually beginning in the mid-afternoon and lasting until the evening meal. Yemeni *qat* from the highland areas around Sana'a is the preferred variety; longtime connoisseurs purchase their *qat* from specific regions and even particular growers based upon criteria that are difficult for the nonuser to assess or even comprehend. For *qat* to be considered good (fresh), it must be less than half a day old. In the past, this factor required (and produced) prodigious feats of transport by only the most rudimentary means in order to supply the major urban towns, as well as Aden and some of the East African towns with substantial Yemeni populations—all in a country without roads and with some of the most difficult terrain around! One consequence is that good *qat* has become horrendously expensive: a few twigs of excellent quality Wadi Dhahr *qat* cost upward of $20–$25 in Sana'a, which is only about an hour away, and it is not uncommon for an afternoon's *qat* chew to cost in excess of $50 per person.

Even if *qat* is not particularly dangerous as such commodities go (it is possible to drive cars, operate heavy machinery and electrical hand tools, etc., while chewing it without fear of loss of life or limb), it does create a substantial drain upon the financial resources of the people who use it. Traditionally, the farmer who raised the plant did not chew it, nor did the majority of the rural population (perhaps because they could not spare either the money or the time). But the custom, which is deeply rooted in the social life and mores of the country in general, has probably expanded from its concentration in a few urban areas because of greater disposable income levels among rural families. It is now estimated that in North Yemen, 91 percent of the men and 59 percent of the women regularly chew *qat*.

Nearly every reform program drafted for and by North Yemen has mentioned the habit and proposed various means for reducing consumption, promoting a "return" to coffee growing (which assumes that coffee trees have been replaced by the *qat* shrub—an allegation that has not been proved), subsidizing alternative crops, or directly taxing the raising and consumption of *qat*. None of these reform programs has succeeded, nor is any likely to unless and until a cash return of similar quantity and speed can be gained from an investment in any of the alternatives. Furthermore, the old problem of transporting the *qat* leaves quickly has been substantially alleviated through the recent construction of a multitude of smaller feeder roads in the region, as well as the availability of four-wheel-drive vehicles, which can negotiate the difficult terrain. One alternative crop has met with success, however: in some of the areas around Sana'a, there has been a remarkable growth in the amount of acreage devoted to the growing of table grapes. There is a sizable demand for this product, which can be met with a relatively small investment, and there is an immediate cash return from the Sana'a market.

Qat seller in the Sana'a market. Photo copyright by Martin Lyons. Used by permission.

Contemporary Cultural Trends

It is, of course, the human landscape that has undergone the greatest amount of change since the revolution of 1962; in fact, it has probably changed in ways that are still too subtle for the casual visitor or the social scientist to precisely describe or analyze. It is important to remember that the people of North Yemen did not undergo any colonial experience (the era of Ottoman control is not even analogous), nor did they have to cope with various economic and social challenges to their traditional values and social system until very recently.

The result is that these Yemenis demonstrate an amazing openness, receptivity, and friendliness toward foreigners, foreign ideas, and foreign technology. In their rush to discard the restrictions (of all types) the imams had imposed, they welcomed all the goods and services the West (most especially) had to offer. But the challenges the Yemenis have encountered to their traditions and their society since the revolution have been monumental, in part because these challenges have been telescoped and concentrated into such a short period of time. The first signs of a reaction have already begun to appear, and the day may not be too far off when North Yemen joins its regional neighbors in a virulent outbreak of xenophobia in a desperate attempt to retain at least some of the country's traditions and indigenous ways as it searches for some stability in a world in which North Yemen is rarely more than a footnote.

Domestic Industries and Crafts. Like other countries with an overwhelmingly rural population, most craft activity in the past was for immediate household or community consumption, i.e., metalwork, ceramics, baskets, etc. Urban crafts, usually for the middle and upper classes, tended to consist of more ornate or expensive goods, and many were designed to show the owner's wealth, e.g., expensive textiles, jewelry, and silver or gold decoration on everyday items such as belts. These generalizations are valid for North Yemen as well, but recently there have been some changes.

First, there has been the near total collapse of the domestic textile industry. Although there are still a few small producers of the heavy, all-cotton cloth for which the Tihama region was famous, most of the textiles available in the country today are manufactured in India, the People's Republic of China, or Japan, often in local design patterns. The finer types of cloth (similar to Western lace and crocheted material) are nearly unobtainable.

Second, the domestic metalworking industry has also almost completely disappeared. Although one can still find a few craftspeople in the Sana'a *suq* ("market"), most of the items they used to make (e.g., scissors and tools of various types) have been replaced by Eastern or Western goods, which are cheaper and, sadly, better in their workmanship and effectiveness than the very traditional and relatively crude designs that are part of North Yemen's heritage.

Third, one of the few industries that has managed to hold its own is knife making. The manufacture of *jambiyya*s continues unabated, but even here there have been significant changes: for example, the blades are rarely, if ever, made in North Yemen any longer, being imported from Pakistan or Japan instead. The ancillary industries—making the scabbards (from local woods covered with locally produced and tanned leathers) as well as the varieties of leather and cloth belts produced to hold them— also continue successfully.

Fourth, one of the few industries that has increased in importance has been the making of baskets and similar containers. Although the local people now generally use plastic or metal containers of various kinds instead of the traditional baskets, the tourist trade has provided a replacement market. Often in the colors and patterns associated with East Africa (especially Somalia and Ethiopia), baskets are now made in nearly all Tihama villages.

Fifth, the design and manufacture of the semicircular plaster and glass vitrines that the Yemenis like to have over their windows and doorways continue to flourish. In the past as well as now, these vitrines have been a means for local artisans to express their sense of shape and color, and the variety and beauty of these expressions of local taste easily catch the eye of visitors to North Yemen.

Sixth, but by no means last in importance, a thriving new local industry, a genuine example of contemporary folk art, has developed: the design and manufacture of the metal doors Yemenis use on their new houses—to the courtyards, on the streetside of shops, etc. The ingenuity of design and the colors and complexity of the work are absolutely staggering in their variety and execution. This new industry is a fertile field for a survey of changing art styles and the tastes of a rapidly changing culture.

The Arts. In most countries with a largely illiterate population, there are other means for both education and transmission of cultural traditions, and in North Yemen, the oral tradition continues to be very strong. Nearly every tribe and village has its poets and the Yemeni/Arab version of the "minnesinger" who can recall the history and traditions of the area and its people (and can catalog their victories and defeats). Poetry remains a major form of expression as well as of artistic creativity, and it is often used for political and other social purposes, e.g., when satirical or even derogatory verse is composed to attack an opponent or, alternatively, to assist in the amelioration of some conflict or dispute.

Metal doors for sale along the highway.

Unlike many other Arab countries, North Yemen has retained a strong dance tradition. Usually performed by men, with the *jambiyya*, the dances have historical, tribal, and social significance and are rarely accessible to the outsider. Music, on the other hand, tends to be performed on command for weddings and similar occasions, but by low-status groups.

The country's literary tradition is quite strong, but it tends to focus on the same general fields as all of Arab literature: poetry and historical accounts and records. At the moment, there are no widely recognized writers of the novel, the short story, or similar literary forms.

Archaeological investigations of the past decades have uncovered a strong sculptural tradition; some of the sculpture (in both stone and metal) demonstrates uniquely Yemeni forms, and some just as clearly shows the influence of Greek forms and designs. This type of art, however, was not a feature of the Yemeni cultural scene under Islam. On the other hand, the tradition of decorative and illustrated calligraphy, which did flourish throughout the Islamic period, has provided the background for a whole new school of Yemeni artists, who have also been influenced by Western concepts of design, color, and perspective.

For the outsider with some knowledge of North Yemen, perhaps the most striking characteristic of the country today is how little the traditional culture has been affected, at least so far, by some of the events and developments since the revolution. In the rural areas, the Yemenis have fiercely resisted attempts by some of their instructors (usually Egyptians, though there are many Arabs of other nationalities who act as advisers and consultants) to change their language, their social patterns, and their general way of life. On the other hand, in the major cities (most especially Sana'a), one can clearly see the effect of these same influences: an increasing bureaucratization of public life and an "Egyptianization" of the mechanisms of government agencies and bodies. It seems fair to say that North Yemen has so far shown an amazing resilience in the face of the multitude of foreign influences to which it has recently been subjected; on the other hand, the persistence and sheer magnitude of such an onslaught has led to the development of various fundamentalist and ultranationalist movements in other countries, and it is as yet not at all certain that North Yemen will not experience some of the same in the future.

NOTES

1. Hans Steffen et al., *Final Report of the Airphoto Interpretation Project* (Zurich: Swiss Technical Co-operation Service, 1978), esp. Part One, "The Physical Setting," pp. 3–29.

2. Yemen Arab Republic, *Statistical Year Book 1985* (Sana'a: Central Planning Organization, 1986), p. 31.

3. Manfred Wenner, *Modern Yemen 1918–1966* (Baltimore, MD: Johns Hopkins Press, 1967), pp. 29–30.

4. On the religious divisions in the population, see the following: Wenner, *Modern Yemen*, pp. 30–37; R. B. Serjeant, "The Zaydis," and A.A.A. Fyzee, "The Isma'ilis," both in A. J. Arberry, *Religion in the Middle East*, vol. 2 (Cambridge: Cambridge University Press, 1969), pp. 285–301, and 318–329, respectively; Reuben Ahroni, *Yemenite Jewry* (Bloomington: Indiana University Press, 1986); Yosef Tobi, "Histoire de la communauté juive de Yemen au XIXe and XXe Siecles," in Joseph Chelhod, *L'Arabie du Sud* (Paris: Maisonneuve et Larose, 1984–1985), 2:119–137; and Aviva Klein-Franke, "The Jews of Yemen," in Werner Daum, ed., *Yemen* (Innsbruck: Pinguin; Frankfurt: Umschau [1988]), pp. 265–280 and 297–299.

5. A good introduction to the role of the tribes in contemporary North Yemen may be found in Paul Dresch, "Tribal Relations and Political History in Upper Yemen," in B. R. Pridham, ed., *Contemporary Yemen* (London: Croom Helm, 1984), pp. 154–174. See also Joseph Chelhod, "L'organisation tribale," in Chelhod, *L'Arabie du Sud*, 3:39–62.

6. Among the more important contemporary studies of this fascinating subject are Werner Dostal, "Traditional Economy and Society," in Daum, *Yemen*, pp. 336–366; Tomas Gerholm, *Market, Mosque, and Mafraj* (Stockholm: University

of Stockholm, 1977); and Joseph Chelhod, "L'ordre sociale," in Chelhod, *L'Arabie du Sud*, 3:15–37.

7. On various aspects of the legal system of the past, as well as the changes currently taking place, see S. H. Amin, *Law and Justice in Contemporary Yemen* (Glasgow: Royston, 1987); Joseph Chelhod, "Le System Juridique Traditionnel," in Chelhod, *L'Arabie du Sud*, 3:127–181 [three essays]; and the works of Brinkley Messick, incl. "Kissing Hands and Knees: Hegemony and Hierarchy in Shari'a Discourse," *Law and Society Review* 24 (1988), pp. 601–623, and "Transactions in Ibb: Economy and Society in a Yemeni Highland Town" (Ph.D. dissertation, Princeton University, 1978).

8. It is possible that this situation was, in part, owing to the fact that the word for the traditional code in southwestern Arabia is *shari'*; in the more inaccessible areas of North Yemen, where tribal independence was valued more highly than any ideology (often including Islam), perhaps the similarity of the two words and the consequent potential for confusion accounted for the continued vitality of tribal law at the expense of Islamic law—especially the idea of collective responsibility and the concepts of collective punishment.

9. The architecture has appealed to many visitors and specialists, so the pictorial literature is quite large. Perhaps the best of the pictorial introductions is provided by Fernando Varanda, *Art of Building in Yemen* (Cambridge, MA: MIT Press, 1982); more analytical treatments are found in Suzanne Hirschi and Max Hirschi, *L'Architecture au Yemen du Nord* (Paris: Berger-Levrault, 1983), and Lucien Golvin and M.-C. Fromont, *Architecture et Urbanisme* (Paris: Editions Recherche sur les Civilisations, 1984).

10. On clothing in the highlands of North Yemen, see Martha Mundy, "Sana'a Dress 1920–1975," in R. B. Serjeant and R. Lewcock, eds., *Sana'a, An Arabian Islamic City* (London: World of Islam Festival Trust, 1983), pp. 529–541.

11. On the role of women in North Yemen, the most important works to consult are Carla Makhlouf, *Changing Veils* (London: Croom Helm, 1979); Cynthia Myntti, *Women and Development in Yemen Arab Republic* (Eschborn: German Agency for Technical Cooperation, 1979); Susan Dorsky, *Women of 'Amran* (Salt Lake City: University of Utah Press, 1986); and Gisela Frese-Weghoeft, *Ein Leben in der Unsichtbarkeit* (Reinbek/Hamburg: Rowohlt, 1987).

12. The literature on the Yemeni diet remains relatively slight, though some important studies have been undertaken. The most important contemporary sources are Annika Bornstein, *Food and Society in the Yemen Arab Republic* (Rome: Food and Agricultural Organization, 1974), and the *Yemen Arab Republic National Nutrition Survey 1979* (Washington, DC: USAID, 1979)—a study conducted by the Yemen General Grain Corporation, the Ministry of Supply, the Ministry of Health, and the U.S. Department of Health and Human Services and the Agency for International Development; see also R. B. Serjeant, A. Qaryah, and A. Bornstein, "Sana'a Food and Cookery," in Serjeant and Lewcock, eds., *Sana'a*, pp. 542–558.

13. Probably no subject has produced as much literature and debate concerning North Yemen as *qat*. Although the literature on this subject cannot be

adequately covered here, the three most important works to consult, in terms of both treatment and bibliography, are John G. Kennedy, *The Flower of Paradise* (Boston and Dordrecht, Neth.: D. Reidel Publishing Company, 1987); Shelagh Weir, *Qat in Yemen* (London: British Museum, 1985); and, Armin Schopen, *Das Qat* (Wiesbaden: Franz Steiner Verlag, 1978).

3

Economic Problems
and Prospects

Until the revolution of 1962, North Yemen had one of the least developed economies in the entire world. This situation was, at least in part, the result of a deliberate policy decision on the part of the imams, who wished to keep the country aloof from the outside world, and as a consequence, they brought North Yemen closer to autarky than any other state in the mid-twentieth century.

Then, as now, the economy was dominated by agriculture: North Yemen has the most fertile land on the Arabian Peninsula, and agriculture is the traditional occupation of the population. Moreover, it was the obvious sector to emphasize in the imams' desire for autarky, since it is the sector least amenable to foreign manipulation and intervention, as well as the one in which North Yemen has the clearest marginal advantage.

Since 1962, agriculture has remained the most important aspect of the country's economy, but in that sector and in other sectors of the economy, there have been many changes. This chapter presents a brief summary of those changes as well as a look at some of North Yemen's economic problems and prospects for the future.

THE AGRICULTURAL SECTOR

The production of basic foodstuffs continues to be the primary occupation of a majority of the population. Moreover, agriculture is the only real source of foreign exchange earnings and will probably be the basis of the future wealth of the country (despite the recent discovery of oil).[1]

In the 1980s, agricultural activity directly or indirectly employed more than 80 percent of the population. In many instances, however, this activity—though often sophisticated, appropriate to the terrain and local factor endowments, and essential to the economy—is neither particularly efficient nor productive. Since the revolution, the government has either obtained funds from foreign donors or itself funded various programs aimed at diversification and development. Such efforts have, until recently, taken second place to efforts at industrialization, however, and the result has been that the percentage of the population engaged in agriculture has declined, as has this sector's contribution to the gross domestic product (GDP). A number of factors and problems must be distinguished in order to present an accurate picture of the current situation.

Traditionally, the Yemeni farmer practiced the dual strategy of risk aversion and subsistence production; in other words, he sought to produce a small surplus as a result of his farming, but this surplus was primarily designed to protect him (and his family) against future failures (owing to drought, crop disease, etc.) rather than to be used to purchase goods. He also raised a few animals for dairy products, meat, transport or draft purposes, and perhaps clothing. Because of heavy taxation, he had little incentive to substantially increase his production of either crops or animals, much less experiment with different strains or breeds when those he knew were appropriate to the conditions he had to cope with.

The most important variables, of course, have always been the fertility (quality) of the soil and access to water (which in North Yemen is available from different sources—rain, spring, spate, wells, etc.). One of the most striking features of the Yemeni countryside, as already indicated, is the widespread terracing, which covers the sides of nearly every hill and mountain throughout the western half of the country. These terraces were established in an effort to cope with the two major variables. Terracing is a way to retain fertile soil (often of volcanic origin), and that fertility has been preserved through the centuries by careful composting practices employing both animal and green manures. Terracing also makes possible a conservative use of the available water supply, which is carefully channeled and retained as much as possible for multiple use. In other words, the terraces make possible excellent drainage, soil retention, and ecologically sound land practices, and they have elicited profound respect from foreign agronomists and hydraulic engineers alike.

However, the fact that one has developed a sophisticated mechanism for agricultural purposes does not guarantee that the agricultural techniques themselves will always be successful. In North Yemen, the single most important variable is rainfall, for more than 85 percent of the arable land is dependent upon the weather for its water supply.[2] When a drought occurs, there are usually no alternative sources of water, so the terraces tend to deteriorate and previous investments in the other factors of production are also lost (e.g., the composting, the drainage channels, and often even the work animals). Droughts sometimes last more than five years, but they do not occur with any regularity or predictability. One of

Terraced hillside: an agricultural coping technique.

the most serious droughts in modern times took place during the civil war (1962–1970), and it had a major impact upon the ability of many mountain tribes, who supported the imam, to supply themselves. The only alternative source of fodder and food (as well as animals in some instances) was the republican government, which had access to external resources. That government was therefore able to use its ability to provide needed supplies as a lever to gain tribal support.

Exactly how much arable land is there? Since no cadastral survey has ever been undertaken, there is no precise answer, and the experts have offered wildly different estimates. The World Bank currently classifies 25 percent of the total land area as agricultural, i.e., land that is regularly cultivated, marginally cultivated (only in years of good rainfall), or covered with woody vegetation (which can be harvested for fuel). The remainder is classified as rocky, mountainous, semi-arid, or scrub grazing land. That percentage amounts to about 1.5 million hectares (3.7 million acres), of which fewer than 250,000 hectares (617,000 acres) are irrigated.[3]

North Yemen's 1981 agricultural census indicated that field crops accounted for at least three-fourths of all production, with sorghum and millet accounting for 80 percent of all the cereals grown (all are consumed locally). Sorghum has been the traditional rural staple; its grain is used in porridges and bread, and the stalks and other remnants provide food for cattle as well as fuel for the Yemeni household oven (the *tannur*).[4]

A number of significant changes have occurred in the agricultural sector since the end of the civil war, the most important being the change from subsistence agriculture in many parts of North Yemen, the concomitant introduction and increased production of nontraditional food crops, and an astronomical increase in the use of diesel-powered pumps to provide water.

Food Crops

Although agricultural production accounts for about 35 percent of the GDP, North Yemen is incapable of producing sufficient foodstuffs to feed its population at the present time. The explanation for this somewhat unusual state of affairs is a fairly complex one, and the reasons help to illustrate a number of unusual features of the Yemeni economy in the 1980s.[5]

One reason is that transportation continues to be difficult. In many, if not most, areas of the country, there are still no real roads (in the sense of all-weather links that can be used by motorized vehicles) between the producing areas and the domestic market. In fact, many villages are still accessible only by foot or by animal power; even four-wheel-drive vehicles are incapable of maneuvering on many of the narrow and stony paths that were the standard links of the past. There has been some improvement in the road system, but much remains to be done to link the producing areas with the major markets. This is the reason why the people in most areas of North Yemen, when queried about priorities for government assistance programs, consistently list roads among the top priorities (along with schools, clinics, and a reliable water supply).

Another reason why North Yemen must still import foods, and it is related to the first one, is that the rural distribution and marketing system is still largely the same as in the days of the imams. In the past, the entire country (with the exceptions of Sana'a, Ta'izz, and Hodeida) was serviced by a network of market towns that were open for business only one day a week. Merchants, traders, craftspeople, etc., moved from town to town in the span of a week (spending the same day of the week in the same town each week). Buyers and sellers from the immediate vicinity of each such market town thus participated in the economy (by buying or selling) only one day a week. This tradition, of course, was the result of the population distribution pattern, the geography, and the lack of roads. As new roads are built, especially feeder tracks, and as communications in general improve, merchants and traders are opening facilities in all areas of the country, and many markets now operate on a daily rather than a weekly basis.

Another factor is the dependence of most agriculture on regular (natural) rainfall, but as pumps become more prevalent, this dependence is decreasing in some areas. This change has enabled farmers to start truck farms in the vicinity of major urban areas, offer new crops, and expand the production of other varieties. It has also, it is worth noting, brought about some changes in land ownership patterns and the income levels of individuals associated with the production, distribution, and sale of foodstuffs.

The mass emigration of adult males to find work in other countries, which took place in the late 1970s and continues to a lesser extent, also has had an effect on food production. Another, and for the moment the last, reason is the relatively high cost of the factors of production in North Yemen in comparison with their cost in the countries that now provide most of the food North Yemen imports; examples include wheat from the United States, beef from Australia, and chicken from France. For an amazing variety of foods, the cost of an imported item (including transportation costs as well as the often high customs duties) is lower than the cost of the equivalent item produced at home.

Generalizations concerning agriculture in North Yemen are difficult because of regional, geographic, and demographic variations. There is, however, one generalization that is possible and relevant: There has been a historical shift in the locus of agricultural activity in the past 2,000 years, and this shift appears to be continuing. Archaeological, archaeo-agricultural, and paleographical evidence appear to show that agriculture some 2,000 years ago was centered in the eastern highlands—where the great pre-Islamic kingdoms were located. In more recent times, the center of agricultural activity has moved rather methodically westward. Until fairly recently, it was located in the central highlands, especially in the plains around Ibb and Dhamar, as well as in the southern uplands around Ta'izz. Since the revolution, it appears to be moving further westward into the foothills and onto the Tihama.[6] This slow but perceptible process is having an impact on the relationship between the various regions of the country and their economic and political strength in domestic affairs (although the discovery of oil in Ma'rib Province will markedly enhance that area's position in internal jockeying for government services and perquisites).

The major agricultural regions of the country may be quickly listed, along with their characteristics:[7]

1. The northern highlands (from Sana'a north to Sa'dah). Here the soil is of limited fertility, rainfall tends to be erratic, and a dependence upon wells has developed in recent years. The major crops are cereals (sorghum, millet, wheat, and barley) and a few fruits (primarily grapes) and vegetables (for the urban markets); here also is the center of livestock raising—sheep, goats, and cattle.

2. The south-central highlands, centered around Ibb. This area is one of the two best agricultural areas in the country because of its broad, open plains and more regular and extensive rainfall. It is the mountains on the western edge of this plateau that are extensively terraced, and these produce cereals, vegetables, and some pulses.

3. The southern highlands, centered around Ta'izz and extending southward. Here there is almost always abundant rainfall, and the percentage of cultivable as well as marginal land (which can be brought into production in years of high rainfall) is higher than anywhere else. Major crops are cereals, pulses, potatoes and other vegetables, fruits, and some coffee and *qat*.

4. The western slopes of the highlands, from Hajjah in the north through Mahwit (northwest of Sana'a), down through Manakhah, and south. The steep ravines and valleys of this area are nearly all terraced and are primarily cultivated with cereals, coffee, and *qat* (in the higher elevations). The valley floors, which have rivers and often very fertile soil (which has washed down from the terraces), are usually planted in sorghum, though extensive areas are now given over to bananas, papayas, melons, and a range of similar subtropical and tropical fruits, all for local markets.

5. The eastern slopes of the highlands. Here the emphasis is upon livestock raising, though some villages have sufficient water to raise some cereals and vegetables. The primary problem is that as the demand for meat increases, and the local population attempts to meet that demand, more and more animals are grazed on what was, from the outset, only marginal, scrub-covered rangeland. In a textbook example of the exploitation of a natural resource beyond its carrying capacity, livestock production has decreased, and a substantial part of the land has been denuded of all vegetative cover, thus leaving it open to massive erosion during the irregular (but usually torrential) downpours.

6. The Tihama, which may be divided into two distinct sub-regions: (a) the area closest to the coast, which has almost no rainfall, only scrub growth for a very limited number of grazing animals, and a socioeconomic orientation toward the sea and its resources; and (b) the area closest to the foothills, which is blessed with fertile soil and relatively abundant water. The first contains large alluvial fans formed by deposits carried by the streams from the highlands; the second benefits from the streams themselves and an extensive system of wells that tap the underground sources (which ultimately, of course, derive their supply from aquifers that are fed from highland sources). The crops in the second region are cereals (sorghum, millet, sesame), a few vegetables (mainly tomatoes), and dates. There has also been an increase in the past few decades on the raising of tobacco, cotton, and other vegetables for the urban markets.

The various development programs the government has supported, encouraged, or sought from foreign donors are designed to diversify and further develop this portion of the Tihama plain.

Cash Crops

The two most important cash crops in Yemen are *qat* and coffee. *Qat* has been discussed earlier (Chapter 2) in connection with Yemeni cultural patterns, but traditionally, at least since the sixteenth century, coffee was the most important crop, in that it provided the major part of foreign exchange earnings and it put North Yemen on the international map.

Yemeni tradition places the discovery of both coffee and *qat* at the same place: al-Udayn ("the two twigs"), between Ta'izz and Ibb. Although most Western literature repeats an absurd and fanciful account of its discovery by an Ethiopian goatherd (originally promoted by an Italian writer), it would appear that the coffee plant is native to the highlands of Ethiopia, North Yemen, and Kenya. In fact, many scientists have noted the similarity in the geomorphology, flora, and fauna of these three countries and suggested that this correspondence is the result of their having been part of the same landmass until the Great Rift Valley developed, which includes the Red Sea basin.[8]

It appears certain today that the discovery that the beans of the coffee plant have an effect upon the human central nervous system was the result of a deliberate search for elixirs which would produce (or facilitate) visions, presumably thereby giving the individual greater or easier access to manifestations of the godhead. In North Yemen, this search for such elixirs was undertaken by members of the Shadhili Sufi order, which had major concentrations of members in southwestern Arabia in the Middle Ages. Apparently, one of the order's shaykhs, who lived in Mocha in the late thirteenth or early fourteenth century, seems to have stumbled on the technique for making a cup of coffee, with the result that the drink was for long known as Shadhiliyya.[9]

By the year 1500, the consumption of coffee was a widespread habit on the Arabian Peninsula; shortly thereafter, because of trading and commercial contacts, its use spread to western and central Europe. Despite attempts (in both Arabia and Europe) to prevent its spread and use (theologians in both regions condemned it as being related to alcohol), coffee was soon in great demand almost everywhere. For a brief time, North Yemen had a monopoly on its trade and sought to enforce and retain this monopoly by preventing the plant from leaving the country. The major port through which the coffee was exported was Mocha, and it is from that city that the variety grown in North Yemen derived its name. In Western markets, the name Mocha (Mocca) is synonymous with particularly good coffee; in the United States, this type is usually combined with beans from Java (whose plants, incidentally, were smuggled there directly from Mocha in the sixteenth century) to make the Mocha-Java variety that is found in specialty shops.

Nearly all of the world's languages derived their word for the beverage from the Arabic *qahwa*, but the Yemenis have their own terminology and also prepare the drink differently. After the beans are harvested, the Yemenis separate the husk from the bean and prepare the beverage known as *qishr* from the husk. The bean itself is sold, and the drink that is made from it (after it has been ground to a fine powder) is known as *bunn*. Whether or not this unique method of preparing coffee is the result of a desire to have the advantages of coffee as a beverage while still being able to market the bean is unknown.

In any event, coffee was North Yemen's largest source of foreign exchange for a long time—in the 1930s, the annual export was in excess of 10,000 tons—but today's production is only around 3,500 tons per year. One reason for this substantial drop is that quality control measures deteriorated, and although a ready market existed, Yemeni coffee became uneven in quality so that purchasing it became risky. Recently, the government has sought to cope with this problem and has undertaken measures to restore the prestige of the Mocha variety in the major Western markets. A second reason is that the rate of return, not to mention the speed with which the grower obtains that return, has also deteriorated. Since coffee and *qat* sometimes compete for the same land and the rate of return as well as the speed thereof is far higher for *qat*, some growers have replaced older coffee trees with the *qat* shrub. On the other hand, as some recent research has shown, there is no evidence that healthy coffee trees have been uprooted and replaced with *qat*, and there is evidence that the vast expansion in *qat* plantations has often been on land that was previously marginal (often facilitated by the low cost of some modern tube wells).[10]

Despite the decline in quantity and quality, coffee still ranks second in terms of (visible) foreign exchange earnings. The amount earned from the export of *qat* is not recorded; although *qat* is still sent to South Yemen (despite efforts by that country to eliminate its use and cultivation) and across the Red Sea, government statistics on these exports are not particularly reliable—not because of government manipulation or reluctance to report accurately, but because of a long tradition on the part of *qat* traders and dealers to operate outside government control. Nevertheless, it is quite likely that besides being the major domestic cash crop, *qat* ranks in the first five as an export crop as well.

Nonfood Crops

The two major nonfood crops of North Yemen are cotton and tobacco.[11] Although introduced into the country on a commercial basis only since World War II, cotton rapidly became the major cash export crop; by the mid-1970s, production was nearly 30,000 tons per year. A precipitous decline in the price of cotton severely hurt this part of North Yemen's economy, however, and by the mid-1980s, production was down to about 4,200 tons—a small increase from the disastrous yields of only 2,000 tons of a few years earlier. The Spinning and Weaving Corporation, a government enterprise established to use the cotton crop, was at one time the largest industry in the country—in terms of persons employed as well as in the value of its production. At one time, it was hoped that locally made cotton goods would eliminate the demand for foreign textiles, but the country simply could not compete in terms of the variety of materials or styles, and often in terms of price as well. This industry nevertheless remains an important component of domestic industrial development.

Tobacco growing increased as the result of an effort to take advantage of the soil and climatic conditions of the Tihama (although some forms of tobacco has been grown in North Yemen in other areas). In recent years, no doubt owing to the skyrocketing demand for cigarettes in the developing areas generally, tobacco has surpassed cotton in importance (now about 7,000 tons per year). Since this crop is amenable to industrial farming (i.e., highly mechanized) techniques, one may expect that the acreage devoted to it will increase, despite its disastrous effects upon the soil.

Animal Husbandry

Nearly all of North Yemen's smallholders, tenant farmers, and agriculturalists have traditionally raised some livestock as well. Camels, donkeys, and cattle provided the major source of energy prior to electrification, and they are still used as draft animals (on the terraces and small holdings) to provide power for wells, and for personal transportation. In part, of course, they are also raised for the milk and meat they contribute to the people's diet. Sheep are also raised to provide milk and meat as well as wool and hides. In recent years, chickens—as layers as well as for meat—have become the major additional source of protein for most of the Yemeni population (indeed, the first foreign fast food chain to open in North Yemen was Kentucky Fried Chicken).

Perhaps the single most important factor to affect the animal husbandry sector was the prolonged drought of the late 1960s: it has been estimated that as much as 25 percent of the country's livestock was lost during this period. Since that time there have been many efforts (by foreign donors) to improve the existing strains of the major food animals, but unfortunately, many of these efforts have met with very indifferent success (although more recent efforts have been more successful). For example, attempts by the British Overseas Development Ministry to cross the European chicken (characterized by greater egg productivity as well as a meatier carcass) with the Yemeni chicken ran into problems because of the ferocity of the local variety—the first imported males were pecked to death.

Under the imams, and for many centuries prior to the current one, the raising of high-quality horses was a proud tradition in North Yemen, especially in the south-central highlands around Ibb, and there was a great demand for these animals from central Arabia as well as other countries. The civil war, however, practically eliminated horse raising as an industry. Most of the horses were sequestered by the republican government for use by the army, and the remainder were almost all slaughtered for food during the drought and its attendant period of starvation in the highlands. Government statistics still listed horses under animal stock into the 1970s but no longer do so, and there does not seem to be any organized effort to restore the horse-raising industry.

Although not actually a part of animal husbandry, North Yemen's honey used to be highly prized for its quality and taste, and beekeeping was a widespread and well-known part of Yemeni agriculture. Although the industry suffered a drastic decline during the civil war, the contemporary traveler will once again see apiaries throughout the highlands. Although there is no government program to support beekeeping, the renewed demand for Yemeni honey may mean that more farmers go into that business, especially to satisfy local demand for another *baladi* (domestic) product.

This review of North Yemen's agricultural resources shows that the situation is far from wholly depressing; indeed, the country's agricultural riches are quite substantial and clearly amenable to expansion and improvement. Like many other countries of the Third World, however, the possibilities were not either recognized or considered important by many of the earlier political leaders, who were more intent upon industrial investment and expansion. As a later section, which concentrates on how the government has sought to develop the economy since the revolution, will show, however, there has been a pronounced shift in emphasis since the late 1970s.

THE INDUSTRIAL SECTOR

Although a few enterprises—public and private—trace their origins to the prerevolutionary period, major efforts toward industrialization have occurred only since 1962. All of the major firms that have any impact on the domestic economy today—in terms of either employment and productivity or as import-replacement operations—date from the period after the 1962 revolution. In monetary terms, these industries contribute about 50 percent to the GDP; in employment terms, their contribution is minimal (perhaps 5 percent of the total, i.e., fewer than 50,000 jobs). If one adds two of the major growth industries of the 1980s, transportation and construction, the sector employs another 85,000 to 100,000 persons, about another 10 percent of the total.[12]

Like many new governments in the Third World, the post-revolutionary leaders began by emphasizing a program of industrial development as the best means to bring about economic development and an increased standard of living. Furthermore, it was expected that domestic industry would decrease the country's dependence upon foreign imports. Unfortunately, although there are a few notable success stories, progress generally has not been as rapid as either the government or the population probably hoped, for a number of rather obvious reasons.

First, once again the mountainous terrain plays an important role. The geography of the country, combined with government policy in the past, resulted in a rudimentary domestic transportation network, and the immense cost of building roads, even feeder tracks, and the difficult social issues which must be confronted before construction can even begin (i.e., whose land will be sacrificed for the roads) are important barriers to the expansion of the domestic economy, including the market for industrial goods.

Second, the level of technical and industrial skills among the population is low. Although this particular problem could be ameliorated through the development of a school system, that is easier said than done. To develop an effective educational infrastructure requires a large investment in personnel as well as buildings and ancillary materials. The government's resources are simply not adequate, and the task of starting almost from square one means that the process will be a slow one. Important progress has been made—the number of schools and instructors increases each year, and there is now a national university in Sana'a— but it will be many years before the educational level of the population is adequate. (For the Yemenis, "adequate" means Yemenis are capable of carrying out all the significant administrative and other duties that foreign nationals, especially Egyptians, have been fulfilling.)

Third, the relative costs of the other major industrial inputs—power (energy), water, and land—are extraordinarily high. Furthermore, the supplies of power and water are unreliable. Electricity, for example, is subject to periodic disruption, though this particular problem will probably decrease in importance as the number of generating plants increases and the national grid is improved. Nevertheless, the fact that electricity costs on the average four times per kilowatt what it does in the industrialized countries is a major deterrent to the development of industry.

The supply of water varies significantly from area to area throughout the country, and one of the cities with the greatest attraction to industry because of its size and wealth, Sana'a, is one of those with the most precarious water supplies. Furthermore, the hydraulic engineers have been suggesting recently that the large number of tube wells and the lack of effective water conservation measures are depleting the known groundwater reserves at a rate that is rapidly lowering the water table.

Land prices have reached such levels that it is probably impossible to amortize a land purchase in any reasonable amount of time. For example, although agricultural land sells for perhaps as little as the equivalent of $11,115 per hectare ($4,500 per acre), there are many instances in which land on a major road or in an urban area has been sold for more than $617,500 per hectare ($250,000 an acre). There were even some land purchases in the early 1980s at more than $6.175 million per hectare ($2.5 million per acre)—higher than land on New York's Fifth Avenue, Zurich's Bahnhofstrasse, or Paris's Champs Elysées.[13]

Fourth, high labor costs make it difficult if not impossible for North Yemen's industry to effectively compete with other countries. Although other Third World countries have managed to attract industries from the First World as a result of inexpensive, trained labor, North Yemen's labor costs are invariably equal to, if not higher than, those in nearly every other Middle Eastern country or those in many southern European countries (e.g., Spain and Italy).

The Yemeni worker has developed an enviable reputation as reliable, industrious, and quick learning. If nothing else, the fact that hundreds of thousands of Yemeni males have been willing to leave their homeland to earn additional income (discussed in the next section) says something about their willingness to engage in manual labor, and even hard physical labor, for extended periods of time away from their families and country. But the readiness of many young Yemenis to leave for work in the Gulf states, or even in Western Europe or North America, in the effort to increase their income has increased the cost of labor in North Yemen itself. Highly skilled Yemeni laborers in such important areas as carpentry and masonry earn upward of $85 a day, thereby largely eliminating the need to emigrate in the search for higher income. (On the other hand, many Yemenis who have emigrated have cited as a major advantage of emigration the fact that with no access to *qat* in other countries, a far greater percentage of their earnings can be saved for use at home.) The emigration of laborers has had one important side effect: The North Yemen government has had to import foreign labor in order to undertake some of the development projects and construction activities it has funded (and construction battalions have also been brought in by some of the foreign donors, e.g., China, to undertake the projects they have donated).

Despite all the problems, the number of new industrial enterprises in some areas is astronomical. Although the sectors in which these enterprises have been started are rather limited, they have made a significant impact on the domestic economy; most of them are concentrated in metalworking (for example, the making of doors and frames), carpentry, small-engine and automotive repair, the manufacture of building materials (cement blocks, stonework, etc.), and trade. To some degree, of course, these businesses reflect the skills that laborers who emigrated and have returned acquired abroad, though in many cases the Yemeni economy (in both financial and social terms) is not ready for the skills that Yemenis have learned in the Gulf states and elsewhere. For example, there is no great demand for, or interest in, linoleum-floor laying, nor is there any great demand for lettuce pickers or artichoke harvesters.

At the present time, the most successful of the industrial enterprises in North Yemen is undoubtedly the series of government ventures that were created as import substitution industries in the 1970s: the Yemen Biscuit Company (now a major earner of foreign exchange, largely because of exports to South Yemen); soft-drink manufacturing firms; a dairy (producing a variety of milk products); and similar firms.

EMIGRATION OF WORKERS

The really significant growth in the Yemeni economy, at an average annual rate of more than 5.6 percent, began in the mid-1970s,[14] and it is quite possible to argue that the most important engine of this growth was the rapid increase in the rate of emigration during this period. Emigration has been a characteristic of the population of the southwestern corner of the Arabian Peninsula for more than 3,000 years.[15] The comparatively mild (temperate) climate, the regular rainfall, the high percentage (and absolute amount) of arable land appear to have been conducive to producing a rather large population, and the "surplus population" has always emigrated. At times, particularly in the distant past, this emigration seems to have been undertaken by whole clans and tribes (some of which are found today in Oman and Saudi Arabia). At other times, it has been on a largely individual basis (with some famous Yemenis found in various places in the Islamic world at different times). There have been variations in population and emigration, and these are the subject of some dispute: some writers attribute them to climatic changes; others are more inclined to attribute them to technological, sociological, and even political factors (associated with various regimes, leaders, or changes in the prevailing ideology).

The modern period of Yemeni emigration may be divided into two phases: from the middle of the nineteenth century to the end of the country's civil war (1970) and from 1970 to the present. In the first phase, Yemeni emigration took place to the following areas: (1) Aden, Djibouti, and other major urban centers in the lower Red Sea region; (2) East Africa, especially former Tanganyika, Kenya, Ethiopia, Sudan, and Uganda; (3) the Far East, especially Java and Sumatra, Indochina (primarily around Saigon), and India; and (4) the West, especially Great Britain (Wales) and the United States (the Detroit area, primarily Dearborn). During this period, most of the emigrants were from the Shafi'i areas of the country.

With the end of the civil war, the dramatic rise in the price of oil during the first half of the 1970s, and the resulting economic boom in Saudi Arabia and the Gulf states, the pattern and the magnitude of Yemeni emigration began to change. Whereas in the roughly 100-year period prior to the early 1970s the total number of Yemeni migrants might have amounted to perhaps 200,000, that figure was now reached and exceeded in the space of less than a decade. Although it is likely that we will never know exactly how many Yemenis migrated during the peak years (roughly 1973–1979), it has often been alleged that at the height of the exodus perhaps more than 1 million Yemenis were working in Saudi Arabia and the Gulf states alone.

In 1975, it was estimated that 1.23 million Yemenis were employed abroad in all countries, a significant proportion of the total population of North Yemen. Of that number, it was estimated that some 600,000 or so were employed in the peninsula states; the remainder were in other countries in the Red Sea region, Western Europe, and North America, where they continued to think of themselves as Yemenis and had every intention of returning home at some point in the not-too-distant future.

Consequences of Emigration

The consequences and implications of such large-scale emigration have been the subjects of considerable theoretical interest and some empirical studies. There is widespread agreement that it has had some significant consequences—for North Yemen as well as the receiving countries—but very little agreement on what those consequences might be or what their significance might be for the future of North Yemen and its economy. For example, at the height of the exodus, some scholars suggested that the thousands of Yemeni workers in Saudi Arabia essentially held that country's economic development "hostage"; others argued that the Saudis could send the Yemenis home whenever they chose, thereby wreaking potential havoc on the economy and the social conditions there—in other words, Saudi Arabia held North Yemen "hostage" rather than the other way around.

Further debates have been occasioned by the large sums of money the Yemeni migrants have remitted home, and these debates have produced all of the following arguments, assertions, and consequences:

1. An acute labor shortage developed in North Yemen itself, in both the agricultural areas and the urban areas. As a result, the government was forced to import labor from Korea, the Philippines, etc., in order to get needed infrastructural work done. In the rural areas, it led to an increased role for women, both in their financial responsibilities as well as in actual field work, but not necessarily an improvement in their status.

2. Because the emigrants sent back more than $1 billion in some years and there were also very limited opportunities for local investment, a horrendous inflation occurred in those few investment areas that did exist (land, construction) and the bride-price as well as in the price of all imported commodities.

3. There was an unbelievable escalation in the availability of consumer goods. At first, these goods were what Westerners tend to call necessities—better clothing, furniture, other household goods, and a better diet—but a wide range of other commodities soon became available: foreign and gourmet foods, electrical-generating equipment (trekked into remote villages to supply the power for color televisions, video recorders, etc.), motor vehicles (many utterly inappropriate for the conditions of the Yemeni transportation system), and imported wares which destroyed many of the local industries and crafts. Plastic replaced the beautiful traditional baskets, aluminum replaced the traditional pots and cooking utensils, and nylon and other synthetics replaced cotton and wool. AK-47s replaced handmade rifles as well as the more traditional Springfields and Mausers, Pepsi-Cola and other similar sugar-water drinks replaced juices, Wonderbread and its analogues replaced the traditional breads, etc., etc.

4. There was also a slow but definite stimulus to the development of local entrepreneurs and small businesspeople, as they used savings from foreign employment in order to open their own shops and businesses (often in locations far removed from their traditional tribal, familial, or previous economic locales).

5. The availability of large sums of money in many small villages was often channeled (usually through traditional local cooperative mechanisms) into infrastructural improvements (such as the construction of a school building, a rudimentary water system, or a new feeder road), all decided upon and implemented with little or no government participation or support.

6. Opportunities for social mobility substantially improved. Elements of the society that had been locked into particular occupations and status rankings because of their birth now had the economic wherewithal to effect change, which was usually accomplished by using remittances to purchase land or to establish a different business. Such change often involved moving far from the traditional residence, usually to the urban centers of Sana'a or Ta'izz, where a person's former social ranking was usually unknown or likely to be ignored if the new business was a success.

7. There was a tremendous stimulus to the growth and availability of *qat*: individuals who previously could not afford to participate in chews more than once or twice a week now managed to participate four or five times, or even every day of the week. This spread in the use and distribution of *qat* also contributed to improvements in the transportation as well as the marketing systems of the country; it thus, indirectly, also helped to improve the market for other cash crops, including the many new varieties of fruits and vegetables that began to appear with regularity even in smaller villages and towns. It also contributed to an increase in government revenues, as the government sought (often successfully) to concentrate the marketing of *qat* in specific localities, where it could more easily be taxed.

8. The remittances contributed to maintaining if not exacerbating the split between the rural and the urban populations of the country. The national banking, credit, and commercial systems were all tied to the major urban centers, and the rural areas had no access to any effective assistance programs in their efforts to keep pace with the changes in consumption patterns as well as the overall changes in the nature of the economy.

9. Last, and in this case perhaps most important, the changes made the Yemeni economy almost completely dependent upon the oil-exporting states of the peninsula as a source of foreign exchange with which to cover the skyrocketing domestic demand.

The extent of this dependence began to dawn on the government and the various donor countries in the early 1980s as the demand for Yemeni labor in many of the peninsula states declined. The causes for the drop in the demand are many, but they include, one, the participation of Yemenis in various social movements, especially in Saudi Arabia, that sought to change the social, economic, and especially politico-religious nature of that state (e.g., the participation of Yemenis in the abortive occupation of the Grand Mosque in Mecca in 1979). Two, the demands of Yemeni workers escalated as far as salary, living conditions and similar aspects of their employment were concerned. And three, as revenues from oil escalated dramatically, the Saudis tended to contract for more and more monumental development projects, often from major Western firms specializing in turn-key projects. These firms generally negotiated labor contracts with major Asian firms, which could provide cheap and reliable laborers who would never wish, or be able, to participate in movements for change, since they were neither Muslim nor Arab. For the same reasons, these laborers could be completely isolated from the Saudi population. In fact, by the middle 1980s, most construction labor on such development projects in Saudi Arabia consisted of South Koreans, Filipinos, and other Asian nationals.

Comparison of Yemeni Emigration with Experience of Other Countries

The developments that have occurred as a result of the emigration have, of course, interested academics as well as policymakers. Studies of the Yemeni economy since the early 1970s have helped to clarify our understanding of the consequences of mass emigration; in another sense, however, these analyses have also highlighted how limited the scholarly coverage of Third World countries really is.

In some respects, the North Yemen example bears out the findings from other states that have had a similar experience. The population is better housed, better clothed, and better fed than was the case in the past (as a result of the remittances). In a country where the standards for such matters were arguably among the lowest in the world, this improvement is a significant accomplishment if one considers that most of it took place in the space of less than a decade. Furthermore, consumption levels have risen dramatically; many if not most Yemenis can afford (or at least buy) nearly all of the marginal goods and luxuries: electronic equipment of all kinds (television sets, cassette players, video recorders, calculators, digital watches, etc.), motorized vehicles (from the most expensive Mercedes-Benz sedans through the Hondas, Toyotas, and four-wheel-drive Land Cruisers down to the lowliest motorcycle for teenagers); foods of all varieties (frozen, canned, and fresh) from nearly all continents; textiles and clothing from countries as disparate as the United States and the People's Republic of China—the list is unending.

Nevertheless, there are some developments, conditions, and expectations that were predicted from the experiences of other countries that have not taken place, and these are worthy of note. First, there is no evidence of any widespread consolidation of landholdings. Even though land was (and still is) the best and most worthwhile long-term investment in the country, land ownership appears to have become more concentrated in only two areas: parts of the Tihama and the southern uplands. This rather limited consolidation is probably the result of a dramatic escalation in land prices and the fact that individuals and families who previously had held no land were intent on obtaining some of their own whenever remittance income made that possible. Most observers doubt that there has been any significant change in the pattern of land ownership from the past; on the other hand, it is worth noting that we know very little about who owns the land or about what has happened to some of the larger state holdings of the past.

Second, there has been no widespread increase in the mechanization of agriculture. Although even the casual visitor will see heavy agricultural machinery in some places (notably in areas of the Tihama and some of the areas around Ibb and southward), the first great rush to mechanize has abruptly slowed. In many places, large tractors and similar equipment were purchased—often as a status symbol—and later discovered to be irrelevant or inappropriate for most holdings (i.e., the terraces and holdings that cannot be easily reached by any form of motorized equipment).

Third, the remittances have failed to stimulate any real economic development. Many previous studies of what might occur in North Yemen were predicated on a long-term, labor-exporting/capital-importing situation. What appears to have developed in North Yemen, however, is that this situation is ending (after only a very few years), which will entail some serious consequences for the economy and the society. In fact, by the middle 1980s, there were already signs that these unpleasant consequences were on the horizon. The first of the two most important ones concerns changes in the links with the Saudi Arabian economy (for the moment, the Yemeni economy remains closely linked to the Saudi one). As many visitors to North Yemen are aware, there are areas of the country in which the preferred medium of exchange is the Saudi riyal; in addition, there continues to be a significant flow of industrial and consumer goods into North Yemen from Saudi Arabia without payment of various luxury or excise duties, which deprives the central government of needed revenues while perpetuating the perception that it does not control its own economic destiny. Related is the sensitive issue of the rights of Yemenis in Saudi Arabia (which have been curtailed in recent years). No one—in Saudi Arabia or North Yemen—can forget that the Saudis have for many years provided substantial foreign aid and budgetary support for the Yemeni government, and it is widely believed that there are multiple strings and conditions associated with this support.

The second important consequence is that as work opportunities for Yemeni emigrants continue to diminish, in line with the decrease in oil prices and a concomitant decline of construction and infrastructural development in the Gulf states and Saudi Arabia, there will be an even greater decline in the remittance flow than already exists. The long-term effects of this trend could be disastrous for North Yemen. The amount of money available for the vast program of development in the remoter towns and villages, all of which has been almost completely funded by remittance income, would decline, and any inability to continue and/or complete projects already under way could prove politically dangerous. In addition, there would be an inability to pay for the labor that is needed to keep the rural economy afloat—i.e., for field labor and for labor involved in transporting goods to local markets—and an associated decline in the market for *qat*, which today is essential for the maintenance of many of the more marginal fields, terraces, and other rural agricultural facilities.

There would also be an inevitable erosion of the agricultural base of the country. Since the latest generation is largely engaged in nontraditional employment, the traditional agricultural methods (of land retention, composting, water supply and distribution, etc.) are being neglected or ignored at a time when the government is unable to intervene with an adequate program of rural credit, assistance, training, and marketing assistance because of a lack of qualified personnel and financial resources. It is conceivable, on the other hand, that a mass return of emigrants would mean that a large percentage of them might return to their home villages and traditional pursuits. However, it seems more likely that, as has been the case in other countries, they would prefer the urban centers and the entrepreneurial possibilities there.

All of the above imply what could be the most disastrous effect of all: a mass return to a local economy utterly unable to accommodate the returnees in terms of jobs or meaningful employment (even in traditional roles in the rural economy). I suspect that no one in any policymaking position in the North Yemen government would like to dwell seriously on the long-term effects of such a development on the contemporary political system. The possibilities listed would inevitably have a disastrous effect upon the presently remarkably vital private sector—in terms of services, manufacturing, and all the other activities that are traceable to the remittance flow—and the return of a large number of emigrants would seriously tax the very fragile set of institutions and the limited infrastructure that have recently been put into place. It might then be the case that emigration will become no longer a choice but a necessity. That change would do far more harm to the traditional social fabric, as well as to the current set of economic and political institutions, than it is comfortable to contemplate.

Instead of remittance income promoting the development of the domestic economy, it would be more accurate to suggest that there has been a near-total collapse of self-sufficiency. As already indicated, domestically produced foodstuffs cannot in most instances compete on the open market against foreign imports. Furthermore, the mass emigration that began in the 1970s has largely eliminated the labor supply that might have effectively kept domestic productivity in various sectors competitive.

And last but not least, nearly all the newly created import substitution industries cannot compete with foreign products.

The implication would seem to be that the Yemeni economy is in a state of near collapse and that a disastrous future awaits the Yemenis, but such an outcome is not necessarily the case. First of all, the Yemenis have shown amazing flexibility as well as resourcefulness over the years. Second, the country's allies and groups that have provided assistance in the past would not be willing to have the current system undergo any radical change without some serious attempts at assistance. Third, and perhaps most important, the Yemeni government recognizes many of these problems, and it has programs and plans for coping with them (to be discussed in a later section).

LANDHOLDING

The question of land ownership and tenure is of especial interest to scholars and analysts of all aspects of North Yemen because, as for so many other countries, it is one of the most important factors in understanding aspects of the country's social, economic, and political systems and processes. However, because of the importance of the regional differences in North Yemen, there are no generalizations that are valid throughout the country. Furthermore, the subject is an extremely sensitive one—inquiries often elicit suspicion and hostility—and since we have little hard data, we are forced to make generalizations that are of doubtful validity in specific instances.

Apparently the first efforts to determine landholding patterns were undertaken by Imam Yahya in the 1930s, and once again by his son Ahmad in the 1950s. (It is possible that the Ottomans attempted to accomplish the same purpose, but I am not aware of any such records.) Additional efforts were made immediately after the 1962 revolution, but the most sophisticated and extensive studies are the ones undertaken in 1980 by the UN Economic Commission on Western Asia (ECWA) and in 1981 by the Yemeni government itself.

There are three basic legal categories into which land can fall: (1) *mulk*, which is privately owned; (2) *miri* or *amlak*, which is either state owned or communal; and (3) *waqf*, which is land held in trust, usually for religious purposes (though private trusts are also possible). Although there are some significant regional differences, land ownership appears to be divided roughly as follows: between 15 and 25 percent is *waqf*, 2–3 percent is communally held, 2–4 percent is state owned, and the rest is *mulk*.[16]

The 1981 survey showed that there were some significant regional differences in the landholding pattern.[17] First, land ownership tends to be in small parcels; specifically, the percentage of land that is in parcels of over 10 hectares (25 acres) is very small; only in Hodeida Province, for example, is there a significant percentage for holdings of over 10 hectares (about 12.5 percent). In Mahwit Province, on the other hand, there are no holdings in excess of 10 hectares at all. Generally speaking, the largest holdings appear to be in Hodeida and Hajjah Provinces, and the largest percentage of smallholdings (down to less than one-quarter hectare [0.6 acre]) is concentrated in Ibb, Mahwit, Ta'izz, and Dhamar Provinces. These smaller holdings in the highland provinces may reflect the fact that many of the holdings are in the form of terraces rather than broad fields. Furthermore, these are the provinces with the highest percentage of arable land.

Second, in Hodeida Province, nearly 80 percent of the land is privately owned. The other extreme is Dhamar Province, in which only about 40 percent is so owned; Mahwit is the only other province in which the percentage of privately owned land is less than 50 percent. Furthermore, land in the Tihama tends to be much more highly concentrated (i.e., in the hand of a relatively few large owners).

Third, most of the land that belongs to the state is, oddly enough, in the Tihama, probably because a good deal of this land belonged to the last imams. Exactly how much land eventually devolved to the imams is not known, but it has been estimated to have been as much as 2–3 percent of the country's total (which would equal about 70,000 hectares [173,000 acres]). These lands were, of course, confiscated after the revolution, but the real question is, Who owns them now? Clearly some of the land was earmarked for government-initiated development schemes, for example, land along the Wadi Surdud (Sardud). Whether some of the land was allocated to government ministries, given or rented to the tenants, or taken over personally by some of the revolution's leaders and added to their own holdings is unknown.

Fourth, the major problem with landholdings in North Yemen is that they tend to be highly fragmented because Islamic rules of inheritance dictate that land be divided up among all the beneficiaries, including (though not in the same proportion) the female ones. The 1981 census showed that throughout the country, there is a pronounced tendency for there to be multiple parcels per holding; that is, each unit (family or clan) has a number of different (noncontiguous) parcels obtained through various inheritances. Again, there are some variations among the provinces; for example, the lowest average number of parcels per holding exists in Hodeida Province (2.7) while in highland Dhamar Province, the average is 6.8 parcels per unit.

Fifth, one of the most sensitive political issues is data on sharecropping and whether or not it varies from province to province in any statistically significant fashion; for example, is the incidence of sharecropping related to the emigration rate from different political subdivisions? From the data that are available, it would appear that Hodeida Province has the lowest incidence of sharecropping (around 7 percent) while, interestingly, the rate is highest in some of the highland provinces (e.g., Mahwit, where the incidence is said to be in excess of 20 percent). This result appears a bit odd if one considers the tradition of the independent *qabilis,* which allegedly characterizes such provinces as Mahwit, as well as the size of holdings.

On the other hand, the available data do not show the existence of a large, landless peasantry, since many farmers rent land even when they also own some (as is common in the United States as well). An important note here: all *waqf* land available for cultivation must be rented, and it is possible that this fact skews the data.

Exactly what has happened to land tenure since the dramatic rise in remittances is a question we do not have an answer for. We do know that there have been dramatic increases in the price of land, but what we do not know is how much land has changed hands or whether or not there has been any appreciable consolidation of holdings as a result of the remittances. As already pointed out, land is one of the few investment possibilities open to people who have sizable remittances to spend, but that fact does not make it legitimate to conclude that there has been any significant change in the patterns that were visible in the late 1970s and early 1980s (or whether, indeed, these are very different from those that existed earlier).

For the moment, major conclusions concerning land and its relationship to other significant social and economic issues in contemporary North Yemen remain impossible. Current knowledge does not permit us to make any supportable generalization relating land and its ownership to the political characteristics of the country and its several regions, tempting and interesting though such speculation might be.

THE NATURAL RESOURCES SECTOR

Forestry and Forest Products

Although Yemen has some of the last remaining sizable stands of trees left on the peninsula, they cannot be considered forests in any meaningful sense of the term. First, they are neither maintained nor managed as forests, i.e., as renewable sources of wood products such as timber or pulp; second, they do not consist of the types of trees that are normally used for building material (those were logged off in the early 1970s when the building boom began); and third, they are not sizable enough to fit the Western European or North American requirements for a forest. The result is that North Yemen must import to meet its rapidly growing timber requirements, and generally speaking, the imports come from Southeast Asia, with smaller amounts from northern Europe, West Africa, and the Western Hemisphere (North America).

The progressive denuding of the remaining stands in North Yemen continues a tradition that began centuries, even millennia, ago. The most important side effect, of course, is increased runoff as less and less vegetation exists either to absorb rainfall or to protect the soil from erosion. This process was probably why the agricultural terraces were developed, and it has also resulted in the only real agricultural land in the riverine valleys and alluvial fans where the highland rivers empty into the Tihama. It is also highly likely that this erosion from the surrounding mountains is the source of the soil found on the broad plains in the provinces of Ibb and Dhamar.

There is some awareness of the forestry problems in some quarters, but the level of commitment, both in terms of human and other resources, precludes the chance of real success regarding reforestation. Many earlier attempts have failed because of a lack of maintenance or an inappropriate selection of trees for the project.

Fisheries

Most foreign aid donors and advisers have suggested that North Yemen should more effectively exploit the resources of the Red Sea. In fact, the country's fishing industry is in a very rudimentary state of development because of two factors. One, most fishing is done by individual entrepreneurs with relatively unsophisticated equipment (especially their ships) and a lack of capital to obtain newer and more efficient equipment. Two, most of the major markets are too far from the coast to be able to sell the fish fresh, and the markets need to be further developed if investments in equipment and processing plants to sell the fish in some other form are to be economic.

Although the highland people have no tradition of consuming fish, precisely because of the transportation/geographical barriers between the coast and the central plateau in the past, a market has slowly begun to develop. In part, this change is owing to the various foreigners in the major mountain cities, who have in turn helped to establish seafood as a comestible for the Yemenis themselves. With the development of modern rapid road transport (and even the occasional shipment via the domestic airline), the coast could easily meet future demand. In the meantime, however, most fish is consumed in the Tihama, with only a small portion filleted and salted for consumption elsewhere. Effective means for fast freezing parts of the catch are in the works.

Current estimates of the amount regularly brought to market total about 18,000 tons per year; nearly all of the catch is pelagic (i.e., mackerel, tuna, and related species). Recent surveys of the shellfish resources of the Red Sea near North Yemen, i.e., shrimp, lobster, and bivalves, indicate that their potential is probably not as great as originally thought. Still, with adequate equipment, better preservation, and better marketing techniques, all the offshore resources ought to be able to produce a harvest in the neighborhood of 25,000 tons per year without endangering any of the species that are currently valued (either by the Yemenis or foreign consumers and markets).[18]

Mining and Minerals

Beginning in the 1950s, Imam Ahmad became interested in finding out whether there were commercially exploitable mineral deposits that could be used to add to the country's (and his) meager income. For this reason, Ahmad granted a number of concessions to oil companies and asked other firms to survey the value of other mineral deposits (for example, the obvious copper deposits in the mountains west of Sana'a). It was not until 1985, however, that exploitable deposits of any minerals were discovered; in that year, high-quality oil was discovered in the area around Ma'rib by the Hunt Oil Company.

As of the late 1980s, it was not yet clear exactly how much oil had been found, but the success of Alif One, the name of the field, has led to further exploration, as well as to the granting of additional concessions—both to Hunt Oil (and its partners) and to some other oil firms (including the Compagnie Française des Pétroles, British Petroleum, and Exxon)—in both the Tihama and the highlands. The first oil began to flow through the newly completed pipeline on 9 December 1987, and production reached around 200,000 barrels per day during 1988, about the same rate of production as some of the smaller producers in the Organization of Petroleum Exporting Countries (OPEC). The oil was expected to bring in about $600 million per year, about the same amount as the reduction in the rate of remittances, with the important difference that the income from petroleum would go to the government directly.

It was hoped that the field would eventually produce about 400,000 barrels per day and would thus cover about half of North Yemen's current domestic needs, thus substantially decreasing the country's dependence upon its powerful northern neighbor for its energy requirements. In fact, the pipeline and its associated refinery are major additions to North Yemen's financial security at a time when other aspects of the economy bode rather poorly for the future.[19]

Until the discovery of oil, three other commodities in this category were of importance—salt, cement, and marble—and these mining activities are still valuable. Unquestionably the most important is the rock salt facility at Salif on the Red Sea coast, for which estimates of the total exploitable amount exceed 25 million tons. For many years, nearly all of the salt quarried there was sold to Japan, and a relatively insignificant amount was used by the fishing industry as a preservative for fish sent to the highlands. In the late 1970s and early 1980s, production varied significantly from year to year: sometimes as little as 70,000 tons, sometimes more than 100,000 tons. Because the facility had benefited from extensive investment by the North Yemen government as well as by the Kuwaiti Fund for Arab Economic Development (KFAED) in the early 1970s, it was a considerable shock when the Japanese ended their purchases in 1975, alleging that the Yemeni salt contained an intolerably high level of mercury contaminants (compounds to which the Japanese had become particularly sensitive). Part of the slack appears to have been taken up by the USSR, but even in the mid-1980s, the mine was not exporting what it had in previous years, nor what it was capable of.[20]

The government-owned Cement Corporation, located at Bajil in the Tihama to take advantage of nearby limestone deposits, was originally part of the Soviet Union's aid program to North Yemen in the 1970s. Although an important part of the economy, the plant does not begin to meet domestic needs; even with recent expansions it provides less than 45 percent of current demand. It is, as a result, high on the list to receive additional investment for expansion, and the government plans to also expand another plant in 'Amran.[21]

In terms of overall contribution to the gross national product (GNP) within the mining category, the quarrying industry is the most important. Various kinds of stone have long been an important component of the Yemeni architectural style, and of these, marble—in its many forms (including alabaster)—is of greatest importance. Alabaster and marble, often in various pastel tints, are found in deposits throughout the highlands, especially north of Sana'a, and these deposits have been quarried since ancient times. The demand for quality stone is very high, in part because of the preference for retaining the traditional style in contemporary construction. The lower-quality alabaster deposits are usually ground into a powder for alternative uses, very similar to those of gypsum—another mineral that is being increasingly mined.

One of the side effects of the high demand for quality stone, especially stone that has been fashioned into usable facing blocks, is that the myriad archaeological sites throughout the country, many of which are in astoundingly good condition after 2,000 years, have become an obvious source of such blocks. In the late 1970s and early 1980s, a stonemason could make more than $85 per day by cutting locally quarried granite, but the maximum number of properly faced blocks produced per day was

Thula: a highland Yemeni town.

rarely more than half a dozen. This very high cost, combined with the other expenses connected with transporting the stone to building sites, led to more and more illegal forays into the archaeological sites in the search for cheaper blocks. By the early 1980s, many of the sites had been reduced to rubble despite the best efforts of the government to protect them from stone thieves and other treasure seekers.[22]

DEVELOPMENT PROGRAMS AND PROJECTS

In order to accomplish a number of social and economic as well as political goals, the various governments of North Yemen since the revolution have undertaken and directed a great variety of development programs and projects. In part, they have been designed to deal with precisely the kinds of present and future problems that have already been outlined.

As in other developing countries with limited resources, the implementation and success of such programs depend upon a significant degree of foreign assistance. This assistance is not, however, limited solely to financial aid; it includes planning and personnel assistance as well. In an effort to demonstrate financial responsibility, a high level of commitment, and a willingness to use domestic resources (in order to continue to be eligible for further assistance, North Yemen has attempted to coordinate its development of the country through a series of plans of varying duration. There have, in fact, been four to date: the Three-Year Development Plan, covering the fiscal years (FY) 1974–1976; the First Five-Year Plan, covering FY 1976–1981; the Second Five-Year Plan, extended by one year to cover 1982–1987; and the Third Five-Year Plan, 1987–1991. (Beginning in 1981, the Yemeni government shifted its statistical record-keeping to an annual basis that corresponds to the calendar year instead of the old fiscal 1 July to 30 June year.)

Each of these plans has had different orientations toward the economy, different priorities, and different expectations concerning funding sources, and each has had to meet a different set of requirements and conditions laid down by participating donor countries as well as UN agencies and international funding bodies (e.g., the World Bank). Nevertheless, there are some areas of concentration, some sectors, some types of projects and concerns that continue to appear, and these give us a good idea of Yemeni priorities.

Every survey of North Yemen that has been undertaken—by the U.S. Agency for International Development (AID); by the Germans, the French, the British, the Italians, the Swedes, and the UN; as well as those by the Yemenis themselves—produces the same list of four items that are of overwhelming importance to the population: (1) easier access to clean water, (2) access to health care—both in the form of clinics and information, (3) access to education, and (4) more roads. Although the order of preference may vary from region to region as a result of recent developments, the overall concern with these items does not.

Water

The water issue really concerns readier access to safe water supplies. The water resources of North Yemen suffer from a number of problems. One is that much of the water is contaminated—either by *giardia lamblia* or similar organisms or by fecal bacteria and disease organisms; another is that many of the reasonably potable water supplies are located far from the settlements and an inordinate amount of time and labor must be spent to obtain water (especially for the women who are primarily responsible for the work). Obviously these two problems are related.

Another of the problems associated with this demand for easier access to safe water is that there is no adequate system for coping with the consequences of an improved supply system. Most towns and villages in North Yemen do not have any sewage treatment system, much less an adequate method of disposing of the vastly increased amounts of gray (nonpotable) water that are engendered. The result is that nearly every settlement is facing mounting problems concerning sewage, supply, and, least expected, drainage. In Sana'a, for example, the last problem has reached close to crisis proportions, since that city's inadequate drainage system has resulted in significant damage to the foundations of major architectural monuments as well as to the centuries-old houses in the core of the ancient city (an area that is on the list of World Heritage Sites and therefore supposed to be retained as is).

Furthermore, there is no nationwide systematic program to deal with these problems. Providing piped, potable water is done on an ad hoc basis, and results depend upon the level of interest and the resources available in any given locale and the difficulty and expense involved in obtaining the necessary pipes, labor, and required equipment (i.e., back-hoes, graders, etc.). Partly because of cost, the pipelines are usually laid on the earth's surface, which leads to later problems of contamination and water loss.

Last but not least, remittance money has made diesel pumps more widely affordable, and the sinking of motorized tube wells in every region of the country has had the effect of significantly affecting the water table in many areas. Fossil supplies are being used for both human consumption and irrigation, as well as for more frivolous purposes such as endless car washings.

It is worth noting that water and the legal rights surrounding water are important parts of Muslim law, a fact that has affected the development of water resources as well as some of the economic development programs and plans. Under Muslim law, all Muslims are entitled to share equally in water that is to be used for drinking and for ablution (prior to prayer). Therefore, one finds public access to wells throughout North Yemen (as, for example, in many of the back streets of Sana'a). On the other hand, water that is to be used for irrigation may be limited (if it is derived from such point sources as a stream or spring). One result of this provision is that very complex arrangements, many of them centuries old, have been designed to allocate water as equitably as possible. The British Overseas Development Ministry discovered, when it did one of the essential surveys for the North Yemen government on water resources, that villages and families were able to produce documents going back hundreds of years to validate claims to a certain amount of water at a given time.

There are also some instances under Islamic law when it is possible to own water: first, in the de facto sense, as when one purchases a bottle of drinking water in the local supermarket, and second, when one digs a well on one's own land. Although one cannot alienate the right to water from the right to the land on which it is found, it is possible to rent water so derived. But every Yemeni wishes to have his own well, without having to share its output with anyone else or having to rent water from someone else, in order to have a drinking supply and enough water for his animals, fields, etc.

There are concepts within Islamic law that could be used to place a limit on the expansion of such well digging, especially when it threatens a resource Muhammad said was held in common by all Muslims. So far, however, the government has shown neither the inclination nor the desire to use its police powers to place limits on access to the country's (rapidly dwindling) water supplies. The result is a dangerous dropping of the water table in some areas, especially in and around Sana'a. It seems almost inevitable that water—the right to obtain, use, and distribute it—is likely to become a major public policy issue in the future.[23]

Health Care

The country's population and government are in agreement that health care is already a major public policy issue. By far the majority of the population has no consistent access to any form of modern medical services, whether in the form of a general-purpose clinic or of even a paraprofessional (not to mention doctors); and prerevolutionary statistics placed North Yemen at the lowest level in the world in terms of life expectancy and infant mortality. This low level was the result of conditions that are being ameliorated slowly but generally still exist: appalling sanitary facilities, which tend to promote and spread a variety of communicable diseases, most of which are lethal to small children; a near total lack of unpolluted water for human consumption; dietary customs and patterns that practically guarantee under- and/or malnutrition on a national scale, and curative practices that in the main are either useless or dangerous.

In the past, the traditional sanitary mechanisms among the urban population of the highlands were adequate; indeed, they were even ecologically sound, given the low humidity and constant exposure to sunlight in conjunction with the rudimentary health provisions that Islam promotes with respect to personal cleanliness. However, many of those provisions were observed only infrequently, and often those associated with personal cleanliness were performed in the same general area as urination and defecation, and in the wrong sequence. Over the years, lack of knowledge and extensive use degraded even those sources that Islam requires to be pure, i.e., water used for personal ablution associated with the rituals of prayer.

A miscellany of health problems arose from various practices found throughout North Yemen but particularly in the rural areas (where around 98 percent of the population lived until after the revolution). Domestic animals were housed in the lower floors of the houses, to provide heat as well as warning of intruders, and although their manure was mainly used in the fields, some of it was used as fuel. The processes involved in the gathering, application, and use of that manure were not conducive to personal cleanliness, as the dung was collected, shaped, and dried, which promotes the spread of disease organisms. Very few houses had an interior source of water or an interior latrine, and by far the majority of the population used whatever temporary protection from the public eye was available, which means that an incredible variety of areas have been (and continue to be) used as public latrines.

The important thing that many observers have noted is the people's readiness and willingness to adapt to modern standards of hygiene when these are either explained or made available. Health problems are, in other words, not the result of rejecting modern ideas and techniques; indeed, as in other Third World countries, such ideas are highly valued because they have demonstrated their effectiveness in cutting down disease and pain. Rather, the problems continue because of difficulties associated with obtaining the necessary funds, building the necessary facilities, finding and paying for the necessary practitioners, and perhaps most important of all, obtaining the necessary supplies of clean water, since that appears to be the critical factor in many instances.

Little improvement was accomplished during the civil war, but since that time, a number of programs have been undertaken; regretfully, these have been implemented only in part or intermittently because the Ministry of Health, the various clinics, program offices, educational facilities, and personnel positions have all been inadequately funded. In fact, the government has clearly understood what the four primary areas demanding support and development are (maternal and child health care, health education, nutritional programs, and school personal health care training), but the First Five-Year Plan (1976–1981) did not assign them a very high priority (despite rhetoric to the contrary). As a result, the standard list of constraints on improvement in the health care field prevailed; lack of funds to build and maintain the physical facilities; lack of funds to attract and keep the personnel who have the necessary training and expertise; a tendency to locate services and programs in the areas of highest population concentration (the major urban areas) and to slight the overwhelming majority of the people (who live in the rural areas); a lack of adequate knowledge about local diseases, their incidence, origins, and vectors; and no adequate groundwork to obtain cooperation and participation from the people in health care programs.

Even this abbreviated list does not do justice to some of the problems. North Yemen was one of the countries that was the focus of a highly controversial campaign in the late 1970s and early 1980s to limit if not eliminate the efforts of baby-food producers to promote breast-milk substitutes among the illiterate and highly impressionable rural population, which was trying to "be modern." The country was also the target of reform groups trying to stop the "dumping" of outdated and banned drugs from the developed areas at the same time that necessary and appropriate medicines were unavailable or in limited supply. (Yemeni pharmacies still regularly offer for sale a variety of pharmaceuticals that have been banned in the West because of their side effects and/or toxic nature.)[24]

The Second Five-Year Plan (1982–1987) recognized many of these problems, and it substantially raised the priority given to health care improvement throughout the country.

One of the ironies is that North Yemen has a long tradition of folk medicine and an elaborate herbology that is at least potentially capable of contributing to the pharmacopoeia of developed countries. Consider, for example, that the first Western visitors to the area found the Yemenis in effect inoculating themselves with blood from individuals who had survived smallpox long before this technique was developed in the West. Consider, as another example, that one scholar was recently able to count hundreds of complex herbal and plant medicines for the (successful) treatment of some of the country's indigenous ailments and diseases.[25] One of the problems in improving the health care has been that the contemporary medical planning process—whether carried out by the government or by donor agencies—utterly ignores the cultural patterns, habits, attitudes, traditions, and practices, as well as the ancient medical lore of the rural population, instead of attempting to adjust and adapt modern methods to the given set of circumstances.

At the same time, it is evident to even the casual visitor that superficial information about various modern techniques and medicines has spread rather widely: on more than one occasion, Western women have been asked almost immediately upon their arrival in the rural areas if they have any spare contraceptive materials. The converse problem, unfortunately, also exists: for too long, uncaring, inadequately and/or improperly trained personnel have prescribed or given a variety of dangerous or ineffective drugs to an impressionable and receptive population, so Westerners are also asked whether they have extra supplies of various narcotics, toxic chemicals, and other inappropriate drugs.

Fortunately, the future looks brighter. Besides the greater emphasis upon these matters in the Second Five-Year Plan, there is in the works a World Bank/International Development Association grant which will reorganize and strengthen the Ministry of Health as well as all its programs and subsidiary responsibilities. It does seem legitimate to hope that, with the cooperation of the United Nations and the various donors, there will be some significant improvement in both the quality and the scope of rural medical care in North Yemen. In addition, there is an increasingly positive attitude among a good portion of the rural male population, who perceive an increase in the quantity, quality, and access to medical care as positive, not just for themselves, but for their wives, sisters, and children as well.

Unfortunately, though, the major endemic diseases in the country are not easily or quickly amenable to eradication. Gastroenteritic diseases (including amoebic dysentery) are the most common, followed by malaria, bilharzia (schistosomiasis), tuberculosis, and the standard childhood diseases (measles, etc.). As the reader can imagine, the distribution of these diseases varies with the region of the country. Malaria, for example, is not found in the highland regions at all, whereas schistosomiasis is found almost exclusively in the highlands.

Education

North Yemen was a center of Islamic education in the medieval period when scholars came to the area from as far away as Spain in the West and China in the East to study, particularly at the "university" in Zabid (where, it has been alleged by some scholars, it is likely that algebra had its origins). Education then, within the framework that existed at the time, was highly valued. Furthermore, there were a number of theological seminaries for the Shafi'i school of law, which similarly attracted scholars from distant lands.

However, such education and the value placed thereupon was essentially associated with those towns that had institutes of learning. Generally speaking, the rural and agricultural population had no access to an education outside of that provided by the *madrasah*, the school associated with the village mosque. Such learning/education consisted primarily of learning the Quran; it rarely provided training in reading and writing since instruction was usually oral and emphasized rote learning and memorization of sections of the Quran.

The result is that North Yemen came to rank among the lowest of the countries of the modern world in terms of literacy. Most observers suggest that the literacy rate under the imamate was less than 2 percent, although I am convinced that at least insofar as literacy in the Quran was concerned, and with respect to being able to write one's name, the figure was considerably higher. Still, there is little doubt that literacy in the broader sense was extraordinarily low, especially in the rural areas.[26]

Both under the imamate and now, the rate is higher in the urban areas. For example, according to the somewhat dated 1975 census figures, it would appear that the literacy rate in the three major cities is about 50 percent today but only about 12 percent in the rural areas. The national average is about 15 percent, but if that figure is divided by sex, about 30 percent of the male populace is literate and only about 3–4 percent of the female population. Furthermore, there is the typical Yemeni division between areas of the country: literacy in Sana'a and Ta'izz Provinces is at least twice that in the more rural provinces of Mahwit and Hajjah.

Apparently the desire for education has always been high, perhaps because of the traditions established by the institutes of learning of centuries ago. Although under the imamate there were fewer than 1,000 primary schools (invariably associated with the local mosque) and fewer than 10 secondary and similar preparatory schools, and individuals interested in obtaining a real education had to go to Aden or Egypt, the *demand* was evidently there. It is of some importance that as soon as possible, the revolutionary government took over the Quranic schools, created a modern curriculum, and established a nationwide system of primary education. Despite such efforts, the access to education and the quality thereof still vary considerably from region to region.

The problem is not, in a word, a lack of desire or will but a lack of resources—both financial and human. Because of the lack of adequate teacher-training institutes, resources, and investment in education in the past, North Yemen today is essentially forced to rely upon foreign (expatriate) teachers, the overwhelming majority of whom are Egyptians. Generally such instructors are financed by other Arab states as a form of foreign assistance, whereas Yemeni teachers are paid by the North Yemen government itself. The problem with this arrangement is that there is no incentive for the government to decrease the number of foreign instructors, because their use saves the government desperately needed monetary resources for other purposes. (It has been estimated that there are about 17,000 non-Yemeni teachers in the Yemeni school system, and of these about 14,000 are said to be Egyptians.)

This reliance upon foreign instructors has a number of side effects, and even though they may be necessary as the country seeks to expand educational opportunities and save precious resources, these effects are not all positive. For example, a definite Egyptianization of certain aspects of Yemeni life is taking place, which may be seen in the operations of public agencies, certain attitudes, and certain speech patterns. One example is the increasing reluctance to have boys and girls educated together, which in most areas was previously not at all opposed by the Yemenis. Since there are signs of an increasing reluctance to accept Egyptian models, and even to having children taught by expatriate Arabs, this particular "problem" may solve itself.

The other problem is that the lack of Yemenis as role models in the first exposure to education does not produce high incentives to remain in school as a mechanism for improved status or as a means to achieve socially valued things. In other words, the first experience with public education in many areas of North Yemen is perhaps more likely to produce vague feelings of alienation rather than integration into the national culture and its goals. Furthermore, since so many different donors and agencies are participating in the effort to upgrade and expand the educational infrastructure, there is an almost inevitable overlap in some instances, friction in others, and even the use of wildly inappropriate techniques, materials, and books in some cases.

The situation, which is often chaotic, fraught with various kinds of administrative and financial problems, and made more difficult by attitudes and orientations that have their origins in a bygone era, should not be taken to mean that rural Yemenis are either ignorant or unwilling to be educated, or even that they are xenophobic. The traditional life-style of the rural population did not require literacy or formal education. What skills and knowledge were required by the occupations or professions were acquired through on-the-job training and one-to-one instruction in the essentials (often the system closely resembled the old European guild system). There was considerable respect for the individual who could read and write and handle situations in which such skills were necessary, i.e., in formalizing important contracts, in drawing up confirmations of specific rights, in formalizing a written appeal to the authorities if a personal appeal was either impossible or too difficult, and last but not least, in providing access to others to the Quran and the commentaries upon it. At the same time, there was little value placed on education for girls. In the first place, the specific knowledge the girls required for their functions/roles in society (cooking, making clothing, making utensils, cleaning, getting water, assisting in various agricultural tasks, etc.) was obtainable at home. In the second place, there was no time, much less opportunity, for girls to attend any kind of formal schooling. Last, there were no public functions that girls could carry out which would require any formal education.

At the present time, many of these constraints are no longer operative or as important as they used to be. Furthermore, Yemeni attitudes with respect to roles for women are not nearly as conservative as those elsewhere on the peninsula, and it is not at all unusual to see Yemeni women in a variety of public roles (including holding office in municipal governments). The result is that there are increasing opportunities and therefore increasing demands for education for all members of society, including women. Nevertheless, women are not perceived as the equals of men and are not likely to be so for some time to come.

The government's programs, though short of what is desired or even needed, have made a considerable impact. The literacy rate in the urban centers is at least respectable and increasing, and adult literacy programs are popular and hugely successful. At the same time, by the middle 1980s, the number of primary schools in the country had risen to over 4,000, and the number of secondary and preparatory schools to over 400; the number of teacher-training institutes and specialized institutes of other kinds was around a dozen. And, largely as a result of assistance provided by Kuwait (through KFAED), North Yemen now has its own modern university (in Sana'a), with faculties of arts, science, commerce, law, and education, and schools of medicine, agriculture, and engineering are soon to open. By the middle 1980s, the university had more than 6,000 students, nearly 20 percent of whom were female (though less than half of those were Yemenis). It had become possible, for the first time in hundreds of years, for a Yemeni to get a decent and complete education in his or her own country—no mean achievement in the space of only fifteen years.

The number of institutions that offer an alternative form of secondary education has also increased. In the early 1980s, the government reported the existence of 300 religious schools, administered by the Ministry of Religious Affairs of Awqaf, and these schools served nearly 50,000 students. It is, in other words, still possible to obtain the traditional education that will enable one to qualify as a *hakim* (Islamic judge), a *qadi* (learned scholar), or an *alim* (religious scholar, almost a theologian in the English sense). The fact that so many citizens are still obtaining an essentially Islamic education is important, even though most of them will later attend institutes of Islamic learning in other countries (e.g., al-Azhar University in Cairo).

Roads

The importance of improving roads in North Yemen is to increase access to the wider world in terms of people, goods, and ideas. Roads, in other words, are perceived as the mechanism by which both individuals and communities are able to participate in the outside world. The symbolic and real value of roads in the country is not readily understood by people who are not familiar with the imamaic period or the geography of the country.[27]

Under the imams, there were no real roads in the modern sense of the term. Although the Ottoman authorities constructed a rudimentary road from Hodeida to Sana'a, the remnants of which are visible at a number of places along the new road, it was not until the 1960s that modern road building came to North Yemen, i.e., roads designed and built to be used by automobiles and trucks without four-wheel drive.

In 1961, the People's Republic of China constructed the first paved road between Sana'a and Hodeida (the present road), which immediately revolutionized transport between these two cities. First, it produced a 50 percent drop in the fee for the transport of goods between the two cities;

second, it shortened the trip from a two-day average to less than four hours; and third, it served as a major impetus to trade and commerce all along its path. New settlements of tradespeople and merchants sprouted, and a significant diversion of the coffee trade took place as growers and middlemen shifted to the new road. Shortly thereafter, in what was clearly an example of competition between the major powers, the United States constructed a gravel-surface road from Mocha through Ta'izz to Sana'a (over two very difficult passes), and the Soviet Union completed a paved road from Hodeida to Ta'izz, thereby effectively linking the three major cities.[28]

In the 1970s, some other larger towns (e.g., 'Amran and Sa'dah) were added to the network, and the task of building secondary and feeder roads was begun. Although only rarely paved, and often very poorly maintained owing to the difficult terrain and the horrendous expense involved in obtaining the necessary grading and road-building equipment, these lesser roads soon had an immense impact on the economy and the life-style of the population. (It should be noted, however, that although everyone wanted to have such roads and tracks, it was not always easy to obtain universal support for their location, as such roads had to be, of course, subtracted from the landholdings of someone or some tribe.)

In fact, the new roads have almost completely revolutionized the rural Yemeni economy. In the past, most economic activity was carried out in the market towns that existed throughout the countryside, and specific locations acted as "hosts" to market activities on specific days of the week (so, for example, everyone knew that on Friday Suq al-Khamis was the place to go to buy, sell, trade, etc.; on Saturday, the same activities would have to be carried out at another town, about a day's walking time away, and so on throughout the week until the whole cycle began again). If one were to stumble on one of these market towns on the wrong day, it would appear to be an abandoned village with its market stalls, pens for animals, quarters for merchants, and facilities for travelers still intact. Each of these towns was a neutral area and had overseers to protect participants, guarantee the accuracy of weights and measures, and prevent price fixing and other undesirable activities (including violence).

The construction of roads has dramatically affected this ancient system (which has not, however, disappeared completely). Permanent, all-weather roads have facilitated the growth of new settlements along their routes, and sometimes these have usurped the activities of the older market towns. These new markets tend to be linear developments along the new roads (e.g., al-Maghrabah, which grew up where the track to Manakhah joins the new road between Hodeida and Sana'a). These new settlements are just that: they are no longer limited to marketing activities but rapidly become new towns. Furthermore, they have promoted the growth of a cash economy, which has replaced the largely barter and credit system that used to exist.

At the same time, the overall improvement in transportation has meant that far more foreign, nonessential, and luxury goods have made their way into the market (demand for which has been stimulated by the remittance flows). There has also, of course, been an increase in the variety of standard goods, giving the Yemenis a far larger selection from which to buy than was ever the case in the past. Furthermore, and of considerable interest for what it tells us about the other changes taking place in the society, a vast range of new services are being offered. In al-Maghrabah, for example, after the first restaurants, coffee houses, and groceries opened, there suddenly appeared *two* dry-cleaning establishments. Conversely, some of the older services are disappearing—praise singers, for example, are far rarer than they used to be—as such low-status occupations are no longer in demand and their traditional purveyors find alternative employment.

As suggested above, the new road system is also responsible for improved access to ideas, for it made possible access to electricity (whether from the national grid or the electricity generated by individual entrepreneurs in remote villages who brought in a diesel generator and began selling electricity to their neighbors) and the subsequent introduction of television. Whether the programs are Egyptian or Western in origin, they have introduced the Yemenis to values, goods, services, and behavior patterns that were utterly inconceivable only a short time ago. Roads, in other words, have helped to promote economic as well as social change, and many Yemenis continue to see both of these ends as highly desirable. It is worth noting, however, that there is another element that sees these changes, and the decline in traditional values, orientations, and behavior patterns, as being ultimately responsible for the disappearance of the "real" Yemen.

ECONOMIC DEVELOPMENT

Local Efforts

Probably the most interesting and important activity associated with economic development at the local level in North Yemen actually began during the last days of the imamate, when some local notables in Hodeida decided to undertake some development projects for that city, using only local funds (and some gifts and donations from overseas Yemenis), without reference to the imam. During the mid-1960s, a couple of other towns followed in Hodeida's footsteps; in the early 1970s, with the new government's encouragement, this new manifestation of the long tradition of localism blossomed into a national movement. These local development associations (LDAs) were, in fact, part of an indigenous movement whereby people employed whatever financial, equipment, and personnel resources were available to try to provide needed services and facilities the government was unable to supply.

The republican government, understanding the economic and development value of these bodies, sought to coordinate and assist this movement. By the mid-1970s, there were more than a hundred such LDAs, and they had been melded into a national organization, the Confederation of Yemeni Development Associations (CYDA), by an individual who recognized their potential political and organizational value (as well as their economic development value): Col. Ibrahim al-Hamdi, who became president of CYDA.

During the late 1970s and early 1980s, the LDAs were, in fact, responsible for a substantial percentage of the development schemes in the four priority areas, though certainly not all (and according to at least one observer, not even a majority). However, as was perhaps inevitable in view of the financial, organizational, and miscellaneous economic and political problems that North Yemen faced during these years, there were problems of coordination, planning, financing, and implementation of the various projects and programs designed to develop North Yemen. In the mid-1980s, a massive reorganization of local administrative and development mechanisms took place (at the behest of the president, Ali Abdullah Salih). The most important aspects of this change were that CYDA was elevated to a cabinet-level organization and that the LDAs themselves were fused with local administrations for government projects and programs into local councils for cooperative development (LCCDs). These new bodies were supposed to have more authority over local projects and their implementation (probably a necessary and desirable change), but at the same time they came under increasing government control (probably an inevitable change), as the government sought to gain a greater measure of supervision over development projects. At the same time, of course, the government of Ali Abdullah Salih was also cognizant of the political potential of these local associations.[29]

National Efforts

Economic development programs on the national level are usually designed to "attack" certain specific sectors of the economy, and the various programs usually fall under one of the four main headings used by the Yemenis: agriculture, human resources, industry/manufacturing, and the public sector (i.e., the development of the administrative machinery that will facilitate the achievement of the goals in the other sectors).[30]

Of these four sectors, agriculture is perhaps the most important for the economic future of the country, and assistance for improvements in the agricultural sector has been provided by a staggering array of multinational (UN) agencies and national governments of countries of every conceivable political orientation: the United States, West Germany, the United Kingdom, the Soviet Union, the People's Republic of China, the Netherlands, etc., as well as a number of Arab states (e.g., Kuwait, Saudi Arabia, and the United Arab Emirates).

The range of projects is at least as diverse, but nearly all have been influenced by the rural development strategies that were set forth during the 1970s, promulgated and advocated in the main by a variety of scholars in the United States and Southeast Asia. As a brief summary of those strategies, it is more useful and easier to produce an increase in disposable income (in broader terms, in the GDP) by initiating marginal increases in efficiency and productivity at the rural level (where the overwhelming majority of the population lives) than it would be to produce the same increase by initiating change in the urban areas. Moreover, such increases would benefit those people most in need of them (and such strategies would accord with the directives of such bodies as AID and the various UN agencies).

As a result, a number of major regional projects have been started, as for example, the Tihama Development Project and the Southern Rural Uplands Development Project. These seek to assist the rural population by introducing new and improved seed strains, improved water supply systems, better storage and transportation mechanisms for crops, better marketing strategies and techniques for available surpluses, and similar benefits. At the same time, some of the donor states provide assistance to establish new local industries, primarily of the import substitution type (such as a domestic dairy industry), or to significantly improve the local breeds of poultry, cattle, and even sheep and goats. Some projects that are absolutely staggering in their scope have undergone feasibility studies, but many of these are being proposed and/or considered solely (or at least primarily) because of factors unrelated to economic development, such as national prestige or historical associations. Into this category one would have to put some of the proposals to develop all aspects of one of the major western wadis (the Wadi Mawr) and the decision to build a new Ma'rib Dam in order to provide water for the development of the Ma'rib region (paid for by foreign donors despite recommendations by various Swiss and German engineering firms that the project would be largely useless as well as horrendously expensive).

The Yemeni government often has a double motive for accepting such offers of assistance from foreign donors. First, their presence, especially in some of the more remote areas of the country, serves to make the local population aware of the central government and of the facts that it has resources at its command and major programs that it seeks to implement. Indeed, the government is strong or influential enough to have non-Yemenis come in to assist it in carrying out the services it seeks to provide. If the program or project is successful, the central government can accept responsibility and thereby increase its influence and prestige in these areas dramatically—something the republican government has found it difficult to do in many areas of the northeast and northwest. If, on the other hand, the project fails, the government has still shown that it has the power to command foreign resources, yet it can disavow responsibility for specific failures by laying the blame on the foreigners who actually undertook the work.

Second, such projects, whether they are successful or not, serve to increase the influence of the central government in several other small but important ways. One of these is the increased income that is generated and can often be taxed (even if only indirectly); another, the likelihood that a program will tie the affected area into the larger economy is rather high, which increases the political and economic influence of the central government (which is still not in complete control of the country).

It should also be noted that local development efforts (in any of the four areas mentioned) are sometimes started by local bodies with the full knowledge that they do not have the funds, the equipment, or the human resources to complete the project. At some point, they turn to the central government and use various mechanisms and arguments to persuade the government and its bodies to either complete the project or take over its implementation. It is, in other words, a conscious effort to get access to the government's greater resources. From another perspective, it is an example of the periphery influencing the center, a fascinating addition to the perennial debate on such matters which only a very few social scientists have either described or understood the implications of.

In view of the above, it should not be surprising that there is precious little coordination concerning the various projects which are sponsored by the various donor states and agencies, and donors complain of over-lapping, conflicting, and even contradictory responsibilities, projects, and goals in the many areas of North Yemen that are outside the major urban areas. On the other hand, they appear to be completely unaware of the kinds of political, economic, and regional issues the central government must cope with if it is going to continue in power.

Nevertheless, the Yemenis have established a body, the Central Planning Organization (CPO), for the purpose of coordinating development planning and programming. However, instead of assuming that the CPO has a rather good understanding of the country's problems, including the government's responsibilities and priorities as well as the range of domestic pressures, foreign donors generally assume that its personnel are uncaring or unaware of the conflicts and problems that arise as a result of the plethora of donors, projects, and programs. As is made clear elsewhere in this book, no government in North Yemen, forced to cope regularly with a complex set of domestic and foreign influences and pressures, could survive for more than a week if it were as ignorant and as obtuse as many foreign donors suggest.

Five-Year Plans

The most effective way to judge the changing priorities and concerns of the government is to compare the various multiyear plans to date. The agricultural sector, which, as was suggested above, is probably the key sector in the future, has been treated very differently in the plans thus far.

The first plan (the Three-Year Development Plan for 1973-1974–1975-1976) was essentially an ad hoc program; it did not cover the various bilateral assistance programs and did not even attempt to cover all aspects of the public sector and its impact on the pace of change. The primary emphases were improvements in communications (ports as well as roads) and education, expansion of the cement plant at Bajil, and promoting new industries and a variety of municipal improvement schemes designed to make government more effective (as well as to give its operations a better image). Foreign assistance provided some 75 percent of this plan's funding, but the Yemenis also gained valuable information and experience in how to set up and implement major development projects and plans.

The second plan, the First Five-Year Plan (FY 1976–1981), was far more ambitious and far more of an integrated effort to develop the economy. Divided into twelve basic categories, 7.5 percent of investments under the plan (i.e., aside from private investment) was to be allocated to agriculture. Unfortunately, as the government's own reports indicate, only 38 percent of the amount planned for the agricultural sector was ever expended and/or implemented. The result was that the average annual growth rate of agriculture during the period of this plan was only about 1 percent, quite likely all of it engendered from the private sector, while the GDP rose at an average annual rate of nearly 7 percent.

The third plan, the Second Five-Year Plan, covered the years 1982–1987 and had as one of its objectives increasing agriculture's share of the GDP at an average annual growth rate of 4.2 percent. In order to accomplish this growth rate, 13.6 percent of total investments was to be allocated to the agricultural sector, far more than under the previous plan (see Table 3.1).

The second plan expected to raise and spend a total of nearly 30 billion Yemeni riyals (YR), which was equivalent to about $6.6 billion at

TABLE 3.1   Government Expenditures by Categories 1985 (in millions of riyals)

Public services		1,814.0
Public administration	995.2	
Public security	818.8	
National defense		2,485.3
Education		1,561.3
Health		231.9
Social services		139.6
Economic services (agriculture, mining, construction, transport, electricity, water, sewage, etc.)		206.6
All other (including interest on public debt)		84.4
Total		6,523.1

Source: Yemen Arab Republic, Statistical Year Book 1985 (Sana'a: Central Planning Organization, 1986).

the old exchange rate (the one in effect when the plan was drawn up). Government statistics indicate a staggering 88.4 percent of the capital for investment during the First Five-Year Plan period had come from remittances, with loans from abroad (8.5 percent) and net capital transfers (3.2 percent) making up the remainder. For the next plan, the government recognized that remittance flows had dropped from their previous highs, and consequently it expected that foreign loans would have to make up 46.1 percent of the capital for investment, with gross national savings and other income from abroad contributing most of the remainder (47.2 percent). As the government's own report admitted, "these latter sources are unreliable since they are subject to fluctuations in the labor markets of neighboring countries," a remarkably frank admission of the dependence of North Yemen's development on its peninsula neighbors.[31]

Since such a high percentage (nearly half) of the government's own sources of revenue were precarious, the plan inevitably had some serious weaknesses. Consider that during the previous plan period, the government had derived 60 percent of public revenue from customs duties, 33 percent from taxes on industrial and commercial profits (many of which are government-owned enterprises to begin with), and only 7 percent from taxes on wages and salaries. The first category is, of course, the most problematic one. If the government depends too much on customs duties, there is no incentive to develop import substitution industries since they would, in effect, decrease government revenue (at least in the short run). Furthermore, if customs duties are set too high, some unique circumstances that characterize North Yemen are relevant and could be affected. For example, the extensive border with Saudi Arabia is extremely porous, and North Yemen has become ever more dependent upon budgetary support from the Saudis to cover the lack of government revenues (with which, presumably, one provides the goods and services the population demands as well as paying for national defense and internal security). When duties are too high, the Saudis react by smuggling in goods and/or by reducing the amount of budgetary support—both responses have, in fact, occurred.

The government's problems do not stop there. As an example of the government's honesty as well as the sophistication of its analyses, the Second Five-Year Plan discussed such important issues as population growth. Undoubtedly to the government's shock and dismay, it had discovered that during the First Five-Year Plan period, the population growth rate had been a staggering 3.4 percent instead of the expected 1.9 percent. Although this increase was undoubtedly an indirect indicator of the success of some of the programs designed to improve health and sanitation, it also significantly affected the success of the first plan in producing real increases in per capita GDP as well as in real per capita income (private final consumption). Specifically, the population growth rate had dropped per capita income from a planned growth of 6.3 percent to a real increase of only 2.5 percent; it had similarly dropped per capita private final consumption from a planned growth rate of 4.1 percent to a real one of only 2.3 percent. Unfortunately, the Second Five-Year Plan did not support any public sector programs to slow down the population growth rate, despite the obvious interest throughout the country (especially among women) in contraceptive information and techniques, in part because North Yemen, like most other nations, tends to equate the size of the country's population with its ability to influence other countries (and its political power).

Other aspects of the later plan were also a reaction to, or an elaboration upon, some characteristics and results of the previous one. For example, in the First Five-Year Plan period, there was a substantial decrease in cereals production (owing, of course, to the vast increase in imports of cheaper foreign cereals) and also a disastrous decline in cotton production (because of the worldwide decline in demand for cotton), but there were some respectable increases in vegetable, potato, fruit, and tobacco production, as well as an astronomical increase in poultry production. It is not surprising, then, that the Second Five-Year Plan sought to promote increases in cereal production (particularly wheat, the demand for which had risen sharply as people demanded more American-style white breads) to eliminate one of the major drains on the government's severely limited foreign exchange reserves.

Similarly, some developments in the industrial sector led to changes in the later plan. For example, the government-owned Yemen Company for Industry and Trade (YCIT)—the country's largest company—was slated for a large increase in its food and beverage processing activities, presumably to decrease the drain on foreign exchange and improve the balance of payments. Overall, in fact, the Second Five-Year Plan overwhelmingly concentrated its resources on large increases in three sectors: mining and quarrying, manufacturing, and electricity and water. The first was expected to have an annual growth rate of 12 percent, probably because of the Yemeni belief that the country has commercially exploitable deposits of copper, iron, cobalt, lead, and some other minerals (an assertion most foreign analysts dispute). Manufacturing was expected to have an average annual growth rate of 13.5 percent, and significant investments were directed toward those government-owned enterprises that had had considerable success, such as the biscuit factory, the aluminum products factory, the soft drink division, and the plastics, foam, and ghee factories (all of which are part of YCIT); the cement plants in Bajil, 'Amran and Mafraq; the tobacco and matches company; and the cotton corporation. Electricity and water were projected to grow at an average annual rate of a staggering 25 percent, on the assumption that they are essential to the growth and development of all the other sectors of the economy.

It is clear, then, that no major restructuring of the economy was planned for 1982–1987. On the other hand, although agriculture was destined to receive nearly twice as high a level of investment as under the previous plan, the primary emphasis of the government continued to be on greater increases in the role of manufacturing, construction, and domestic financial institutions. Whether, in the eventual final summary, actual investments and programmatic assistance resulted in the changes desired will, of course, take a couple of years to determine.

According to the Central Planning Organization, percentages of planned expenditures in the Third Five-Year Plan period (1987–1991) were as follows for each sector: agriculture, 8.0; industry, 29.7; construction, 0.5; housing, 8.0; trade, 5.1; transport and communications, 12.5; banking and finance, 0.8; and services, 5.7. The 29.7 percent in the industrial sector was to further break down as: manufacturing, 8.9 percent; electricity and water, 6.7 percent; and mining, 14.1 percent. The total anticipated investment in Yemeni riyals for the Third Five-Year Plan period was 38,582,000.

OTHER ECONOMIC ISSUES AND PROBLEMS

The Tax System

Part of the central government's financial difficulties lies in the fact that it is unable to collect all of the various taxes that have been imposed

TABLE 3.2 Sources of Government Revenue 1985 (in millions of riyals)

Direct taxes		967.0
Zakat (all types)	211.3	
Profits (on wages, salaries, commerce, etc.)	755.7	
Foreign trade taxes		2,540.5
Customs duties on imports	1,862.5	
All other	678.0	
Taxes on goods and services		492.5
On tobacco, fuels, soft drinks, etc.	286.7	
On transport & motor vehicles, cinema, etc.	205.8	
Total tax revenues		4,000.0
Nontax revenues		1,331.1
Revenue from government properties	748.7	
Revenue from government operations	582.4	
Total government revenue		5,331.1

Source: Yemen Arab Republic, Statistical Year Book 1985 (Sana'a: Central Planning Organization, 1986).

and are due—like most developing states, North Yemen manages to collect less than 40 percent of the amounts payable. The difficulties, as well as the expense involved, in collecting direct taxes tend to make them a relatively unimportant source of government revenues. For example, in 1985, the sources of government revenues were foreign trade taxes, 48 percent; revenues from government properties and operations, 25 percent; direct taxes, 18 percent; and taxes on goods and services (indirect taxes), 9 percent (see Table 3.2).[32]

In keeping with North Yemen's past and its Islamic heritage, some of the direct taxes that are levied are Islamic in origin: the zakat, which takes many forms and which in some respects resembles the medieval Christian tithe. In fact, there are four basic zakat taxes: (1) al-'ashur (the "tenth"), which is a tax on agricultural produce; (2) al-mawashi, a tax on animals/livestock, which, however, is not levied unless and until an individual has a certain minimum number of animals (40 sheep, or 30 cattle, or 5 camels, for which 1 sheep would be due); (3) al-batn, a "wealth" tax of 2.5 percent per annum, which is generally self-imposed; and (4) al-fitrah, essentially a kind of "poll" or poor tax, the receipts of which are committed to such social enterprises as orphanages.

There are, in addition, some more-specialized sales taxes. For example, the muhaddar is a sales tax of 30 percent on the sale price of qat, and there is a 5 percent tax on various grasses and fodder used for animal consumption. The amam is a tax collected by the shaykh in charge of a *suq* on animal sales in the *suq,* and similar imposts are considered legitimate sources of local (and sometimes national) revenue.[33]

Foreign Trade

Although historically much of North Yemen's wealth and influence was the result of trade, such is no longer the case. In recent times, Yemeni merchants and entrepreneurs have played an important role as middlemen and suppliers for a variety of goods in the Red Sea and Gulf of Aden regions, as well as down the coast of East Africa, but not on the scale of the past.

The post–civil war period has, in fact, seen some major changes in North Yemen's trade relations with the rest of the world. First and foremost, its trade pattern is now as skewed as that of most countries undergoing (and promoting) economic development along essentially Western lines. On the one hand, its imports of nearly all commodities (food, machinery, equipment, chemicals, textiles, electrical and electronic goods, etc.) are overwhelmingly from the countries of Western Europe, North America, and Japan. Oil has been overwhelmingly imported from the country's regional cohorts who are members of OPEC and/or OAPEC (the Organization of Arab Petroleum Exporting Countries). Imports from non-oil-exporting developing states consist primarily of building materials, foodstuffs, labor, and miscellaneous items.

On the other hand, its exports are overwhelmingly skewed in the direction of its regional cohorts on the Arabian Peninsula and the Red Sea littoral. There is, of course, a demand among the industrialized states for North Yemen's prized Mocha coffee (when it is available in sufficient quantities and the quality control mechanisms have been effective), and those same countries have also provided the major market for North Yemen's cotton, hides, and skins. A survey of the country's primary export categories/goods, by value, shows the following breakdown: cotton and cotton products, 51 percent; coffee, 18 percent; hides and skins, 14 percent; and all other (mostly baked goods), 17 percent.[34]

The foreign trade problem North Yemen faces is evident when one compares the amount spent for imports with the amount received for exports (see Table 3.3). Clearly, the country has a staggering foreign trade imbalance. In the 1970s, the problem was not too great because the remittances from the Yemenis abroad made up most of the difference. Indeed, in fiscal years 1975-1976 and 1977-1978, the remittances from expatriate workers more than covered the deficit; they allowed North Yemen to have a surplus in its net balance for those fiscal years. But, as the government's own figures also show, the amount of these remittances began to decrease so that by the early 1980s, the deficits had sharply

TABLE 3.3   Foreign Trade (in millions of riyals)

Year	Imports	Exports	Trade Balance	Net Transfers (Remittances)	Net Balance
1964	22.9	4.9	−18.0	negl.	−18.0
1969	157.8	18.0	−139.8	42.0	−97.8
1974–75	981.0	52.9	−928.1	858.0	−70.1
1975–76	1,706.9	50.0	−1,656.9	2,057.0	+400.1
1977–78	6,194.9	33.4	−6,161.5	6,350.7	+189.2
1979	6,806.5	61.7	−6,744.8	6,118.4	−626.4
1981	7,340.4	216.6	−7,123.8	4,444.2	−2,679.6
1983	8,082.0	44.0	−8,038.0	5,600.7	−2,437.3
1986	7,699.5	153.0	−7,546.5	5,867.2	−1,679.3

During this period, $1 = YR 4.55; 7.44 (85), 9.31 (86)

Source: Yemen Arab Republic, Statistical Year Book 1976–1977, 1980, 1982, 1986 (Sana'a: Central Planning Office, 1977–1987).

increased. In fact, by 1982, the deficit had reached 33 percent of the GDP, and the government was financing the deficit with loans from the Central Bank.

In the early 1980s, the government was faced with more than simply a decline in remittances; there was also a decline in the rate (amount) of assistance being provided by other governments as well as international bodies. The result was that the country began to have deficits in the balance of payments. By 1983, the deficit had reached such alarming proportions that the government was forced to take unusual measures. Wage restraints were imposed (an unpleasant and difficult thing to do in an economy that has had relatively high inflation for a number of years, and particularly painful in view of the kind of domestic and foreign problems that dominated the scene at the time), and development spending was reduced (creating similar problems as well as raising the issue of credibility). The government also instituted some new programs to increase revenues (increases in some taxes and duties as well as employing better collection techniques, etc.). These measures did succeed in significantly reducing the deficit, because one of the effects of the measures outlined above was a decline in imports. Nevertheless, the total decline in the net foreign assets of the Central Bank amounted to nearly $900 million in a span of only three years (1980–1982).[35]

In 1984, the government prepared a foreign exchange budget for the first time and also adopted an import-licensing system. In addition, it took a step many foreign analysts and Yemeni economists and businesspeople had been urging for some time: it lowered the official rate of exchange between the dollar and the Yemeni riyal, from its old rate of 4.56 YR to $1 to 5.8 YR to $1. This change led to further reductions in imports for 1984, and for the first time real growth in North Yemen dropped sharply. Further reductions took place in February of 1985 (6.5 YR to $1), and by 1987, the rate had dropped to more than 10 YR to $1. By mid-1990, it had dropped even further to 18 YR to $1.

All of the problems raised some serious questions. First, would the government still be able to implement the Second Five-Year Plan at the levels and to the extent originally planned? In fact, the distribution of resources underwent considerable revision as a result of some of the problems outlined above. Overall, actual investment under the plan fell about 30 percent short of planned expenditures, for essentially two reasons. First, the economy was unable to absorb the large capital outlays and investments because of the lack of an adequate infrastructure, and second, unplanned events, such as the massive earthquake of December 1982, both disrupted the developing infrastructure and, of course, required a significant adjustment in the amount (and percentage) of investment directed at housing.

Nevertheless, plans for the Third Five-Year Plan began in 1986, and the whole was approved in late 1987. Probably the most important change from the previous plans was the renewed emphasis on the development industry and the concomitant reduction in the priority given to domestic agriculture (which was reduced from receiving 13.6 percent in the second plan to only 8 percent in the third). Once again, it was anticipated that foreign aid would cover a significant portion of the planned investment (though not as much as the 40 percent in the previous plans).

Second, in the past, North Yemen received an amazing variety and number of loans, grants, assistance and credit packages, program supports, and related mechanisms designed to provide help in a wide array of sectors and activities. As the Second Five-Year Plan indicated, Yemen expected to continue to receive such largesse—in part because of its strategic location, in part because of the unique political situation in which it finds itself. The problem is, if North Yemen is widely perceived as being able to receive significant income from oil exports, will the various donors continue to be willing to provide the kind of assistance upon which the economy, and especially the development programs, have become so dependent?

CONCLUSION

It is difficult at this point to be very optimistic about North Yemen's economic future. At the same time that it appears that oil may provide some desperately needed additional income for the government, the array of problems associated with the balance of payments, the lack of any other exploitable natural resources, the evident decline in the demand for expatriate workers, and the dependence upon Saudi Arabia for budgetary support (subventions designed to keep North Yemen as a dependable buffer against South Yemen) seem almost insuperable. Ironically, it is almost inevitable that the people, individually and collectively, will continue to demand more and more goods and more and better services as the pent-up demands of the decades of imamic rule continue to dominate. Furthermore, it is difficult to accept many of the gloomy analyses as one walks through the markets of North Yemen and sees the variety of goods available and the hordes of people scrambling to buy them.

NOTES

1. A good general survey of the subject and of the changes taking place is Richard Tutwiler and Sheila Carapico, *Yemeni Agriculture and Economic Change* (Milwaukee, WI: American Institute for Yemeni Studies, 1981).

2. Consortium for International Development, *Agriculture Sector Analysis* (Sana'a: 1981), p. 50.

3. World Bank, *Yemen Arab Republic: Development of a Traditional Economy* (Washington, DC: 1979), p. 91.

4. Yemen Arab Republic, Ministry of Agriculture, *Summary of the Final Results of the Agricultural Census in Six Provinces* (Sana'a: 1981).

5. Yemen Arab Republic, *Statistical Year Book 1986* (Sana'a: Central Planning Organization, 1987), p. 380.

6. W. C. Overstreet, M. J. Grolier, and M. R. Toplyn, *Geological and Archaeological Reconnaissance in the Yemen Arab Republic 1985* (Washington, DC: American Foundation for the Study of Man, 1988), vol. 4.

7. Nearly every analyst of North Yemen has created a set of categories to characterize the country's geographic features. Among those who have been widely cited for their efforts are Hans Steffen et al., *Final Report of the Airphoto Interpretation Project* (Zurich: Swiss Technical Co-operation Service 1978), Part One, pp. 3–4, and Horst Kopp, *Agrargeographie der Arabischen Republic Jemen* (Erlangen: Palm & Enke, 1981), pp. 176–223.

8. For a brief summary, with additional materials, see Steffen et al., *Final Report*, Part One, pp. 5–7.

9. On various aspects of coffee, see M. W. Wenner, "Mocha and Coffee," *Middle East Forum* 40 (Autumn 1964), pp. 11–14, and Ralph Hattox, *Coffee and Coffeehouses* (Seattle: University of Washington Press, 1985). For annual production figures, consult Yemen Arab Republic, *Statistical Year Book*.

10. Shelagh Weir, "Economic Aspects of the Qat Industry in North-West Yemen," in B. R. Pridham, ed., *Economy, Society, and Culture in Contemporary Yemen* (London: Croom Helm, 1985), pp. 73–75.

11. Information and data for this section are drawn from: Yemen Arab Republic, Statistical Year Book 1986, section on agriculture, pp. 91ff.

12. Ibid., section on industry, pp. 111ff.

13. Personal communication to the author from Jon Swanson and Thomas Stevenson (for Sana'a and 'Amran, respectively). More official data may be

obtained from the Yemen Arab Republic's Central Bank Research Department and its *Financial Statistical Bulletin* (appears irregularly). It should be noted that the recession of the late 1980s brought about a commensurate decrease in prices both demanded and paid.

14. *World Development Report 1989* (Washington, DC: World Bank, 1989), p. 166. (The figure for the 1970s is even higher; the figure given is for the period 1980–1987, for which period the data are more reliable.) See also *International Financial Statistics 1989* (Washington, DC: International Monetary Fund, 1989), pp. 744, 745, and the special report in the issue of 5 May 1986.

15. On all aspects of Yemeni emigration, see Jon Swanson, *Emigration and Economic Development* (Boulder, CO: Westview Press, 1979); the various essays on the subject in Jonathan Friedlander, ed., *Sojourners and Settlers: The Yemeni Immigrant Experience* (Salt Lake City: University of Utah Press, 1988); and Günter Meyer, *Arbeitsemigration, Binnenwanderung, und Wirtschaftsentwicklung in der Arabischen Republik Jemen* (Wiesbaden: Reichert Verlag, 1986).

16. Kopp, *Agrargeographie*, pp. 130–134, provides percentages of different types of ownership in different areas of the country; the figures given in the text attempt to provide a rough national average; on pp. 135–149 Kopp describes and analyzes the categories in greater detail.

17. All data in the following analysis are drawn from Yemen Arab Republic, *Summary of the Final Results.*

18. Consortium for International Development, *Agriculture Sector Analysis,* p. 79.

19. On the new oil industry and its various implications, see "Refined Prudence," *South* (April 1988), pp. 33–35; "North Yemen Faces the 1990s," *Middle East* (May 1988), pp. 23–26; and, "Oil Makes Better Neighbors," *Middle East* (August 1988), p. 32. Regular updates are published in the Economist, *Country Profile* (the Yemens and Oman), which appears quarterly.

20. *Middle East Economic Digest,* 11 June 1977, 2 December 1977, and 23 May 1980; for recent production levels, see Yemen Arab Republic, *Statistical Year Book 1986,* p. 113.

21. On the production and expansion of the cement industry, see *Middle East Economic Digest,* 12 October 1979; 9 October 1981; 15, 22, and 29 October 1982; as well as Yemen Arab Republic, Central Planning Organization, *Second Five-Year Plan, 1982–1986* (Sana'a: Central Planning Organization, n.d. [printed in the U.S.], Chapter 4.

22. Yemen Arab Republic, Central Planning Office, *Summary of the First Five-Year Plan* (Beirut: Central Planning Organization, 1977) and *Second Five-Year Plan;* see also the CPO's Annual Reports of the plans.

23. On various aspects of Muslim water law and water problems in general, consult the works of Daniel Varisco, in particular, "The Adaptive Dynamics of Water Allocation in Al-Ahjur, Yemen Arab Republic" (Ph.D. dissertation, University of Pennsylvania, 1982), esp. Chapters 6, 7, and 8 (on sources, principles of water allocation, and water allocation mechanisms), pp. 183–290.

24. Dianna Melrose, *The Great Health Robbery: Baby Milk and Medicines in Yemen* (Oxford: Oxfam Public Affairs Unit, 1981).

25. Armin Schopen, *Traditionelle Heilmittel in Jemen* (Wiesbaden: Franz Steiner Verlag, 1983).

26. On the various aspects of education, educational institutions, and literacy, consult A. Faroughy, *Introducing Yemen* (New York: Orientalia, 1947), esp. pp. 23–27; Yemen Arab Republic, *Summary of the First Five-Year Plan*, p. 27, which gives the illiteracy rates at the time as 74.4 percent among males and 97.7 percent among females; Peter Clark, "Aspects of Education in the Yemen Arab Republic," in Pridham, ed., *Economy, Society, and Culture*, pp. 172–177; and Horia Mohammad al-Iryani, "The Development of Primary Education and Its Problems in the Yemen Arab Republic," ibid., pp. 178–189. See also Section 6 of the Yemen Arab Republic, *Statistical Year Book 1986*, pp. 165–210, for current statistics; the most complete set of data for the 1970s is in Steffen, et al., *Final Report*, Part One, pp. 109–122. The most complete analysis of the problems of education as of the 1970s is in Eastern Michigan University, *Education Sector Study* (Sana'a: EMU, 1979).

27. Although Yemenis believe that roads have great importance, there have been surprisingly few studies of their impact—both economic and political. The first such study was by Brigitta Mitchell, *Yemen Arab Republic Feeder Road Survey* (Washington, DC: World Bank, 1978). Consult the Yemen Arab Republic, *Statistical Year Book 1986*, p. 136, for data on the rate of growth of the road system from the revolution of 1962 to the present.

28. The U.S. road, which was a major engineering feat, was not paved until a few years later. It became clear that the people considered it a second-class road, which reflected poorly on U.S. aid and technological expertise.

29. World Bank, *Yemen Arab Republic: Urban Sector Report* (Washington, DC: 1981).

30. Ragaei el-Mallakh, *The Economic Development of the Yemen Arab Republic* (London: Croom Helm, 1986), provides a very useful overview of various aspects of the characteristics of the country's economy and the development programs proposed for the various sectors.

31. Yemen Arab Republic, *Second Five-Year Plan*, p. 56.

32. Yemen Arab Republic, *Statistical Year Book 1986*, pp. 330–332.

33. Ibid.

34. Compiled by calculating an average from export data provided by the Yemen Arab Republic, *Statistical Year Book* for the years 1974–1985. The data do not reflect the amount or significance of *qat* exports.

35. Yemen Arab Republic, *Statistical Year Book* for the years 1973-1974 to 1986.

4

Before the Republic

Much of the preceding discussion about the various aspects of North Yemen has implied that an understanding of today's issues and problems requires an acquaintance with the country's past. In this chapter, I consider this past, beginning with the ancient city-states of 2,000–3,000 years ago and ending with the end of the civil war in 1970.

THE PRE-ISLAMIC PERIOD

The precise significance of North Yemen's contributions to a general history of the Middle East remains a matter of considerable debate and speculation, primarily because our knowledge of Yemeni history in the pre-Islamic period remains limited. As archaeological, paleographic, and other records come to light, it should be possible in the not-too-distant future to effectively integrate North Yemen into a more comprehensive picture of Middle Eastern history specifically and human history generally.

Some of the previous efforts to place Yemeni history into the wider context of human history have given it an inordinately influential position; for example, it has been suggested that the original birthplace of the peoples who later achieved renown as the Dilmun Culture, as well as those who were later called Phoenicians, was in the area of contemporary North Yemen. In fact, some Western and Yemeni scholars have tended to hyperbole in their accounts of North Yemen's history and role in the ancient world, most notably, H. St. John Philby, who has located and attributed many of the most important developments of the ancient world to the area.[1]

Early Empires

Among contemporary scholars, the most important distinction is between those who accept what is known as the "long chronology" and those who accept the "short chronology." The key difference is which century (even millennium) before the birth of Christ important empires and events are placed. The long chronology places the origins of major Yemeni empires into the era around 1000 BC; the latter group of scholars, headed by the French scholar Jacqueline Pirenne, argue that the origins and development of the major Yemeni states and empires did not take place until around the fifth century BC.[2]

There is almost complete agreement on the names and the rough sequence of the major political entities that existed in the area we today know as North Yemen. Most of these names, however, are known only to specialists and therefore have not (yet) been included in more general histories of the Middle East. Only one seems to have indelibly impressed itself on the consciousness of Westerners, both scholars and laypeople: the Sabaean Empire, often more widely recognized in its Hebrew version, Sheba. It is, of course, primarily known because one of its queens, known as Bilqis to the Arabs, allegedly traveled to the court of King Solomon (Bible, 1 Kings 10; Quran, Surah 27:22–44). Since the traditional date of Solomon is around 1000 BC, her visit would tend to support the long chronology. On the other hand, although the story probably accurately reflects some joint trading or economic link between southwestern Arabia and the region of ancient Palestine, there is no independent evidence of its accuracy, its date, or the individuals involved. Perhaps modern archaeological investigations will provide us with additional information. Several empires (to use a modern political term) existed in southwestern Arabia, and distinctions among them may be made on the basis of any one or more of several criteria: language; geographical area; period of ascendancy; their major cities (and the evidence associated with them); and their influence on contemporary North Yemen (and the latter's perceptions of their importance).

On a few points the scholars agree. For example, it seems clear that the areas these empires controlled had adequate arable land and water (something that is no longer true today). In fact, throughout the eastern part of North Yemen, there is abundant evidence of a highly organized system of water retention and distribution: there are ruins of dams and barrages of various sizes throughout the region as well as networks of sluices and channels. Only one, however, has achieved any real fame, the "great dam" at Ma'rib, which was originally constructed sometime during the sixth century BC and "burst" in the sixth century AD. It was, as its remnants clearly show, a monumental engineering feat. The actual dam was hundreds of meters wide, and its sluices and water distribution network extended for more than 1,500 meters (4,900 feet) on both sides of the river bed. Its sheer size, the beauty of its stonework, and the sophistication of its design have attracted admiration ever since, and its fame helps to explain the decision to build a new dam in the same area.

Economic Bases

The second point of agreement among the scholars concerns the basis of the wealth of these city-states/empires. First and foremost, in terms of their contribution to economic wealth and political success, are frankincense and myrrh.[3] The other items that were of importance were generally not local products; rather, they were gathered by "Yemeni" merchants and traders in such places as East Africa and southern Asia. In other words, the knowledge of the seas and the winds the merchant sailors of these empires possessed allowed them to establish a monopoly over the trade of a large number of commodities that were highly valued by the peoples of the Mediterranean basin. Among these commodities were aromatic woods, spices of many kinds, various precious and semiprecious stones, exotic timber, fine textiles and raw silk, ostrich feathers, ivory, horns and similar animal products from East Africa, dyestuffs, and herbs.

Of all the commodities, however, it is clear that frankincense and myrrh were the most important. It is difficult for us today to conceive of the importance attached to these two products in the ancient world, although some idea of their value may be gained from the fact that in the Bible they are ranked with gold in the triad of gifts brought to the Christ child by the Magi. (It is of some interest in this regard that the early Christians all thought the kings who visited the Christ child came from southern Arabia precisely because they brought frankincense and myrrh as gifts.) Apparently the demand for these two forms of incense always exceeded the supply, and since both were used for medicinal purposes as well as for ceremonial functions of various types (including funerary), the demand remained strong for many centuries.

The source of these two commodities is in each case a small tree that grows only in southern Arabia and in a few areas on the East African coast (around the Horn of Africa). In order to protect their monopoly over both production and transportation, the states of southern Arabia resorted to techniques that have been used throughout history. They propagated various myths and legends concerning their sources, including naming the area where the majority of the trees were located "the valley of death" (Hazarmaveth in the Bible; in Arabic, Hadhramawt); they searched the harvesters daily to protect against illegal smuggling and exports; and they sought to prevent any sales outside the "consortium" of growers and marketers by tightly controlling the routes used to get the products to market. Remnants of these defenses and control arrangements are still visible today.

The monopoly of transportation was rigorously maintained by controlling all the collection points and requiring all caravans to follow specified routes through the eastern part of contemporary North Yemen until they merged into one near the present frontier between Yemen and Saudi Arabia. It may be assumed that entrepreneurs who sought to use alternative routes were dealt with harshly. Often, control over transportation passed to allies just north of the present-day Saudi province of Asir, and these allies carried the goods to the areas controlled by the Nabataeans, an Arab people located in what is today northwestern Saudi Arabia and southern Israel. All along this Incense Road, there are still signs of this trade—ruins of caravansaries, warehouses, cisterns, distance markers, graveyards, etc.—which bear witness to how lucrative, extensive, and long-lived the trade was.

The Incense Road was used in preference to the sea for a number of reasons, first and foremost among them being the fact that the land route was more reliable. The Red Sea is notably lacking in good harbors and is well-known for the treachery of its winds and currents. At a time when vessels and provisioning were considerably less dependable than today, a land route that offered specific sites for water, food, rest, and defense was much to be preferred. (Later this decision to ignore the potential for sea transport meant that the Red Sea was controlled by others, notably the Romans.)

It was, then, a combination of the agricultural wealth of the area, its (apparently) adequate rainfall, and the socioeconomic characteristics (and demands based upon them) of the peoples of the Mediterranean basin that made the ancient empires possible; when those factors changed, the states began to decay.

Centers of Power

Exactly who were those city-states, those empires, that dominated the area in ancient times? In order to answer that question, a short discussion of the various methods and criteria by which one characterizes political entities is necessary. For example, one of the important distinctions by which groups are defined is language. If this distinction is valid in the case of southern Arabia, we must return to a division noted earlier (Chapter 2), the one between 'Adnani (northern) and Qahtani (southern) Arabs.

In their language (and presumably their culture), the Sabaean and Himyar Empires were much closer to northern Arabs; if so, perhaps the visit of Bilqis to Solomon represents a recognition of some earlier ties between these immigrants from the north and their northern "relatives," since the evidence indicates that the geographical origins of the population of the Sabaean Empire was in fact to the north. On the other hand, the Minaean, Qataban, and Hadhrami states were characterized by their use of the ancient southern Arabian language—which is a related but lingu-istically quite distinct member of the Semitic language category. It is of some interest that this particular distinction continues to the present day, for in some of the rural areas of both North and South Yemen, one can still find variations in the language that reflect the difference. The best (and probably most obvious) example is the definite article: in northern ("classical") Arabic, the definite article is "al-," whereas in southern Arabic it can be "am-" or even "an-," depending on location.

Another difficulty in identifying the city-states/empires is a lack of knowledge about how they interacted or coexisted. It was long thought that the various empires followed each other in a clear, linear progression, but now it seems reasonably certain that this was not the case. Although some of them retained their independence longer than others, there were times when one or another was politically (militarily) in the ascendant. The one with the greatest fame, the Sabaean, apparently also lasted for the longest period of time—from perhaps as early as 1200 BC to perhaps as late as the fourth century AD—and there were three distinct periods when it was the most important empire (according to the long chronology).

The center of the Sabaean state was in the area of Ma'rib, and that region still has numerous remnants of Sabaean power and wealth besides the great dam. Ruins of temples and other public buildings are found throughout the Ma'rib area, and archaeologists have only recently begun the process of excavating and dating them and their contents.

The center of the Minaean state was in the area of North Yemen known today as the Jawf, in the northeastern mountains; its capital was called Qarnaw (sometimes Ma'in). Because of the difficult terrain and the fierce independence of the area's present inhabitants, it was difficult to gain access to the sites of Ma'in until rather recently. As a result, some of the sites were found to be in far better repair than those of other states, but the ravages of the civil war, stone thieves, and other kinds of entre-preneurs have greatly despoiled them. The other two major states, Qataban and Hadhramawt, were essentially named after their capital and their geographical area of control, respectively. Both are today in South Yemen and are undergoing archaeological investigations (primarily by the French).

The height of Sabaean power and influence appears to have been the reign of Karab'il Watar, around the end of the fifth century BC. In the century after he created a federation among ten different statelets in what is today eastern North Yemen, the great dam was completed, commercial missions were dispatched throughout Southeast Asia and East Africa, a colony was created in Ethiopia (at Axum, which was later to present a major threat to the Yemeni states), and Saba was influential enough to control the land routes to the Mediterranean as far north as Gaza, the northern terminus of the Incense Road, and into the Tigris and Euphrates river valley (which is considered by many scholars to be the original home of the Sabaeans). In the following centuries, other states began to assert (or, in some instances, reassert) their autonomy or independence, especially the Qataban, Hadhrami, and Minaean states. It is for this reason that the Ptolemaic geographer Eratosthenes (273–192 BC) was able to write that the four existed on an equal footing.

The simple fact that a Ptolemaic geographer described these states provides evidence of the growing power of Egypt: its fleets sailed the Red Sea freely and posed a potential threat to the southern Arabian monopoly and its trade routes. It was not, however, until Egypt became a part of the Roman Empire (when the last member of the Ptolemaic dynasty— Cleopatra—married the Roman emperor Antony) that the threat to the southern Arabian states became real. Although the first organized effort to either conquer Saba or ally it with Rome, in the year 24 BC, ended in complete disaster for the Romans (whose fleet and armies were devastated by the terrain, the weather, and Saba's northern allies), Rome continued to try to humble Saba and the other southern Arabian states. The primary motive was, of course, to control the incense trade and end the monopolistic prices the southern Arabian states charged for all the commodities in which they traded. Naturally, these prices were only possible because the Mediterranean states, like Rome, had no access to alternatives and had no products that were as highly valued by the southern Arabians. In the middle of the first century AD, the Romans experienced a monumental stroke of luck: One of their ships became caught in a monsoon and was blown to Ceylon (today's Sri Lanka, known to the Arabs as Serendib, from which the English language gets the appropriate word, serendipity). An important result was the publication of a mariners' guide—*Periplus of the Erythraen Sea*—to the South Asian sources of commodities other than frankincense and myrrh, thus ending that area's monopoly of such goods.

Soon thereafter, Rome took control of the sea routes, and the commercial basis (i.e., trade) of the wealth of the states of southern Arabia began to deteriorate. Although their continued monopoly over the supply of frankincense and myrrh made it possible for them to maintain some semblance of their former wealth and power for another couple of centuries, it was clear that the inevitable decline had set in.

Religion

In some ways, however, developments in another sphere were even more important and may have contributed more directly to the eventual decline and disappearance of the city-states. This factor was the change in the religion of the peninsula as well as of the Mediterranean.[4]

A number of local faiths coexisted in southern Arabia and on the peninsula at the time of these empires; the moon appears to have played an important role in some, and the sun and Venus seem to have also deserved special respect. There was also a multiplicity of faiths in the Mediterranean, and when the Mediterranean ideologies began to penetrate the peninsula, a monumental upheaval began. Although its origins were purely social at the outset, it soon had a tremendous impact in the economic and political spheres as well.

We cannot be absolutely certain, but it appears that Judaism was the first of the Mediterranean faiths to make its appearance on the peninsula. As Jews left Palestine after the destruction of Jerusalem by the Romans in 70 AD, some apparently moved southward and settled in some of the major towns along the Incense Road on the western edge of the peninsula. (Perhaps some of them had already been involved in the sale and distribution of southern Arabian products.) The presence of these communities of Jews in such towns as Mecca and Yathrib/Medina played an important role in the religious atmosphere of the region, and thereby in the development of Islam.

Insofar as the economic history of southern Arabia is concerned, however, the effect of the introduction of Christianity was even greater; in fact, it can be described as devastating. First, after Christianity became the official religion of the Roman Empire (in 325 AD), the demand for frankincense and myrrh plummeted as the pagan rituals that required their use were either outlawed or slowly abandoned. (The amount used by the Christian church itself, e.g., in the censers associated with its own ceremonies, was miniscule compared to previous consumption rates.)

Second, as Christianity spread even more rapidly after it was adopted by the Byzantine Empire, missionaries appeared in Arabia. They were able to win many converts, including among the peninsula's Jewish population, and by the end of the fourth and the early fifth centuries, there were major centers of Christianity on the Peninsula and adjoining islands. The largest of these is said to have been in Aden, known to the ancient world as Eudaemon, and according to local legend, the site of the garden of Eden. The major Christian sites in what is today North Yemen were in Najran, on the border between North Yemen and Saudi Arabia in the Saudi province of Asir, and in Sana'a, which may have had the largest cathedral on the Peninsula. (This cathedral is recalled by the use of the Yemeni Arabic word al-Qalis, derived from the Greek word ekklesia, to describe an area of Sana'a where there is presumed evidence of the cathedral's actual location.)

The appearance of the Christians led to fierce rivalry with the Jews, and in southern Arabia there were frequent massacres and countermassacres on the part of the two groups. (It seems likely that one of the reasons for the population's willingness to accept Islam was the general disgust, among the people who belonged to neither faith, with the behavior of the adherents of these two other forms of monotheism.) As so often happens, outsiders felt it necessary to intervene in defense of their religious cohorts. After a particularly nasty massacre of Christians in Najran (523 AD) by the Jewish king of the (now) Himyarite state, Dhu Nuwas, the Christian emperor of Byzantium requested his nearest Christian allies to intervene and avenge their deaths. As requested, Christian Ethiopians marched into North Yemen in 525, overthrew and killed Dhu Nuwas, and established a short-lived Christian protectorate. (Culturally, the Ethiopians were closely related to the Yemenis since their state, i.e., the one at Axum, had been originally established by the Sabaeans.) In turn, the Jews and their allies requested the Persian emperor to intervene on *their* behalf, and thus North Yemen was for a brief time a Persian satrapy (province)—from about 575 to 628.

ISLAM IN NORTH YEMEN

The spread of Islam into North Yemen is a complex story involving the "sons" of the last Persian governor (i.e., the descendants of the troops that had been sent to defeat the last Christian rulers), a number of prominent individuals related to some of the influential tribes and tribal confederations (e.g., the Hashid), and the remnants of the Jewish and Christian communities.[5] Most historians date the conversion of Yemen to Islam to the personal conversion of the last Persian governor, Badhan, in 628. Within two years, tradition and some evidence have it, more than half of the Yemeni tribes had also converted. Explanations for the rapidity of the spread of Islam include the excesses of the Jews and Christians referred to above and the fact that Islam was an Arabian phenomenon, incorporating into its requirements, ceremonies, and beliefs a large number of Arab traditions, beliefs, and customs.

One cannot say, however, that Yemen was easily incorporated into the new "realm of Islam"; in fact, significant portions of the southwestern corner of the peninsula resisted Islam for a long time. Furthermore, there is some doubt even today whether adherence to Islamic principles in the more remote areas is anything more than a very superficial facade (with tribal law, 'urf, being far more important in the regulation of everyday life). Insofar as this book is concerned, however, North Yemen had essentially been included within the realm of Islam by the middle of the seventh century, i.e., within twenty years of the Prophet Muhammad's death. Yemen's early association with Islam is recalled in a *hadith* ("tradition") of the Prophet, as well as in the tradition that two of Yemen's mosques—the ones in Janad and Sana'a—were begun during the Prophet's lifetime.

During the reign of the first four caliphs, leaders of the Islamic community (from *khalifa*, meaning successor), the remaining Jewish, Christian, and pagan communities in North Yemen were relatively undisturbed. During this period, it was within Islam itself that the disputes occurred, and they led to another very important development in Yemeni history.

In the Islamic community, differences of interpretation of the relevant documents, and of what constituted appropriate practices and beliefs, soon arose, and these differences led to the development of alternative Muslim communities, each of which called themselves adherents of the "real Islam." (It does not seem sacrilegious to suggest that these alternative interpretations often reflected different social and regional interests, as well as different economic and political interests in the new realm of Islam.) The most important of these alternative interpretations was concerned with who were the legitimate successors to Muhammad as leaders of the Muslim community. The adherents of the position that Muhammad's descendants, through his son-in-law and cousin Ali's marriage to his daughter Fatima, took the name Shi'at Ali ("the party of Ali")—the Shi'as of today. It is not possible here to detail the many disputes that racked the community, or the various philosophical and genealogical disputes which led to the tangled skein of murder and countermurder that afflicted the early leadership of the *umma* (Muslim community), but it should be pointed out that Ali himself was one of those who was murdered.

Ali had served as a judge in the area of North Yemen; in other words, he had close ties with the region and probably heavily influenced Muhammad, who delivered himself of a number of very favorable statements about Yemen (e.g., "faith is of Yemen" and "wisdom is Yemen"). Ali's association with Yemen is important because it undoubtedly induced many Yemenis to join the Muslim cause.

With Ali's death, the portion of the Muslim community that wished to have only the Prophet's descendants as leaders of the community (because they were presumed to be imbued with elements of the wisdom and other positive characteristics associated with Muhammad) had to look to Ali's descendants for such leadership. The leadership passed through various descendants until it reached Zayd, who proclaimed himself imam of the Muslim community in 739. When Zayd was killed shortly thereafter, his followers and adherents, incensed that other Shi'as had not come to his aid, fled Iraq and sought refuge as far from the Umayyid (Sunni) caliphs of Damascus as possible, the East African coast. Within a little more than a century, however, they moved their refuge to the mountains of North Yemen, which became a haven for other Shi'a sects as well.

Strange as it may seem, however, the long sequence of imams of the Zaydis who reigned (to a greater or lesser degree) in North Yemen until the twentieth century did not begin with someone from this group of Zaydis. Instead, the line started with one al-Hadi ila al-Haqq Yahya ibn al-Husayn al-Qasim al-Rassi, who was invited to Sa'dah as a neutral arbiter in 897. The dynasty he founded, which is known as the Rassid dynasty, was named after his grandfather, a sixth-generation descendant of Ali and Fatima.

RISE OF THE ZAYDI IMAMATE

Al-Hadi ila al-Haqq Yahya's beginnings in North Yemen were not easy, and his ascent to a position of influence and power among the Zaydis and the northern tribes was a lengthy process. North Yemen at the time, in the ninth and tenth centuries, was a battleground for various forces, including the Fatimids, who later established their own states in North Africa; the Qarmathians, an offshoot of the Isma'ili Shi'as, who had established themselves in the Tihama as well as parts of today's South Yemen; the Isma'ilis, who had established themselves in the mountains of west and central North Yemen; remnants of the Himyar nobility, who aspired to rule the southern highlands; and, of course, the Zaydis themselves.

Imam al-Hadi ila al-Haqq Yahya ibn al-Husayn, during his career as an arbiter and judge of Islamic law, was responsible for an almost infinite number of truces, compromises, settlements, and arbitrations; some of them were fleeting, some of them broken as soon as he departed the scene. Yet his reputation as a just leader flourished and spread. Although unable or unwilling to construct a permanent administrative structure, his influence upon North Yemen was to last for more than a millennium.

> His general objective was similar to that of the primitive Islamic missionaries of three centuries before, with the addition of the imamate concept. He made only a minor dent in the tribal anarchy of the time; but he accustomed the tribal chiefs to the idea that a Zaidi imam was a judicious mediator . . . and the citizens learned to expect Zaidi officials to concern themselves with morality, as their indigenous leaders often did not.[6]

Another important change also took place. The Yemenis, who were accustomed to the notion that power belongs to the one able to seize and retain it, were able in time to accept the important refinement that the seizure of power should be undertaken only by an Alid (a descendant of Ali and Fatima), especially one in the house of Rassi. Additional refinements were added over the years until Zaydi theory eventually developed the lengthy list of requirements enumerated in Chapter 2. Although this does not constitute a political theory in the Western sense of the term, the Zaydi notion of what constitutes legitimacy eventually became a pragmatic combination of a claim to leadership based on descent from Ali and the fulfillment of a specified list of prerequisites (which, it was hoped, would guarantee effective rule).

Nevertheless, it was to be some time before the ideology, the practices, and the careers of some of the prominent successors to Imam al-Hadi ila al-Haqq Yahya ibn al-Husayn became the decisive pattern of political succession, as well as the dominant political force in the Yemeni highlands. In the meantime, North Yemen continued to be wracked by political disputes between the Sunnis and Shi'as as well as between different dynastic and imperial claimants to rule in southwestern Arabia.

THE MIDDLE AGES

In the next centuries, the two most important outside claimants to rule as governors of North Yemen were the Ayyubids and the Rassulids.[7] The first, descendants of Kurds and members of the Salah al-Din (Saladin) family, ruled in the late twelfth and early thirteenth centuries; the Rassulids, whom the Ayyubids originally introduced into North Yemen, ruled for more than two centuries thereafter, i.e., into the mid-fifteenth century.

The Rassulids had their origins in a family that had some Yemeni roots, so they were perceived as being Qahtani (rather than 'Adnani) in origin. Much of the historical material of this period indicates that the Rassulids, despite their heavy taxes and maladministration, were viewed as essentially Yemeni, and therefore different from the multitude of princes, kings, and warlords who had ruled in the previous centuries.

The nature of the Rassulid rule produced effects that continue to be visible in the twentieth century. Their overwhelming reliance upon force, upon military might rather than persuasion or legal principles, to accomplish their objectives (which included strict enforcement of Zaydi precepts) meant that tribal alignments and alliances were perpetuated as a mechanism for resisting Rassulid predations and administration, especially in the northern areas. Tribal alliances, feuds, and rivalries thus also became an important aspect of all later conflicts over succession.

THE FIRST OTTOMAN PRESENCE
AND ITS AFTERMATH

The next major period is, generally, a depressing and monotonous story of maladministration, foreign depredations, oppression, exploitation, and rapacious rulers of various origins; it is not a tale that is likely to edify or produce sympathy for any of the participants (including the Yemenis).[8] This period began with the invasion of North Yemen by the Mamluk rulers of Egypt in 1517, only to be succeeded in 1538 by the Ottoman Turks after they had taken Egypt. During the next three centuries, there were brief occasions when North Yemen was self-governing, including the time (early eighteenth century) when it reached its apogee of influence and territorial extent in southwestern Arabia (until it once again fell victim to foreign manipulation, occupation, and maladministration).

A variety of Middle Eastern and, later, European rulers and states became interested in the trade that used the Red Sea as its major route, and in eliminating the south Arabians as middlemen in the lucrative commerce between the Far East and the Mediterranean. The major commodities involved were spices, foodstuffs, medicinal plants and commodities, dyestuffs, and a variety of luxury goods (such as perfumes and precious stones) as well as manufactured items.

The Portuguese were the first Europeans to enter the Red Sea, and they attempted to control the trade to southern Asia in the early years of the sixteenth century; the attempt of the Mamluks and the Ottomans to resist this encroachment on Muslim lands and prerogatives is a morbid and bloodthirsty tale of duplicity, cruelty, and unprincipled greed. Eventually, the Portuguese succeeded in wresting control of the spice trade from the Muslims and completely reoriented the trade between the Indies and Europe to their new route around the continent of Africa. The result was that the old Red Sea route, in which the Yemenis had played an important role for more than 1,500 years, withered; the income of the Yemenis (leaders and people) declined drastically, and the Ottomans had little reason to continue their presence. The Yemenis themselves managed to agree on one objective, to oust the Turks, and had succeeded in doing so by in 1636. They could not, however, agree on any indigenous replacement who could obtain, much less maintain, any widespread support, and the country sank into a period of petty rivalries and incessant warfare.

For the next two centuries, the only interest anyone evinced in North Yemen was in connection with its coffee: in the seventeenth and eighteenth centuries, the English, the French, and the Dutch were regular visitors to the port of Mocha to obtain the precious beans, and Americans began coming early in the nineteenth century. In time, of course, the Yemeni monopoly was broken, as coffee plantations were established in the colonies of those same countries (in Kenya and Uganda, French Guiana and Martinique, the Dutch East Indies, and Central American states). North Yemen was forgotten.

It was during this period that individual European travelers (as distinct from rapacious admirals and other military personnel associated with the attempts to conquer and control the Red Sea coast and its ports) first began to penetrate North Yemen and report back to Europe about the peoples and sites they found there. Probably the first such visitor to Yemen was Ludovico de Varthema, an Italian from Bologna who traveled in southwestern Arabia in the early years of the sixteenth century; he was followed by a succession of other travelers and adventurers from nearly every country in Europe. The most famous of these was undoubtedly Carsten Niebuhr, a Danish engineer who organized the first truly scientific expedition to North Yemen in the middle of the eighteenth century (he was accompanied by a linguist, a botanist, a doctor/zoologist, and an artist, though he was the only one to return alive). His account of the trip, *Description of Arabia* (1772–1774), is a true masterpiece of scientific description and analysis, and many of its observations remain valid to the present day. It contains information on the most incredible variety of matters: genealogy, social class, religion, diet, clothing, education, poetry and literature, astronomy and the sciences, medicine, etc. Although Niebuhr spent only a few months in the area, his account (and the edited materials of his biologist) kindled an interest in all aspects of North Yemen, which has continued to the present day.

THE SECOND OTTOMAN PRESENCE

In the nineteenth century, perhaps the most important event was the reappearance of the Ottoman Empire as a major influence in the Red Sea region, which included their retaking of North Yemen.[9] This second Ottoman occupation of the area was directly linked to the interests and aims of a number of other powers on the Middle Eastern scene. For example, it was around this time that the house of Sa'ud, based in central Arabia, had its first real impact on events in the Arabian Peninsula, and as its "fundamentalist" warriors took over city after city in the Nejd and Hijaz, it also turned its attention to Yemen. The Saudi seizure of the Hijaz (and the holy cities of Mecca and Medina) brought about a reaction, and the Ottoman Empire sent its most powerful vassal, Muhammad Ali of Egypt, into Arabia in order to suppress this threat to the stability of Islam. As a result, Egyptian troops once again appeared on the peninsula; after they took the Hijaz (in the name of the empire), they retook North Yemen in order to gain a stake in the Red Sea trade for Muhammad Ali.

The British became alarmed at the long-term consequences of an Egyptian/Ottoman presence on the Red Sea (and in the Gulf of Arabia), and they feared that communications with India and southern Asia might be threatened. They therefore asserted their interests by establishing a presence on the peninsula: in 1839, they took over the most important natural harbor and port in southern Arabia, Aden. It was a fateful decision and was to play an immensely important role in events that later shaped the development of North Yemen, relations between it and Great Britain into the middle of the twentieth century, the development of South Yemen, and the borders between the two Yemens.

It wasn't long before Aden began to flourish. Under British administration and benefiting from various subsidies, improved commercial policies, political stability, and much more modern harbor facilities, it soon attracted most of the trade of highland North Yemen away from the traditional Red Sea ports. Those had been allowed to deteriorate, as a result of incompetent administration over many decades (e.g., allowing ships to unload ballast in the harbor itself), and at the same time, they were not in the imam's hands in any event (in other words, there was no great motive for the highland people to use them).

In order to forestall British control of all of the Red Sea, the Ottomans reestablished their authority over the Yemeni Tihama in 1848/1849 and were apparently content to remain there. When the Suez Canal opened in 1869, however, the entire Red Sea once again assumed strategic importance as a major route to Asia. The most immediate effect was that the Ottomans once more expanded into the Yemeni highlands (1872), although they were "invited" to do so by a group of Sana'a notables who were upset and disadvantaged by the economic instability that had developed as a result of the political changes taking place in the Red Sea region.

The standards of imperial rule had improved somewhat since the previous Ottoman presence, and the rudiments of administration, education, health care, communications, transportation, and the like were at least introduced in those areas where the Ottomans were in control. On the other hand, Ottoman taxation was as capricious, exorbitant, and cruelly enforced as it had been earlier; moreover, this second administration was only marginally more just, effective, and sympathetic to Yemeni sensibilities than the first one had been. The inevitable result was that a variety of Yemeni claimants to the imamate attempted to organize a nationwide resistance to the Ottoman authorities. This time, however, because of a conviction that control of North Yemen was essential to control over the Bab al-Mandab (the strait that separates Arabia from Africa and which, in theory, can control access to and egress from the Red Sea) and therefore the Red Sea itself, and that not retaining such control would subject the Ottoman Empire's domains to erosion at the hands of the British (as well as the hands of the French and the Italians), the Ottomans were determined to remain.

During this period, a succession of other scholars—Swiss, German, French, British—also made their way into North Yemen. Most of them visited areas that had not been penetrated by Niebuhr, and they brought back to Europe the first inscriptions and sketches of the archaeological sites associated with the ancient empires—the first evidence that North Yemen contained such archaeological and paleographic treasures.

During the last quarter of the nineteenth century, the uprisings against the Ottomans increased in both number and severity, and now the Zaydis produced a succession of religious leaders with political and military skills of an order that had not been seen in North Yemen for more than 200 years. They were members of the Qasimi family, a part of the Rassid line, a collateral branch of the Hamid al-Din family, which had played an important role on many previous occasions in Yemen's history. In 1890, one Muhammad ibn Yahya Hamid al-Din became imam, and during his tenure, he managed to put together an alliance among the highland Yemenis, which included representatives of nearly all the tribes, regions, and religious affiliations present there—all in the name of a pro-Yemeni, anti-Ottoman policy.

Upon his death in 1904, Imam Muhammad was succeeded by his son Yahya, and the revolt continued. By 1911, Imam Yahya ibn Muhammad's influence and power were such that the Ottoman authorities were forced to compromise, and they signed what was, in essence, a peace treaty between themselves and the imam. Under its terms, the imam was allocated a considerable range of responsibilities in the Zaydi areas of the country but none in the Shafi'i areas. For Imam Yahya, however, the treaty was only the first step in what would be a long campaign to assert the hegemony of the Zaydi imams over their ancient patrimony—a hegemony that he perceived to be political, judicial, economic, and social as well as religious. It is perhaps surprising, then, that in World War I Imam Yahya and the Yemenis were the only Arabs to side with the Ottoman Empire in its war with the Europeans. This alliance can only be explained by Yahya's sincere and complete commitment to Muslim solidarity in the face of an outside, non-Muslim threat to the *umma*; it clearly was not motivated by love for the Ottoman administrators and troops whom he had fought for so long.

INDEPENDENT YEMEN UNDER THE IMAMS

With the end of World War I and their defeat, the Ottomans began to withdraw their contingents from the peninsula. As a result, Yemen achieved de facto independence—the first Arab state to attain it. Unfortunately, it turned out to be unexpectedly difficult to get anyone, especially such powers as Great Britain and the United States, to recognize this independence.

It was not until the mid-1920s that some states decided that they would legitimize a relationship with Yemen, and the first two states to do so were Italy and the Soviet Union. Since their motives for doing so were hardly altruistic, but rather a combination of a desire to embarrass and weaken the British presence in the Red Sea region and to increase their own political and economic influence in what they deemed to be a strategically important area, and since Yemen had little of interest to offer other countries, no widespread or general recognition of either the country or its leadership resulted.

Imam Yahya was therefore left to his own devices, especially with respect to his domestic policies. It was the first time in more than two centuries that a Zaydi imam had had such an opportunity, that is, to implement the policy goals and values that Zaydi Islam advocates. The Zaydis consider themselves to be the only true community of believers (the imam has all the traditional titles associated with his being the caliph of Islam), and the imam saw the situation as one in which the community could act as a unit after centuries of foreign intervention, manipulation, and subjection. Therefore, while attempting to keep the outside world away, Imam Yahya attempted, first, to establish his right to carry out specifically Zaydi policies in those areas under his control and, second, to create a state structure that would continue after his death, i.e., to obtain recognition of his position and his authority throughout the country and to create institutional arrangements that would remain in place for his successor.

During the interwar period, Yahya devoted much of his energy and treasure to consolidating his position as imam of the Zaydis and to obtaining analogous recognition from the non-Zaydis living in the Zaydi districts, i.e., the Jews and the Isma'ilis. He also sought to strengthen his position as temporal king of the rest of the non-Zaydi Yemenis, the Shafi'is of the south and the commercial interests in the urban centers. In these goals, he was no different from many of his predecessors; the difference was that the lack of outside interference and interests enabled him to act decisively and effectively. The result was that by the outbreak of World War II, Yahya's regime was in fact largely consolidated, accepted (if grudgingly), and even operating relatively efficiently and honestly (at least in comparison with the Ottoman period and before). Moreover, it was concerned with enforcing Zaydi precepts.

Whether or not Imam Yahya would have succeeded in accomplishing all of his domestic goals (not to mention his foreign policy goals, such as autarky and driving the British from southern Arabia) if World War II had not occurred is a question we shall never be able to answer. The war drastically altered the entire world, including Yemen, and even Imam Yahya recognized that some accommodations with the changed order were necessary—for example, he agreed to join both the Arab League and the United Nations.

On the other hand, it is important to point out that Yahya had largely achieved his primary aim: to create a Shi'a state that was independent, governed by an imam, and capable of enforcing the principles and doctrines of Islam (as understood by the Zaydis). Such a state had not existed for centuries, and there would not be another one until the takeover of Iran by Ayatullah Ruhollah Khomeini in the late 1970s.

Imam Yahya found it necessary to take some steps toward accepting the industrial, commercial, military, and even social influences that were developing outside Yemen and beginning to impinge upon it. He concluded that foreign, especially military, technology might be useful for his own purposes, but understanding such technology required more extensive education and training, which, by its very nature and extent, also meant exposure to other influences (ideas). The first Yemenis to leave the country for a secular foreign education at government expense went to Iraq in the mid-1930s (wealthy Yemenis had been sending their children abroad for years). Imam Yahya had been displeased with the poor showing of his tribal levies against Saudi Arabia in the war in 1934 in which Yemen had been forced to give up Najran and all of Asir. The imam wished to be able to field a modernized regular army, one that would be loyal to the imam and more successful in the future. When the individuals who had been sent to Iraq for more education returned, they almost immediately became involved in political affairs; in fact, all of them participated in various movements and schemes to modify the imam's system—thus ending Yahya's original scheme to modernize the armed forces.

These military officers were not, however, the only ones who chafed under the imam's restrictions; similar resentment against his policies was especially strong in the southern towns that had some access to Aden, which under British rule had developed into a major metropolis with a cosmopolitan population and sophisticated economy. Inevitably, the small commerce-oriented middle class, joined and supported by a small group of intellectuals, began to agitate for reforms (as well as opening up Yemen to the outside world). Imam Yahya, schooled in the conflicts of the nineteenth century and the way of life of imams of earlier centuries, could not and would not accede to any changes in the way in which he dealt with what he perceived to be the major issues of the time: foreign interference in Yemeni affairs and lack of respect for Zaydi principles especially.

In 1948, a coalition of opponents decided to remove Yahya from his position as imam and to create a "constitutional imamate," but one of the factions decided to assassinate him instead. This act enabled his son Ahmad, an able and shrewd if merciless and often cruel individual who had been his father's major supporter and commander of his forces in the campaigns of the 1920s and 1930s, to weld together a different coalition. This one included the northern tribes, who traditionally supported the imamate; elements of the traditional nobility—i.e., high status families and clans (sayyids)—that had produced imams in the past; and some progressive elements that had been shocked by the assassination. With their support, Ahmad was able to restore the ancien régime with himself as the new imam. For about fifteen years, Ahmad was able to follow essentially the same policies as his father, including permitting Yemenis to study abroad to acquire skills and training he felt the government needed (in military technology and certain types of public-works technology such as electricity, telecommunications, and water management). However, the number and size (in terms of the number of participants) of rebellions against his policies and system began to increase markedly after the mid-1950s.[10]

Imam Ahmad died of natural causes on 19 September 1962 (though his health had been much weakened by disease and the bullets from unsuccessful assassination attempts that were still in his body). He was succeeded by his son, Muhammad al-Badr, to whom he had delegated some limited authority on previous occasions when he had gone to Rome for medical treatment. However, although Ahmad had been able to convince or coerce many of the relevant elements into publicly accepting Muhammad al-Badr as his successor, a traditional Yemeni reluctance to accept more than three members of the same family in a row as imams came into play. (More than once in the past, this tradition had led to civil conflict.) Within a week, elements of the military under the leadership of one of the officers who had been trained abroad attempted to assassinate al-Badr. Although they failed, they did proclaim the establishment of a republic and the end of the imamate (on 26 September) and set about attempting to introduce the reforms and modernization for which their predecessors had advocated and agitated for more than two decades.

It was not to be a peaceful transition. Al-Badr escaped into the northern mountains and led the attempt to restore his regime (just as his father had done)—although al-Badr supported many of the reforms and changes in the economy and the political system that had been demanded.[11] The result was an eight-year long civil war, as partisans of the republic (republicans) and of the imamate (royalists) fought for control of the country.

THE REVOLUTION OF 1962 AND CIVIL WAR

The news that Imam Muhammad al-Badr had escaped with his life from the shelling of his palace in Sana'a, and even more important had managed to make his way into the northern mountains where the Zaydi imams had always had their traditional basis of support, changed what was supposed to be a simple revolution into a lengthy and often bloody civil war. It was not even to be a simple civil war, with clear-cut alternatives concerning Yemen's future political system. Rather, it became an "internationalized" conflict, involving the United Nations, many of the other Arab states (with Saudi Arabia being the most important), and many of the great powers. Furthermore, some actions and policies on the part of some of the participants (notably Egypt) not only violated international law but simple human decency (the use of poison gas), and there were untold acts of duplicity and sheer opportunism and multiple acts of outrageous cruelty (in the treatment of prisoners). The result was thousands of casualties—among the combatants as well as the civilian population—and perhaps the kind of war for which Yemen's medieval past should have prepared the participants.

Factions in North Yemen

Although certain groups chose sides early in the conflict and tended to remain on that side, there were others that changed their allegiance during the conflict. Some did so out of principle, some were influenced by the tide of battle, some were swayed by the amount of the subsidy they received from the respective sides for their support, and some changed because of various real or perceived slights to their honor.

On the side of the revolution, whose supporters soon were called republicans, there were the major intellectuals, who had founded a variety of movements, especially in Aden, and had been calling for reforms for more than twenty years—Muhammad al-Zubayri, Ahmad Muhammad Nu'man, Abd al-Rahman al-Iryani, etc. There were also the commercial and mercantile elements in the towns and cities; most of the Shafi'i population; most of the detribalized population of the towns and villages of the Tihama; the majority of Yemeni workers abroad (in Aden, Djibouti, etc.); and those government workers who were employed in the modernized sector, i.e., members of the army and directors and technicians associated with the public services such as water supply, electricity, telecommunications, and the cotton and tobacco industries.

In addition, at least at the outset, there were those families who opposed the continuation of the imamate in the Hamid al-Din family; these families included the al-Wazirs, the Sharaf al-Din, and some others.

Many of these people, however, once the imamate as an institution appeared threatened, supported the "third force" movement or some similar effort to create a constitutional imamate. And last, but definitely not least, there were the tribes of the central and northern regions who had varying motives for supporting the republic. Probably the most important of these was the Hashid Confederation, under the leadership of Shaykh al-Ahmar. On more than one occasion, his support of the republic enabled it to survive. On the other hand, there were many tribes who changed their loyalty repeatedly; it would not be possible (or even necessary or desirable) to detail the number of times some of these tribes switched sides.

On the side of the imamate, the royalists had a different constellation of forces, and most of them were not as consistent in their support or as intensely committed. First and foremost among them were, of course, those tribes and tribal confederations whose loyalty to Zaydi Islam and the Zaydi imamate could be expected to be the paramount consideration. In general, they included nearly all of the Zaydi tribes of the north, northwest, and northeastern sections of North Yemen as well as some of those in the central highlands, i.e., around Sana'a.

The major additional source of support for the imam came from elements of the population throughout the country that were disillusioned or disaffected with the republic and its policies. This faction included a few loose tribal groupings in the Tihama and some in the region south of Sana'a (in the western mountains).

But, this list is, it must be remembered, largely a description of how the population chose up sides at the outset, and during the eight years of the conflict, there was a constantly shifting set of alliances and new allegiances. Perhaps it would be most accurate to say that throughout the conflict, a majority of the Zaydis supported the royalist side and a majority of the Shafi'is supported the republican side.

Outside Participants

As the war dragged on, the list of other participants grew. Countries in the Middle East and elsewhere saw their interests, their ideological principles, and their objectives in the world arena either threatened or affected by developments in the Yemeni war. The result was that what had begun as a domestic conflict over the form of government developed into an international one between "progressive" and "conservative" forces.

A brief overview of who these other participants were includes, on the side of the republic, the "progressive" Arab states, such as Egypt, Iraq, and Algeria, and "progressive" forces in other areas of the world, i.e., the Soviet Union, the People's Republic of China, and many of their allies and satellites. These countries were later joined by the United States, West Germany, and others that did not want to see their image as supporters of reform, economic development, and struggling Third World countries tarnished.

On the side of the royalists, there were the more "conservative" Arab/Middle Eastern states such as Jordan, Morocco, and Iran. Further afield, Great Britain was the only major Western state to actively oppose the republic. But by all odds, the most important supporter of the cause of the imamate was Saudi Arabia. That country's very location, on Yemen's northern and eastern borders, made it most immediately concerned with the effects of such a drastic change in the political orientation of the country. Furthermore, since the leaders of the republic announced soon after the deposition of the imam that they were also interested in creating a Republic of the Arabian Peninsula, the Saudi monarchy felt personally threatened by the revolutionary activities on its southern frontiers. One other aspect of Saudi Arabia's location was of great importance during the conflict: it was able to transfer arms and money directly to the northern Yemeni tribes without any serious interference. As a result, it may be suggested that only after Saudi Arabia had been convinced to change its policies with respect to providing subsidies and weapons to these tribes that the war could come to an end (though this was not the only relevant factor).

The United States, under President John F. Kennedy, decided to recognize the republic rather early in order to bolster the image of the United States (and Kennedy) as a supporter of reform and progress in the Middle East. At the same time, the United States was also tied, in a variety of ways, to Saudi Arabia—perhaps its major Arab friend in the region—and the United States was Saudi Arabia's major arms supplier. As a result, in 1963, it was U.S. arms, which had been purchased under particularly favorable terms by the Saudis, that wound up in the hands of the imamate's supporters. Furthermore, U.S.-operated training and similar military programs (i.e., in Jordan and the Najran Oasis) provided the royalists with some modicum of training in the equipment as well as in modern military organization. Bluntly put, the United States supported both sides—a position that soon became untenable and cost the United States dearly in prestige and influence for some years thereafter.

As the war continued, new elements appeared. For example, the international community sought some means of either limiting or ending the conflict. In the summer of 1963, the United Nations Security Council authorized the creation of a United Nations Yemen Observation Mission (UNYOM), whose purpose was to disengage the major parties (domestic and foreign) and provide for a peaceful transition to some completely Yemeni government. Frustrated and obstructed in a variety of ways by both of the major foreign participants at the time, Egypt and Saudi Arabia, UNYOM was disbanded in the following year (September 1964).

Steps Toward a Settlement

The means by which a settlement was eventually reached finally began to emerge, as disaffected republican elements and the more modernized elements among the royalists began to move toward each other. The process was clearly an attempt to find a Yemeni solution, and it was, of course, the only possible way for the conflict to end in view of the multiplicity of participants and motives.

This "third force," as it became known, was not at first very successful, and it underwent a number of transformations on the tortuous path of trying to hammer out a compromise that would take into account Yemeni circumstances, interests, personalities, and domestic problems. In fact, it was only when some of the other participants, especially the external ones, decided for one reason or another that they were "fed up" with Yemen—its intrigues, the war's costliness, and the international morass into which they had (willingly) been dragged—that the third force groups began to exert some influence over the course of events.

The first such efforts at compromise were proposed by a group that called itself the Party of God (Hizb-Allah; no relation to the Shi'a faction in Lebanon of the same name in the 1980s), and this group met with some royalists in the Sudan in late 1964. Over the next three years, other such joint meetings were held in Yemen—at Khamir (May 1965), Harad (November 1965), etc.—and other meetings were also held by the two major outside participants—in Jidda in Saudi Arabia (August 1965) and Khartum in the Sudan (August 1967).

It was the Jidda meeting that produced the so-called Jidda Agreement, which eventually became the keystone to Egyptian withdrawal. Since it had been the decision of Jamal Abd al-Nasir (Nasser) to intervene in the Yemeni situation that had precipitated the intervention of so many others, his decision to withdraw essentially provided the signal for others to do likewise. When the Egyptians finally did leave in 1967, it was clear that their economy and military establishment had been dealt severe blows. The total cost to Egypt, in terms of men and material, may never be known; for one thing, the government was reluctant to admit exactly how high its casualties were. (The number of Egyptian troops in Yemen had varied from around 70,000 during some of the major offensives against the royalists to fewer than 20,000 during one of the earlier abortive disengagement agreements.) It was, however, clear that Yemen in the 1960s had become as much of a graveyard for Egyptian soldiers as it had been on previous occasions (e.g., the first century BC, the sixteenth century

AD, and even under Muhammad Ali). On the other hand, the cost of the war for Egypt, widely estimated to have been more than $1 million per day, was in the long run largely borne by the USSR through its generous program of assistance to Egypt during the mid-1960s. Within Egypt itself, some people suggested that Egypt's disastrous defeat in the 1967 war with Israel was at least in part occasioned by the long conflict in Yemen (and the consequent depletion of supplies and trained troops).

Egypt's policies had also incurred the enmity of a majority of Yemeni political figures of various ideological persuasions. Indeed, much of the political activity of the years 1965–1967 was an effort by moderate republicans, disaffected with Egyptian policies, to reach an agreement with their opponents. These efforts were often stymied by a small group of absolutely intransigent and Egyptian-supported Yemenis, such as Col. Abdullah al-Sallal, one of the first leaders of the revolution.

There were also problems within the royalist camp, largely because the imam never seemed to be able to act decisively. Unlike his father and grandfather before him, who had led their forces into battle personally and thereby earned an enviable reputation for courage as well as demonstrating their right to be imam, Muhammad al-Badr delegated such responsibilities. Furthermore, he also seemed incapable of providing effective political leadership and was never able to build a real coalition of interests capable of providing a viable alternative to the programs and promises of the republicans. At the same time, the fact that he was accepting money from Sunnis (the Saudis and the Jordanians) and allowing them to set some conditions on his operations—in other words, he couldn't even exercise adequate control over the funding and arms that were provided—cost him dearly in terms of prestige. That prestige was also diminished by the duplicitous actions of some of the tribal chieftains—including reselling some of their weaponry—which alienated much of the support for the cause of the imamate as an idea and office of high moral purpose. In general, the leadership of the royalist faction was poorly coordinated, poorly exercised, and only irregularly organized enough to present a real threat; ultimately, the royalist effort rested upon the willingness of certain tribes to continue the war.

In the final analysis, it was the year 1967 that was decisive: the Egyptians suffered an overwhelming defeat at the hands of the Israelis, and the British decided to withdraw from South Yemen (i.e., the Crown Colony of Aden and the Aden protectorates), leaving behind an adamantly antimonarchical regime. As a result, the Saudis were faced with the prospect of two revolutionary regimes along their entire southern frontier. No doubt the Saudis decided that accepting a moderate regime in Sana'a was preferable to dealing with two antagonistic regimes at the same time.

The result of the Egyptian decision to withdraw, and the Saudi decision to accept less than a full restoration of the imamate was a stalemate in North Yemen. The rudimentary government apparatus of the Hamid al-Dins began to disintegrate, largely because the most talented and energetic of its members, Prince Muhammad ibn Husayn, resigned as the imam's deputy in the spring of 1969; the only really effective royalist military commander had already resigned in October 1968.

Still, the terrain of the highlands meant the royalists could hold off the republican forces, even if the former could not advance, and desultory battles and disruptions of each other's transportation and supply networks continued. It became clear, however, that neither side would be able to win a decisive and final victory, even after the outside participants had withdrawn.[12]

Compromise of 1970

In the spring of 1970, the Saudis finally decided to encourage negotiations between the two sides (in Jidda). These meetings were attended by senior royalist leaders (but members of the Hamid al-Din clan were excluded), and a number of important officials from the republican side. It didn't take long for an agreement to be reached, to which Imam Muhammad al-Badr gave his approval—thus, at least for the moment, ending the history of the Zaydi imamate in North Yemen. The imam moved to Great Britain, and the process of reconciliation began.

The terms of the Compromise of 1970 produced a unified central government, with royalist officials continuing to carry out whatever limited administrative responsibilities they had in the areas under their control. The Republican Council was expanded to include a royalist member, and three portfolios in the cabinet were given to royalists. In addition, eight royalists were named to the Consultative Council, and others received appointments in the diplomatic service. Although the terms of the agreement (not to mention its mere existence) were opposed by some elements on both sides, the more strident opponents were quietly but firmly suppressed (some were sent into exile) or transferred to responsibilities where they could not effectively interfere with the implementation of the compromise. Two months later, Saudi Arabia and the new Yemen Arab Republic established diplomatic relations, and the long civil war was over.

NOTES

1. H. St. John Philby, *The Background of Islam* (Alexandria, Egypt: Whitehead Morris, 1947).

2. In general, the majority of today's historians and scholars of ancient Yemen accept the long chronology. A summary of the dispute (from the point of view of a defender of the short chronology) may be found in Jacqueline Pirenne, "The Chronology of Ancient South Arabia—Diversity of Opinion," in Werner Daum, ed. *Yemen* (Innsbruck: Pinguin; Frankfurt: Umschau [1988]), pp. 116–122. See also the following works on the country's ancient history: Walter W. Mueller, "Outline of the History of Ancient South Arabia," in Daum, *Yemen*, pp. 49–54; Remy Audouin, J.-F. Breton, and C. Robin, "Towns and Temples—The Emergence of South Arabian Civilization," in Daum, *Yemen*, pp. 63–77; and R. LeBaron Bowen, Frank Albright, et al., *Archeological Discoveries in South Arabia* (Baltimore, MD: Johns Hopkins Press, 1958). An informative, illustrated, and more popular account is Brian Doe, *South Arabia* (London: Thames and Hudson, 1971). On the most recent discoveries, it is worth consulting the annual review *Raydan*, the journal of ancient Yemeni antiquities and epigraphy (published since 1978 by Peeters, Louvain).

3. The significance of this trade tends to be under appreciated today in view of the minimal value of these commodities in current markets. For additional information on all aspects of this important commerce in the past, see Nigel Groom, *Frankincense and Myrrh* (London: Longman, 1981), and J. Innes Miller, *The Spice Trade of the Roman Empire* (Oxford: Clarendon Press, 1969). See also Walter W. Mueller, "Notes on the Use of Frankincense in South Arabia," *Proceedings of the Seminar for Arabian Studies* 6 (1976), pp. 124–136.

4. For a good, short summary, see the two essays by Alfred F.L. Beeston, "The Religions of Pre-Islamic Yemen," and "Judaism and Christanity in Pre-Islamic Yemen," in Joseph Chelhod, *L'Arabie du Sud* (Paris: Maisonneuve et Larose, 1984–1985), 1:259–278, and Jacques Ryckmans, "The Old South Arabian Religion," in Daum, *Yemen*, pp. 107–110.

5. The standard works are Arthur S. Tritton, *Rise of the Imams of Sana'a* (London: Oxford University Press, 1925), and C. van Arendonk, *Les Debuts de l'Imamat Zaidite au Yemen* (Leiden: E. J. Brill, 1960).

6. Robert W. Stookey, *Yemen: The Politics of the Yemen Arab Republic* (Boulder, CO: Westview Press, 1978), p. 94.

7. Henry Cassels Kay, ed. *Yaman, Its Early Medieval History* (London: Edward Arnold, 1892); G. Rex Smith, "The Political History of the Islamic Yemen Down to the First Turkish Invasion," in Daum, *Yemen*, pp. 129–139 (a thorough survey with an extensive bibliography); R. L. Playfair, *A History of Arabia Felix or Yemen* (Bombay: Education Society, 1859).

8. Manfred Wenner, "An Economic History of Yemen: 1500–1948," in Daum, *Yemen*, pp. 322–329; Eric Macro, *Yemen and the Western World Since 1571* (New York: Praeger, 1968); John Baldry, "Al-Yaman and the Turkish Occupation 1849–1914," *Arabica* 23:2 (1976), pp. 156–196.

9. In the nineteenth century, a large number of travelers and other visitors produced accounts dealing with various aspects of the country and its culture as well as with the economic and political changes that were taking place. A good overview of developments is Thomas Marston, *Britain's Imperial Role in the Red Sea Area 1800–1878* (Hamden, CT: Shoe String Press, 1961). Some of the traveler

and scholar accounts that are still useful for an understanding of the country and its development include Eduard Glaser, *Eduard Glasers Reise nach Marib* (Vienna: Alfred Hölder, 1913); Walter B. Harris, *A Journey through the Yemen* (Edinburgh: Wm. Blackwood, 1893); G. Wyman Bury, *Arabia Infelix, or the Turks in Yemen* (London: Macmillan, 1915); A. Deflers, *Voyage au Yemen* (Paris: Paul Klincksieck, 1889); Paul E. Botta, *Relation d'une voyage dans l'Yemen* (Paris: E. DeSoye, 1880); A.J.B. Wavell, *A Modern Pilgrim in Mecca and a Siege in Sana* (London: Constable, 1912); Renzo Manzoni, *El Yemen: Tre Anni nell'Arabia Felice* (Rome: Tipografia Eredia Botta, 1884); Eugen Mittwoch, *Aus dem Jemen* (Leipzig: D.M.G., bei Brockhaus, 1926); and Heinrich von Maltzan, *Reise nach Südarabien* (Braunschweig: Vieweg, 1873).

    10. Manfred W. Wenner, *Modern Yemen 1918–1966* (Baltimore, MD: Johns Hopkins Press, 1967), esp. Chapters 3, 4, and 6; J. Leigh Douglas, *The Free Yemeni Movement 1935–1962* (Beirut: American University of Beirut, 1987).

    11. Imam al-Badr was allowed to escape by the revolutionaries because the man leading them had had his life spared by al-Badr a few years earlier when Ahmed had ordered his death (personal communication to the author).

    12. Wenner, *Modern Yemen*, esp. Chapters 5, 7, and 8. On the war, see Dana Adams Schmidt, *Yemen: The Unknown War* (London: Bodley Head, 1968), and Edgar O'Ballance, *The War in the Yemen* (Hamden, CT: Archon Books, 1971).

5

The Republic

The founders of the new republic were essentially a coalition of reformist military figures, elements of the commercial class, and a wide variety of intellectuals. They faced an incredible number of problems in attempting to bring about the changes envisaged as either necessary or desirable—first in the political and then in the economic and social realms.

There were, of course, very different conceptions of what the "new order" ought to look like, who should direct it, and what kinds of institutions were required in order to make it successful. There were also very different ideas as to what kinds of foreign and domestic policies ought to be followed as well as very different conceptions of what kinds of assistance, and from whom, would be available for both the near and far terms as the republic developed.

Several very specific problems had to be dealt with in order to accomplish *any* of the goals. Among the most obvious of these were first, integrating the tribal elements into the system. The unique position, influence, and characteristics of the tribes in North Yemen are an important part of the contemporary political system and for an understanding of that system (less so the economic, since the tribes should not be thought of as economic units). Second, there was the need to create a new political/government system that would be able to accomplish a number of goals; the two most important of these being integrating the royalists into the new system and creating a system that had some new and recognized basis of legitimacy (to replace the imamate). That basis of legitimacy was generally assumed to be increased popular participation in policymaking through new mechanisms. The third problem was concerned with institutionalization in the broadest sense, that is, to create and staff the variety of administrative, regulatory, and service agencies and bureaus associated with modern governments: finance, justice, agriculture, health, education, transportation, etc.

During the civil war, it had been impossible to create any institutional framework that was not simply an adjunct of the military and its goals.

In fact, while the Egyptians bore the major responsibility for the republic (from 1962 to 1968), all the functions of a modern state bureaucracy and administration were carried out essentially by (and even for) the Egyptians, and then only in those areas that were under the government's control.

Beginning with the phased withdrawal of the Egyptians and the multiple efforts to reach a compromise, there was a transition period, and during this time, a number of experiments were undertaken in the effort to accomplish some of the goals enumerated above. In many respects, however, the first priority was and had to be national reconciliation; this goal involved, to put it bluntly, the elimination of the more extremist elements on both sides, i.e., the most adamant supporters of the imam as well as the most uncompromising supporters of radical policies for a new Yemen and the Arabian Peninsula in general.

On the royalist side, this meant the elimination of the most conservative and uncompromising supporters of the continued existence of the imamate as an institution, as well as the role of Muhammad al-Badr in any future political arrangements. In fact, to all intents and purposes, this faction had already been discredited by the late 1960s, since the most competent and intelligent members of the royalist camp had already begun to participate in various informal and formal discussions with republicans. On the Republican side, the conflict was to prove far more deadly and prolonged. In 1968, during the defense of Sana'a against the last royalist siege, it had been the Left that had organized the Popular Resistance Forces and the successful withstanding of the siege. Moreover, this group had organized itself as the Revolutionary Democratic Party, a kind of umbrella organization to press for reforms and changes. One Hasan al-Amri led the republican forces, which consisted of the moderates and most of the tribalists. Both of these republican groups were prepared to negotiate with the royalists, but it was only after the Left had been dealt a crushing blow that it became possible for the two remaining factions to reach the Compromise of 1970. Once the Compromise had been arranged and actual combat had ceased, it was the task of the new republican/royalist government to cope with the goals enumerated above.

POLITICAL ROLE OF THE TRIBES

The tribe, it must be recalled, is the basic unit of social and political organization in most of North Yemen, and furthermore, the tribes are of immense military importance.[1] But, and this fact is often forgotten, the function of the tribe in each of these aspects of life, and in its relationship to the state and its governing bodies, is very different. Any analysis of the role of the tribes is made more difficult by the extraordinary complexity, as well as the flexibility, of their role and function.

Understanding their role, both during the civil war and in the contemporary political system, requires further elaboration. Up to the reign of Imam Yahya, the vast majority of the tribes of North Yemen belonged to four large confederations, but his campaigns to subject the tribes to his control succeeded in (apparently) permanently eliminating two of these confederations. The two remaining confederations, the Hashid and the Bakil, are the major ones today. (There are also a few smaller groupings of tribes, for example, around Sana'a, and a very loose association in the Tihama known as the Zaraniq). Hashid and Bakil are names of great antiquity, and the genealogies of many of their tribes and families are traced back to the pre-Islamic period. The number of tribes that belong to each of these two confederations is not specific, however; indeed, both the number and the actual tribes vary over time. The variation is owing to such factors as conflicts over land or water or civil or criminal disputes between members of allied tribes, as well as more general issues of policy that may affect them differently (such as the tax rate imposed). To put it another way, a tribe may change its affiliation from one confederation to another as a result of some issue that is of central importance to a tribe's members or leaders; there are few permanent affiliations. The membership of each confederation is determined by a constantly shifting set of alliances, agreements, and affiliations, which are presumed to meet the demands of, and provide benefits for, tribal members.

For many years, writers on Yemen referred to the Hashid and the Bakil confederations as the "two wings of the imamate," implying that without their support (and the warriors they could field), the imamate would have ceased to exist. This observation is not true, as a substantial volume of research that has been undertaken in more recent years has amply demonstrated. In fact, although the Zaydi tribes could, in general, be rallied to the cause of the imamate, *which* tribes responded and *why* was not a simple question of supporting the imamate. In fact, it more often had to do with local issues, the personalities (i.e., of tribal leaders, the imam, and government officials) involved, the role of the sayyids, other pending disputes, etc. In most of the Yemeni literature on the tribes, the imams are depicted as quite ambivalent if not hostile toward the tribes, describing them as the "evil ones" on more than one occasion. This characterization was often the result of significant policy differences between the tribes and the imams, and therefore it represents only a specific viewpoint at a particular point in time; it should, however, serve to make the reader aware of the fact that the tribes have their own interests to protect, their own sets of policies and problems to cope with, and their own sets of enemies and friends. There is no reason to assume or suppose

A gathering of tribal figures (Sa'adah). Photo copyright Martin Lyons. Used by permission.

that there ever would be a universal overlap between their interests and those of the imams, or indeed any government, especially if one takes into account the variations in geography, resources, and population of North Yemen.

As a result, the imams had to develop their own set of mechanisms, sometimes extremely crude and cruel, to cope with the machinations and determined independence of the tribes if the imams were to influence, alter, or even implement their own policies. For one thing, on more than one occasion, the tribes resorted to wholesale sacking of larger towns or villages in order to demonstrate their power and/or opposition to government policy. Indeed, the city of Sana'a was turned over to tribespeople for precisely that purpose in 1948 by Imam Ahmad in retaliation for the fact that the city and its population had sided with the attempt to overthrow the ruling Hamid al-Dins. When Sana'a was threatened once again by the tribes in 1968, the population—remembering the cruelties associated with the 1948 sacking—managed a heroic defense, organized in part by the leftist forces who were later eliminated as an important element in the domestic politics of the republic.

In more recent times, specifically during the reign of Imam Yahya, this effort to rein in the tribes, and furthermore to make them adhere to the Shari'a (rather than 'urf), was undoubtedly the most thoroughgoing and effective of any such effort in many centuries. It was accomplished through a combination of a system of *divide et impera*, financial induce-ments, judicious use of armed forces loyal to the Hamid al-Dins, and a ruthless taking of hostages from the major tribal families and some of the tribal units. However, it was precisely this policy (also followed by Imam Ahmad) that led to the decision of some tribes to support the republic, because Imam Ahmad's policies and means of coping with the growing unrest in the country had led to some rash acts in dealing with some of the major tribal shaykhs in the late 1950s. Foremost among these were the paramount shaykhs of the Hashid Confederation (the al-Ahmar family of Khamir, of the 'Usaymat tribe), the Nihm of the Bakil Confed-eration, the Abu Luhum of the Zaraniq, the Abu Ra's of the Dhu Muham-mad, and some others.

During the civil war, tribes that had affiliated with one side or the other arranged truces between themselves, and in general they employed many of the traditional mechanisms (i.e., *'urf*) in order to limit the destructiveness of the conflict on their territory, for their personnel, and on their livelihood. It is this ability to mobilize large numbers of men for combat, to both contain and participate in conflict, and to control access to, and activity within, their territory that has made the tribes such a problem for governments. Perhaps more important, despite the fact that the tribes have come to play a major role in the politics of the republic, there is no regularized mechanism for their participation in the political life of the country. They have used many of the institutions that have been created since 1970 as the means to influence public policy, and they have succeeded far beyond the expectations of the architects of the republic, and perhaps even their own.

POLITICAL EFFECTS OF THE CIVIL WAR

As already noted, the civil war made it impossible to implement many of the desired changes and reforms, and two other factors, over which the Yemenis had little or no control, also markedly influenced developments after the war ended.[2] First, there was a prolonged drought in the late 1960s, which substantially destroyed the ability of many Yemenis to survive the conflict that raged around them without external assistance (especially food). Even though centuries of self-serving and occasionally malevolent rulers in Yemen had made more than a subsis-tence-level existence improbable for the vast majority of the population, they had at least been able to survive. The effects of the drought of the 1960s, however, coupled with the depredations, military operations, and side effects of the war, were more than the majority could cope with effectively. The fact that the republican government had access to outside sources of supplies and was often able to deliver them to needy areas added considerably to the acceptability and prestige of the new regime.

Second, North Yemen was caught up in the geopolitical ambitions of the Egyptians in the Red Sea region. Although President Jamal Abd al-Nasir acted from a multiplicity of motives in supporting the republic and sending thousands of Egyptian troops to its defense, one of the most important of his motives was his desire to modernize an Arab state in order to make it more capable of resisting the political and economic blandishments, machinations, and manipulations of the Western powers. This desire was an integral part of his scheme to create an Arab power bloc in the world arena.

This modernization required at least some effort toward establishing an institutional infrastructure. Since there were virtually no Yemenis trained and able to lead, or even effectively staff, a modern government system, Egyptians were assigned the relevant tasks. In sum, the civilian as well as the military leadership of the new republic was thoroughly subordinate to the interests and policy aims of the Egyptians until 1968.

Eventually, as noted, Yemenis from both camps began the process of rapprochement, and the Compromise of 1970 was effected. But the end of the civil war meant that a whole new set of problems had to be dealt with. In fact, the enforced republican solidarity—which the royalist threat had made necessary—was the first casualty of the rapprochement. Factions that had previously subordinated their differences in the interest of the republic now had multiple motives, multiple goals, and multiple occasions to differ on a wide range of issues and policies. The Compromise then, in a perverse but understandable way, made some of the domestic conflicts worse, precisely because the threat presented by a potential royalist victory—which had acted as a mechanism to submerge such ideological, policy, and personality differences—had disappeared.

It had of course been difficult, if not impossible, for the republic to begin the construction of a complete administrative infrastructure, a modern economy, and a new political system while it was engaged in a fierce civil war. During those years, the royalists continued a very traditional political system in the northern mountains, which, as the war dragged on, became increasingly ineffective and incompetent as well as dependent upon the largesse and support of the Saudis. The republicans, on the other hand, began to create and attempt to run government agencies and to try to supply the kind of services associated with modern governments. Although their efforts were limited, rudimentary, and largely dependent upon the Egyptians, they did attempt to come to terms with the modern world, and in this respect, they made the royalist system look even more backward.

It was not until after the Compromise—and after the two major outside powers had withdrawn from the arena and allowed the Yemenis to work out a mutually satisfactory agreement—that any real progress on a new political system could begin. The efforts of the republicans up to that point were not irrelevant, however; indeed, the basic outlines of the new institutions and the new framework had been shaped by the republicans during the civil war years, and the people who were to become the major architects and governors of the postwar system began to achieve prominence at that time.

The major architects of the revolution had been army officers, among whom the most well-known to the general public was undoubtedly Abdullah al-Sallal, who had been associated with a number of earlier attempts to alter the political system (and who had been among those sent abroad to acquire sophisticated military skills). However, his subservience to Egyptian interests, the corruption that marred his administration, and his generally ineffective leadership had managed to discredit him among most Yemenis by the mid-1960s. When the Egyptians began to recognize alternatives to al-Sallal among the Yemenis and began their withdrawal, leadership of the republic was transferred in 1967 to a Republican Council, which consisted of three leading figures: Abd al-Rahman al-Iryani, who was chairman; Ahmad Muhammad Nu'man; and Shaykh Muhammad Ali Uthman, a Shafi'i.

This change marked the political ascendancy of moderates among the republicans at the same time that moderates were coming to the fore among the royalists, which made it possible to seriously consider a compromise between the two warring camps. The interesting aspect of this development is that the people who worked for a compromise, and eventually succeeded in arranging one, were traditional civilian politicians. However, the emergence of civilian leadership was not achieved without a price, as the 1968 struggle for control over the direction and leadership of the republic shows. At the time of the siege of Sana'a and its aftermath the political Left consisted of a number of Ba'athi factions (the Ba'ath is a multinational political party in the Arab world), supporters of Jamal Abd al-Nasir, members of the Yemeni branch of the Arab Nationalist Movement (ANM), elements sympathetic to the National Liberation Front (the political group that had succeeded in wresting control of South Yemen from Great Britain), and a collection of rather more radical groups seeking rapid change, most of whom had been associated with the formation of the Popular Resistance Forces (which had organized the defense of Sana'a against the tribal siege).

For better or worse, the moderates succeeded in defeating the Left and purged the Left from every organization and body that could influence or make public policy. Perhaps of greatest importance was the fact that the moderates were all Zaydis while a significant proportion of the leftists were Shafi'is, which exacerbated the level of friction between the two sects for a time. In the late 1970s, a new incarnation of the Left appeared, in the guise of the National Democratic Front, but it too suffered a military defeat at the hands of the tribal forces and political moderates in 1982.

INSTITUTION BUILDING

In one way or another, the primary concern of every republican government since the revolution has been to create, and then expand, the realm/scope of central government control over the country. Ironically, of course, this concern was one of the major motivations of Imams Yahya and Ahmad as well. The problems encountered in trying to reach this goal reflect the effect of the geographic and demographic characteristics outlined earlier—the variations in geography, religion, traditions, life-style, economics, etc.—which have always made governing North Yemen an immensely difficult task.

Inevitably, the primary responsibility for change, and for coherence in the development of policy, has devolved to what Westerners term the "executive branch" of the government. In part, this focus is an outcome of the fact that whatever change took place during the first eight years of the republic took place in a wartime atmosphere (when few countries are willing to accept a large role by an elected legislature and a weak executive). In part, however, it is also owing to the Yemeni traditions of political leadership and responsibility reasserting themselves despite honest efforts to lessen their influence on policymaking.

For the sake of clarity, it makes good sense to deal with the characteristics of the political system from 1970 to the present along traditional Western lines, i.e., the time-honored division into executive, legislative, and judicial functions. Despite the fact that this tripartite division is not always relevant or apposite, it is a convenient means of organizing the material in order to make some crossnational comparisons with regard to both processes and institutions (structures). First, however, it is appropriate to consider the various documents drafted to provide a basis of legitimacy for the system after the Compromise.

The Formal Bases of Government

Obviously influenced by Western traditions and mores, the architects of the new Yemeni republic deemed it essential to produce a constitution, i.e., a written document that would spell out the major characteristics of the new system, its institutions, and its processes. There is little doubt that the emphasis upon "writing it down" was also owing to the fact that there had been no such formal documents or limitations on the power of the government under the imams.

Accordingly, the new government proclaimed a provisional constitution a little more than a month after the overthrow of the imam, on 31 October 1962. It was not, however, a terribly sophisticated document, and it rather clearly rationalized the preeminent role of the Revolutionary Command Council, in whose name the revolution had taken place. Under Egyptian guidance, at a time when the Egyptians had the dominant role in the republic and its institutions, another constitution was announced, on 28 April 1964. Because of this document's very obvious copying of Egyptian models, it was perceived as simply an Egyptian instrument and therefore met with considerable resistance among the more nationalistic republican elements. On 8 May 1965, then, another provisional constitution was announced; the most important difference between this and the previous one being that Yemenis participated in its creation. This difference is probably most clearly seen in the greater emphasis upon creating a civilian political system. For example, the Revolutionary Command Council, the preeminent executive body, was replaced by a three-member Republican Council, and a much broader ministerial system and a Consultative Assembly were both provided for. The last, although purely advisory, was perceived of as a mechanism for political input from a broader range of elements of the population.

This document remained in effect until the end of the civil war, but close to the end of that period, there was a desire to produce a constitution that would be a demonstration of the national reconciliation between republicans and royalists. In 1969, therefore, the Republican Council appointed forty-five individuals to a National Council, which had as its primary purpose the drafting of yet another constitution. This new constitution was officially proclaimed on 28 December 1970, and it was a genuine effort to develop a system that would deal with the perceived problems of the past and create institutions (including elections) which would permit a greater public participation in governance.

The new constitution had a number of interesting features. One, it specifically declared that the Shari'a had to be the source of all legislation (a requirement the conservative elements, including the tribespeople, had long insisted upon). Two, it required that all members of the nation's public bodies had to be practicing Muslims; three, the special role of the *ulama* was acknowledged and accepted; and four, it was stipulated that judges had to be selected from among the religious scholars of the country. (These provisions were, by and large, a reminder and a consequence of the conflict with the Left of a couple of years earlier.)

This constitution was first suspended and then replaced entirely by a new document, which was designed to provide a legal basis for the administration of Ibrahim al-Hamdi. This constitution was announced on 19 July 1974, and although a number of changes have in fact been made with respect to institutions and processes, it is this document that still provides the constitutional basis for the government and the system and processes which operate today. Many of its provisions are similar to provisions in the previous documents, for example, those that refer to the Arab and Islamic nature of the nation, the special role of the Shari'a, and the rights and duties of all citizens.

In North Yemen, then, as in many other states in the developing areas, the constitution is a formal document that attempts to provide some measure of legitimacy for the current wielders of power. It is in large measure a rationalization for the system actually in place, and despite rhetoric to the contrary, it does not provide an effective or enforceable basis for citizens' rights or effective public participation in the making of public policy. In many respects, such constitutions are efforts to evoke or provide a patina of legitimacy more often for foreign consumption, than to be used as accurate descriptions of the domestic political process.

The Executive Function

In the immediate post-Compromise period, there was a return to many of the more traditional Yemeni political and governmental values and orientations. This move was no doubt inevitable: royalists were brought into the government system, and there was a widespread desire to be done with many of the Egyptian models, policies, and institutions. One clear indication of this desire was the continued existence of the Republican Council—a plural executive that was in many respects a reaction to the rule of the imams as well as to the experience with the governments of Abdullah al-Sallal.

The first four years after the Compromise are usually characterized as the presidency of Abd al-Rahman al-Iryani, the chairman of the Republican Council. (Although "president" has not always been used as the official title of the individual who exercises primary executive responsibilities, custom has allocated this title to all of the system's leaders since the Compromise of 1970.)

Although the al-Iryani period laid the foundations for a number of important institutions and aspects of the contemporary political and governmental system, it was increasingly unable to deal with the multitude of domestic and foreign problems in an effective manner. By 1974, the opposition, including the tribal alliances of the north, had lost its patience with the government and its policies (especially for dealing with what were perceived as major threats).

Thus, on 13 June 1974, a bloodless coup took place, and military officers took over the government in a move that was so smooth many people believed it had been planned and organized with the connivance of important figures in the government that was overthrown. Usually known as the "corrective movement," this coup marked the beginning of the institutions and processes that characterize the current state. It also marked the reentry of the military into politics (which was justified by many of the same reasons used to justify military takeovers in other countries), and last but not least, it proved to be the end of the collegial presidency. In other words, the coup marked the reintroduction of the overwhelming power and position of a single individual within the system as the focus of policymaking and executive authority and as the symbol of national unity. I do not suggest that there are no other centers of power that affect public policy, but it does appear that the Yemeni political system has returned to an older pattern, in which a single individual exercises the major role in policymaking.

A survey and analysis of developments since 1974 is best organized around the individuals who have exercised the office of "president" of North Yemen, as these men are responsible for the "executive function" in the contemporary political system.

Ibrahim al-Hamdi: 1974–1977. The army officers who organized the coup of June 1974 were led by Col. Ibrahim al-Hamdi, a prominent figure who had performed both military and civilian functions in the years since the revolution. The officers formed a Military Command Council, and among its first acts were suspension of the 1970 constitution and the Consultative Council, dissolution of an ineffective national political organization (the National Yemeni Union), and, of course, assumption of all legislative and executive powers and duties. The council immediately appointed new government leaders and a new prime minister; all of the individuals appointed to ministries and cabinet-level positions were people who had played important roles in prior governments, and the overwhelming majority were civilians.

It may indeed be argued that the change from a nominally civilian government to an overtly military one was not all that clear. In the first place, many of the individuals appointed by the Command Council were civilian technocrats who had been frustrated in their efforts to achieve reform by the weaknesses of previous governments. Second, figures such as al-Hamdi had played prominent civilian as well as military roles up to that point. He had been commander of the reserves in the early 1970s, but in 1972 he was serving as deputy prime minister. In 1973, he was serving as deputy commander in chief of the armed forces, yet he had also sought and gained the leadership of the Confederation of Yemeni Development Associations (CYDA)—the national association of the Yemeni local cooperatives, which had been organized to promote and fund various development projects.

Al-Hamdi's political skills were extraordinary, and within a few months he had managed to either neutralize or gain the support of practically every major domestic faction. He thus consolidated his position and fashioned a sufficiently strong and wide enough base to enable him to carry out the reforms and objectives he considered important: economic development, elimination of corruption (especially in some of the government bureaucracies), centralization of political control (and the increase in political responsibility that went with it), and an end to the financial/economic irresponsibility and near chaos that had characterized many of the ministries and the projects they were responsible for either overseeing or implementing. In the eyes of most observers, what set al-Hamdi apart from most of his contemporaries was—besides his ambition—his vision of what needed to be done, of where North Yemen needed to go in order to fulfill its destiny, and his unquestioned ability to organize people.

Perhaps his most important purpose was to centralize the political system. It must be remembered that the tribal shaykhs and regional notables had consistently benefited from the highly *de*centralized system that the early efforts at institutionalization had created. Needless to say, that type of system also accorded well with North Yemen's political traditions. But, al-Hamdi's primary goal was to achieve a greater role for the central government in governance and policymaking. In order to accomplish this change, he had to curtail the power of many of the most important political elements in the country, i.e., major tribal shaykhs such as Abdullah al-Ahmar, Sinan Abu Luhum, etc.

One could argue that his balancing act among the various political, tribal, and religious and regional factions and interests was bound to eventually unravel, as such efforts nearly always do. In al-Hamdi's case, he came to rely upon elements in the south and sources of support that were deemed leftist and more actively reformist and supportive of significant change, and from that point his days were numbered. By 1977, Saudi Arabia, nearly all of the northern tribes, and some other elements of the political center believed al-Hamdi was playing a dangerous game with South Yemen and elements in the south of North Yemen. On 11 October 1977, al-Hamdi and his brother (upon whom he had relied heavily for the loyalty of some special army units) were assassinated.

We may never know who was directly responsible: al-Hamdi clearly had enemies at nearly all points on the political spectrum as a result of his three years of maneuvering (and out-maneuvering) the opponents to his policies. Most analysts, and most Yemenis, tend to assume that the people who had the most to gain from his removal and those who were most disadvantaged by the policies he was following were the ones responsible. The first to come under suspicion were the tribal alliances and powers of the north, whose influence in the Yemeni system al-Hamdi had significantly circumscribed (though, of course, not eliminated by any stretch of the imagination). The second possibility was Saudi Arabia, which was clearly very upset by al-Hamdi's moves toward reconciliation and accommodation with South Yemen, and the fact that the assassination took place the day before al-Hamdi was scheduled to meet with some South Yemenis has tended to favor this particular explanation.

Ahmad al-Ghashmi: 1977–1978. Just a few hours after al-Hamdi's death, the remnants of the Military Command Council met and announced that the chief of staff, Col. Ahmad al-Ghashmi, would be its new chairman. He took office declaring that there would be no changes in the policies and goals of his martyred predecessor; in fact, during his short tenure in office, his actions seemed to indicate that he was in basic sympathy with al-Hamdi's policies. On the other hand, the most important fears of the Saudis and the northern tribes were allayed immediately, as the move toward improved relations with South Yemen was terminated, al-Hamdi allies who were in positions from which they could materially influence policy were either removed or shifted to other responsibilities, and relations with Saudi Arabia were perceptibly improved.

Although al-Ghashmi did not overtly devote much of his energy to the development of projects, programs, and plans, which had occupied so much of al-Hamdi's time and effort, he was interested in developing new institutions that might give his regime a measure of legitimacy. So it was, for example, that in February 1978 he appointed a People's Constituent Assembly (PCA) of 99 members to replace the old Consultative Council. He also decided to abolish the Military Command Council, but this latter decision created a major threat to the regime. One of the members of the council had been Abdullah al-Alim, the highest ranking Shafi'i officer in the North Yemen army, and he had had close ties to al-Hamdi and had strong support in the south. The abolishment of the Military Command Council ended his role in the government, and this move was interpreted as a deliberate diminution of the influence of the Shafi'is and the south; al-Alim rebelled. Al-Ghashmi sent his protégé, Ali Abdullah Salih, the military governor of Ta'izz Province, to deal with al-Alim. The latter was unable to effectively rally his supporters, and he committed a major blunder in dealing with some local elements that had sought to mediate his dispute with the central government, thus discrediting himself and his position. Ali Abdullah Salih forced him to flee to South Yemen, thus eliminating the last major al-Hamdi supporter from any position of influence, either civilian or military.

Al-Ghashmi, however, ran afoul of exactly the same two forces as al-Hamdi. He maintained that the tribal elements of the north appeared opposed to all development efforts and wished to continue to be a state within the state, and in the area of foreign relations, he had his own troubles in the south. In fact, overall, al-Ghashmi's tenure was not characterized by any really major changes in al-Hamdi's general policies. He continued the implementation of the First Five-Year Plan, and he did not attempt to undermine or decrease the levels of support from foreign donors for the various development projects (an act that would certainly have produced some major disruptions in the now slowly developing economy). Nevertheless, his tenure in office was brief. Like al-Hamdi, he was assassinated, on 24 June 1978, and also under mysterious circumstances—a bomb exploded in his office as he was receiving an envoy from South Yemen. Although the assassination had its repercussions in South Yemen, where it led to the trial and execution of the country's nominal leader at the time, Salim Rubayy' Ali, the motives and goals behind the assassination were never very clear.

There is very little that can be credited specifically to al-Ghashmi's brief tenure in office, although he was the first leader to have the actual title of "president" since Abdullah al-Sallal (conferred on him by the PCA). In fact, it might be suggested that his relatively short tenure was characterized by little ability to manipulate the various forces whose interplay is ultimately what "politics" in North Yemen is all about. During his brief regime, the northern tribes became more assertive as they attempted to regain prerogatives lost under al-Hamdi, the Hujjariyya region (the southern portion of the country) became increasingly disaffected, and there was a clear inclination to swing closer to the Saudi orbit as the initiatives of al-Hamdi with respect to South Yemen were allowed to dissipate.

Ali Abdullah Salih: 1978– . Because there was no obvious successor to al-Ghashmi (and the Military Command Council had been dissolved), the principals of the PCA put together a Presidential Council consisting of al-Ghashmi's vice-president (Abd al-Karim al-Arashi), the prime minister (Abd al-Aziz Abd al-Ghani), the chief of staff (Ali al-Shayba), and Ali Abdullah Salih. After a brief period of intense political activity behind a facade of stability and peaceful transfer of authority, Ali Abdullah was elected as the new president of the republic and commander in chief by the PCA.

From the outset, foreign analysts as well as many Yemenis were more than happy to point out Ali Abdullah's limitations: He was too young, he was compromised by an alleged association with the death of al-Hamdi, he was thought to be uneducated and unsophisticated, he was inexperienced as far as military affairs were concerned (since he was only a tank commander), he had narrow horizons and no vision of the kind needed for a country with the kinds of problems that plagued North Yemen, and, last but definitely not least, he was associated with a very minor tribe (of the Hashid Confederation). It was thought that this combination of alleged deficiencies would give him little or no chance to obtain any measure of popular support, and his tribal association would be detrimental to his efforts to resolve the problem of rising discontent in the southern areas of the country.

To add further fuel to the discontent in the south, Ali Abdullah's first moves were directed toward placating the northern tribes. He seemed to be more concerned with personal survival and maintaining his new position than with any conscious or deliberate effort to cope with the multitude of problems that existed, the number of which had, if anything, probably grown larger and more serious since al-Hamdi's death.

By the late 1980s, however, it was clear that these original opinions required revision, if for no other reason than that Ali Abdullah had managed to remain in power far longer than any other political leader in North Yemen since the revolution. His ability to balance the complex of forces in the country and to maintain stability slowly but surely drew respect from observers both within and without North Yemen. Furthermore, in a country where about a dozen of the country's ablest and most important political leaders had been assassinated, and an uncounted number of attempts had been made on the lives of others (including Ali Abdullah himself), he had survived and even begun some major reforms. In fact, it could well be argued that in the first ten years of his presidency, Ali Abdullah presided over changes in the economic and social systems of North Yemen that were more significant and far-reaching than anything else in North Yemen in hundreds of years. Moreover, he successfully trod a precarious middle path between the various domestic and foreign political forces with their own agendas for the country. All the while, he managed to promote a degree of political development, which, while too slow in the eyes of many people, had the overwhelming advantage of giving North Yemen a measure of domestic stability, something it desperately needed after the turmoil at the end of al-Hamdi's tenure and the brief rule of al-Ghashmi.

The Development of Administrative Agencies. As already noted, the founding of government agencies designed to provide services and carry out government responsibilities in areas that had previously been the personal domain of the imams was an important priority of the new republic.[3] During the early years of the republic, many of the younger Yemenis who had been trained abroad and were committed to reform of the system chose to return home and become active in the political life of the country. They sought to construct a liberal, socially conscious, and dynamic state that would take the lead in developing and providing the range of social services which are associated with developed, modernized states. Many of these young Yemenis, still only in their twenties and thirties, were drafted to fill major administrative and policy-making positions as soon as they arrived.

However, the near total lack of the requisite personnel, adequate financing, and general infrastructural development (buildings, roads, etc.), not to mention the general insecurity of the countryside and the necessity of coping with the more immediate problems associated with the war effort, made the development of ministries, agencies, and similar kinds of government bodies a very slow and difficult process. In fact, during the civil war, it may be said that the great majority of all efforts to found, fund, and staff administrative agencies and government bodies were dependent upon Egyptian planning and support.

After the Compromise, the first and most important government priority was to deal with the disastrous state of the economy, and the near total lack of any resources. For this reason, there was a long and bitter debate within the government as to whether the country ought to join such international agencies as the World Bank and the International Monetary Fund, and it also meant that the major effort of the al-Iryani presidency would be directed to dealing with economic issues. Indeed, the first post-Compromise governments focused on economic planning, fiscal management, and general economic development.

Among the important initiatives taken during this period were the founding of the Central Bank in 1971 to gain control over the nation's currency (for centuries it had been the Maria Theresa taler, which was minted in Austria and over the supply of which the government had no control). In 1972, the al-Iryani government created the Central Budget Bureau to gain some control over the financial crisis, and it also set up the Central Planning Organization (CPO), which is usually regarded as the most important of the new institutions since it was given the responsibility for the formulation of national development policies and programs. In more recent years, the CPO has prepared budgets, coordinated and supervised the implementation of various projects of the different ministries, and made recommendations to the government as to which foreign assistance proposals and projects are the most valuable—for their contribution to national economic development as well as for their expansion of the central government's role in the countryside.

The individuals who were associated with the CPO during the 1970s were among the ablest and most dedicated of the new technocrats, and many of them have played important roles in the political life of the country since that time. By the mid-1980s, the CPO's prestige and effectiveness were not what they had been, owing to many factors including the lower level of training and skills of its staff, many of whom had been trained in Egypt in the interim and had neither the level of expertise, the

initiative, nor the motivation that had been such outstanding characteristics of the staff in the 1970s.

The other major accomplishment of this period was the formulation
of Yemen's first development plan, (the Three-Year Development Plan),
and for the first time, it established clear priorities among the proposals
that were forthcoming from nearly all quarters concerning what North
Yemen needed most. It also provided a major mechanism whereby some
of the new agencies, including the CPO and the newly created Ministry
of Finance, gained the experience of working together for national goals.

In general, the founding and development of the government agencies and ministries took place as specific problems arose that had to be
dealt with, rather than as part of a fully formulated plan to handle
responsibilities in some preordained order or in accord with available
resources (financial as well as personnel). For example, it was only when
outside agencies provided the requisite funding that the government was
able to create the University of Sana'a (in 1970, with Kuwaiti funding) or
even such bodies as the National Institute of Public Administration (1974).

The Legislative Function

Although no real legislature in the Western sense, i.e., a body of
popularly elected representatives with a clearly defined role and independent powers in the making of public policy, has existed since the
establishment of the republic, there have been a number of genuine efforts
to introduce a measure of public participation into policymaking.[4] The
problems connected with introducing the concept and the reality of such
a measure into North Yemen are many. First, there has been a general
reluctance, especially in the early days of the republic, to allow a situation
to develop that would enable the conservative forces to bring back the
imamate or to abrogate important changes that have been introduced.
Second, all of the basic prerequisites for such a legislative body were
lacking. Although North Yemen, as countries elsewhere in the Arab world,
had traditions of public participation and input into decision making, as
well as electing leaders, there was no tradition or basis for a system of
representative democracy. The first problem, therefore, for the architects
of change was to design a system that would accord with Yemeni traditions, be comprehensible to the population, and not elicit a fierce back-
lash—either from the tribes or the urban leaders—because it was thought
to introduce "un-Yemeni" ideas and mechanisms. This factor was especially important because at the time, there was significant xenophobia
developing as a result of the important role of the Egyptians and the
arrogance with which they controlled every aspect of the republic. Third,
the populace had to be educated with respect to the mechanics of a system

of representation in which their participation, their input, at the *national* level would be seen as important and real. It had always been so at the local level, that is, during the many decades when the hamlets were essentially dependent upon their own resources and leadership for coping with development, government services, and the provision of any amenities.

It was the constitution of 1965 that first provided for some form of "legislative power," as it foresaw the creation of an advisory body, the Consultative Assembly. That provision, however, was never implemented, so the first real effort to provide an institutional framework for a wider input into government policymaking did not take place until the National Council drafted the 1970 constitution.

Aside from the characteristics mentioned earlier, that constitution had two specific provisions with respect to the new political system. First, it continued the concept of the plural executive by retaining the three-member Republican Council, and second, it provided for the creation of a 179-member Consultative Council (to replace the National Council). The membership of this new body was to consist of 20 individuals appointed by the chairman of the Republican Council and 159 individuals who were to be indirectly elected by "electors," who in turn were to be chosen by the male residents of an equivalent number of electoral districts into which North Yemen was subdivided. The elections for these positions were indeed held in March 1971, and the first session of the new Consultative Council took place in April.

It was, of course, inevitable that the council would have a conservative orientation, because a majority of its members were tribal shaykhs and other notables who were the inevitable first choice of the clans and/or the people associated with them in their daily lives. The new council was not technically a legislative body, but it became as powerful as some of the legislatures of the French Fourth Republic. It refused new legislation (proposed by the Republican Council); it refused to ratify budgets, thereby creating some significant domestic problems; and in myriad ways it acted quite independently of the Republican Council and its wishes. Naturally, such actions were only possible because the membership consisted of individuals who wielded political (and military) power that did not depend on any existing government hierarchy or institutional structure or chain of command. These people were also quite capable of either resisting or effectively quashing efforts by the government to enforce the council's rulings and decisions.

By 1973, the Consultative Council had become the symbol as well as the reality of tribal power in the system. Its speaker was Shaykh Abdullah al-Ahmar, the paramount shaykh of the Hashid Confederation. During this period, he maintained good relationships with Saudi Arabia, and it was he and the Hashid who were the recipients of much of that country's subsidies to the northern tribes—as an insurance policy and lever on the orientation and, especially, the foreign policy of the republic.

Most observers of the 1970–1974 period would argue that the domestic instability of this period (represented by rapidly changing cabinets and prime ministers as well as numerous government reorganizations), the tense relationships that persisted with North Yemen's regional neighbors on the north and south, and the financial problems (i.e., no real resources or foreign exchange) made any lasting reform or political institution-building and development unlikely if not downright impossible.

Colonel al-Ghashmi, who succeeded al-Hamdi, had neither the political experience nor the stature of his predecessor, and he therefore seemed more interested in giving his regime a measure of legitimacy based upon popular participation. Accordingly, he appointed the 99-member People's Constituent Assembly, which consisted primarily of urban elements (as opposed to the tribal elements that had dominated the Consultative Council). This membership seemed to indicate a different perspective and perhaps it was an acknowledgment of the fact that at least a small shift in the domestic balance of forces had taken place.

Upon his accession, Ali Abdullah Salih expanded the membership of the PCA from 99 to 159 members, and most of the additional members were drawn from the tribal notables. There is little doubt that Ali Abdullah, being from one of the smaller and less powerful tribes, was deliberately seeking to expand the role of the tribes in order to avoid any feeling on their part that they were being ignored or not sufficiently consulted by his regime.

Still, it cannot be said that Ali Abdullah had no desire to expand the popular basis of his government or that his motives were purely self-preservationist. In 1980, President Salih drafted the National Charter of the YAR, a 120-page document that presented, in five chapters, his views on a variety of national issues. It was, in effect, a laying out of the parameters of political discussion, and despite the opposition of some groups to the views expressed, it inevitably became the framework within which debate concerning goals and policies increasingly took place. In order to promote such discussions, the president created the National Dialogue Committee in May 1980; this was a broad coalition of Yemenis who were given the task of using the charter as a working paper in discussions on future policy (and institutions).

Then, in 1982, President Salih created the People's General Congress (PGC); this was designed to be an instrument of political mobilization and the prelude to the often-promised and -postponed national election to create a Constituent Assembly, that is, a real national parliament. The PGC consisted of 1,000 delegates, of which 300 were appointed by the president, and 700 were elected; these elections, in August 1982, were supervised by the National Dialogue Committee.

In its first session, the PGC created a Permanent Committee, composed of 50 individuals selected from its ranks, to which another 25 appointed by the president were added. In accordance with the provisions of the charter, ratified by the Permanent Committee, Ali Abdullah was appointed secretary-general of the PGC and also appointed to a five-year term as president of the Yemen Arab Republic. The Permanent Committee was to meet on a regular basis (quarterly) between the regularly scheduled sessions of the congress. In effect, the PGC (which held regular sessions in 1984, 1986, and 1988) became a rudimentary party organization (though not officially so labeled) that promoted mobilization and greater participation.

The next step in promoting mobilization and participation took place in July 1985, when an estimated 60 percent of all men and women over eighteen (about 1.5 million people) took part in voting for some 17,507 members of the newly created Local Councils for Cooperative Development (LCCDs). These bodies were to have responsibilities in both the political and economic development spheres: for example, in administering of village development projects and in selecting the electors who were to choose the delegates to the PGC. In 1986, the LCCDs chose those delegates, and the new PGC held its first meeting in Ta'izz, where it elected a new national administrative board for the federation of LCCDs (replacing the old CYDA).

The most important elections, however, took place in the summer of 1988: the long-promised and often-postponed elections for the Consultative Assembly (Majlis al-Shura). This body was to have 159 members and was designed and intended to be a regular legislative body. The elections involved 1,293 candidates in the 128 electoral districts (the remaining 31 seats were to be filled by appointment by the president). The new assembly met for the first time in early July to select its own leadership; shortly thereafter Ali Abdullah tendered his resignation and was promptly reelected to another term as president, this time by the Majlis.

Although the set of structures that had been created between the regime of Al-Hamdi and Ali Abdullah was, if nothing else, confusing and sometimes overlapping and contradictory in purpose and lines of responsibility, some important points should not be missed: (1) the panoply of institutions created indicated a real commitment to the creation of some sort of popular basis for the authority of the regime, and (2) the readiness and willingness of substantial numbers of Yemenis to participate in the elections (including many women) to the LCCDs and the new Majlis indicated a real desire to have the opinions of nonelites heard in the policymaking process.

The Judicial Function

An understanding of the current judicial situation requires a brief introduction to the traditional legal systems of North Yemen.[5] Under the imams, Yemeni society was really governed by two legal systems: (1) the Shari'a, i.e., the Islamic legal system as elaborated and understood by Zaydi religious scholars (the *ulama*), and (2) *'urf*, the traditional tribal legal system as elaborated and understood by the tribal entities. In many respects, the two supplemented and complemented each other. In the northern and tribal areas, *'urf* regulated the conflicts that arose among individuals, families, clans, and tribes over various social and economic issues (including many disputes Westerners would consider "criminal," e.g., assault and battery or murder). Nominal obeisance was paid to the Shari'a in matters of personal status—i.e., birth, marriage, divorce, etc.— as well as in such other "secular" matters as taxation.

Within both systems, the sayyids played an important role. In the tribal areas, they were a protected class and often carried out the highly important role of neutral mediator in intertribal disputes. In the urban areas, they provided the major group from which the *hakim*s (the term for Islamic judges in North Yemen) were drawn—because of their education as well as their descent from the Prophet Muhammad.

There is, however, an interesting and significant difference between the two legal systems, especially in terms of the development of Western legal systems. Zaydi Islam specifically recognizes the right to *ijtihad* (independent interpretation of the basic elements of the Islamic faith), so that Zaydi judges may base their decisions solely on the circumstances, facts, and consequences of the specific case they must decide (in line, of course, with the broad precepts of the Shari'a). On the other hand, *'urf* is, in real terms, completely based on precedent, and tradition and custom are the key elements in reaching decisions. One of the major aims of Imam Yahya had been to expand the sphere of influence and applicability of the Shari'a, that is, to limit the occasions in public and private life when *'urf* was used.

The republic did not at first seek to make any important change in the old system, if for no other reason than it would have been extremely difficult and disruptive to do so and quite probably would have produced even greater support for the royalists. Yet many of the actions of the republic were clearly designed to modernize the legal system, if only to promote the kinds of development and modernization that were considered desirable. Foremost among these actions was the attempt to improve the commercial and investment climate and system (e.g., by providing incentives for foreign investment and participation in the development of the economy). To accomplish this aim, it was believed, required the adoption of secular codes for those sectors that would have regular contact with Western institutions—importers, manufacturers, banks, donor agencies, freight expediters, etc., and even the governments themselves.

Since most of North Yemen continued to operate under the old mechanisms, and probably had little or no need of the newer codes, the secular codes were introduced in the major urban centers in an incremental manner, coordinated and promoted by a special office of the president. In order to facilitate the development and institutionalization of these changes with a minimum of social disruption and conflict, the government brought in a number of Sudanese legal officials as advisers in the later 1970s and early 1980s.

Later in the 1980s, however, the rate of change in the legal sector was the slowest of any aspect of the Yemeni system. The major effort was to produce a sector of public law that would make government officials responsible for the apprehension and prosecution of criminals—whether in such traditional areas as murder or in such newer areas as child abuse, credit fraud, and even traffic offenses (all of these offenses would have been previously handled through the traditional systems of vengeance, reparation, and collective guilt). The fact that the government was accepted as an active participant in the resolution of certain kinds of social conflicts (civil as well as criminal) in the major cities in the 1980s was a major accomplishment, but it was clearly not the norm throughout the country.

MAJOR CONTEMPORARY ISSUES

The definition of what is a major political issue in North Yemen varies with the group affected and the region of the country—evidence that the traditional divisions and cleavages continue to be important. Nevertheless, some broad issue-categories are applicable to the entire country; most are related and are separated here only for purposes of analysis and presentation.

Tribalism

Because tribalism represents, at least in part, an orientation toward outside political authority (which in North Yemen means any activity on the part of the central government), it continues to be a potent political force. It cannot be ignored, and it will not decrease in significance to any real degree in the immediate future. Although the extent of the government's authority has expanded in recent years (so much so that the central government can now put its representatives into such areas as Khamir and the Jawf, something that was inconceivable as recently as the late 1970s when one of the Hamid al-Din princes was still living there) and continues to grow, there are still regions where the government's authority is tenuous and often exists only during the daylight hours. As far as the government is concerned, it would be most unwise if not downright foolish to ignore the opinions and interests of the major tribal shaykhs and the particular tribes (Shaykh Abdullah al-Ahmar of the Hashid, Sinan Abu Luhum of the Nihm, Shaykh Amin Abu Ra's of the Dhu Muhammad, etc.). Furthermore, evidence as late as the early 1980s indicates that the central government would be unable to effectively deal with some major threats to its continued existence and powers (e.g., the 1979 conflict with South Yemen and the 1982 battles with the NDF in the Dhamar region) if there were not an agreement between the government and some of the major (Hashid) tribes to provide government forces with essential support.

In a word, then, anyone wishing to understand the political dynamics of contemporary North Yemen needs to have extensive knowledge of the tribes. It is, however, not enough to simply know the names of the major tribes and their current leaders. It is also essential that one develop some sympathy for their past history, interests, and leaders and to recognize how these have an impact on their current alliances, their current economic and political interests, their current status, and their attempt to deal with what is, even in North Yemen, a rapidly changing set of economic and political conditions.

Domestic Opposition: Religious

Although it first appeared that the revolution would be able to do away with some of the older religious frictions (which were partly tied to economic issues), the outcome was different. In fact, only a few years after the revolution, there were fears that the country might split in two along Zaydi-Shafi'i lines. That particular fear has abated, in part at least because of a deliberate policy of bringing prominent Shafi'is into cabinet and consultative posts where they can influence policymaking, but a different issue has arisen: the reaction of North Yemen to the increased militancy of Islam in other regions.

North Yemen has a number of unusual characteristics as far as its place in the Islamic world is concerned. The most important recent one is that it represents a Muslim country which has removed a religious leader whose theoretical and pragmatic role in the society was such that, in theory, the community could not legally exist without him. Clearly, the Zaydis have managed to do so, and though there are some who yearn for the "good old days," this is a diffuse and politically irrelevant feeling, especially insofar as it applies to the actual return of the imamate (as opposed to vague dissatisfaction with aspects of the contemporary secular government). There are, in other words, few if any people who would wish to return to the days of subsistence agriculture, lack of electricity, no access to education, poor health facilities, no piped water, and a lack of other modern conveniences that have been introduced to much of the population since the republic was declared.

Nevertheless, there is a "Muslim opposition"—of sorts. For example, the Muslim Brotherhood (organized to effectuate a greater reference to Islamic norms in public life) does exist in North Yemen. However, in view of the rather widespread fear and paranoia concerning the Brotherhood that exists in the Western world generally, and in the United States in particular, some comments about the group in North Yemen are in order.

First, the Brotherhood in that country was one of the earliest participants in the movement to reform the imamate; it is not, therefore, perceived by the average Yemeni to be a reactionary organization opposed to modern conveniences or all of the changes that have occurred. Second, the members of the Brotherhood in North Yemen tend to be literate, have a better than average education, and to be modernized individuals in the sense that by far the majority of them are engaged in occupations that are in the modernized sector. Presumably, therefore, they are not overly interested in working for a return to the days of the imamate.

Third, it is important to realize that the Muslim Brotherhood is not a monolithic organization. There are different factions (which all use the same name) with differing views on a variety of social, economic, and even political issues. There are, for example, factions that are overwhelmingly Yemeni and generally supportive of the changes that have taken place since the revolution. There are also, however, extremely conservative factions, dominated by Egyptians who are in North Yemen as teachers and civil servants or supported by Saudi Arabia, and these factions occasionally present the government with a serious problem because of their agitating and propagandizing activities.

The main outlet for the views of individuals, including members of the Brotherhood, who see events, personalities, and developments in North Yemen through the prism of a primarily Islamic orientation is the monthly magazine *al-Irshad* [Guidance]. With a circulation of about 5,000, it has become a widely read journal of opinion if for no other reason, ironically, than it is the only widely available Yemeni publication that does not come under regular government supervision with regard to its content on such sensitive issues as the domestic and foreign policies of the USSR.

Domestic Opposition: Secular

In general, and in addition to whatever tribal and similar traditional opposition may still exist to the republic and many of its policies, the most important center of opposition has been the National Democratic Front (NDF). This group was created in February 1976 when a number of generally leftist organizations, with roots going back to the 1960s, amalgamated. The list included such groups as the North Yemen branch of the Arab Nationalist Movement (ANM), headed by Sultan Ahmad Umar; the Vanguard Party, the pro-Syrian branch of the Ba'ath (Arab Renaissance Party); and the Organization of Yemeni Resisters, which grew out of the forces that helped defend Sana'a during the famous siege of 1968. As the NDF's purposes and orientation became clearer and more well-known, it began to attract an exceedingly eclectic group of supporters and participants who had quite a variety of other (major or minor) grievances against the government, its personnel, its policies, and its institutions (including the army).

Because of its pronouncedly leftist origins, the NDF was the favored mechanism by which South Yemen attempted to influence the policies and orientation of the Sana'a government. Indeed, as a result of this support, the NDF at one point was able to control some significant areas of North Yemen. In general terms, the personnel and material flowed from South Yemen into North Yemen via the Wadi Bana on the border up to (and occasionally on the other side of) the main north-south road of North Yemen around Yarim northward to Ma'bar.

At the height of its influence and power, roughly the late 1970s, the NDF included the following general categories, which provide some indication of the sources of domestic discontent: a number of convinced ideologues of various degrees of leftist thought; some disgruntled military officers of various ideological orientations and religious affiliations who sought to use the NDF for some of their own purposes, as well as those who felt their position and status in the military had not been adequately valued or properly rewarded; a sizable collection of middle-and lower-class elements who resented the continued important social and politico-economic roles of the wealthier elements of the south's social structure; detribalized Yemenis of various tribal and regional origins, many of whom had worked abroad and whose commitment to the traditional class and social structure was minimal, if not downright antagonistic, and who sought a new social system in which their traditional position would no longer matter; and a miscellaneous collection of individuals and small groups with various commercial, agricultural, and trade occupations who felt that the central government's policies and actions were detrimental to their interests and hoped for a new economic order. The NDF had as its own weekly organ *al-Amal* [Hope], which published generally Marxist, anti-Western, and antigovernment analyses of domestic, regional, and international affairs.

In the early 1980s, after a brief set of discussions in which the government and the NDF were said to have come to a general agreement on principles, the government decided to put an end to the NDF threat to the unity of the state and its disruptive activities. (It has been suggested that the decision to do so was owing to heavy pressure from the Saudis as well as some of the major northern tribes, who receive Saudi subventions). After some fierce fighting, particularly near the town of Damt in the Wadi Bana, the combined forces of the government and tribal units decisively defeated the NDF in June 1982.

Although the NDF has been largely eliminated as a significant administrative and military force threatening the central government in a particularly sensitive region, the various opposition strains that went to make it up have not disappeared. In the first place, the intellectual rationalizations and their authors still exist; in the second place, the social discontent and economic grievances have not all been effectively dealt with or ameliorated. In other words, it would not be wise to dismiss the idea that the NDF could make a comeback.

On the other hand, many of the intellectual forces that went into its organization have formed a new organization, the Yemeni Popular Unity Party (YPUP), which seeks to represent some of the same lines of opposition—both intellectual and pragmatic—to the current regime. Whether YPUP will become as much of a threat, or become as much of an ally of the South Yemen regime, as the NDF remains to be seen—and probably depends upon the policies of both regimes in the near term as much as it depends upon the creativity and activism of the group's leaders.

Foreign Policy Issues

There is no doubt as to where Yemen's foreign policy priorities will continue to lie for the immediate future: with its two neighbors to the north and south.[6] The issues in the relationship with Saudi Arabia remain basically unchanged. Saudi Arabia will probably continue to provide economic assistance to both the central government and certain tribes in the north as a means of making certain that North Yemen's regional and international position does not threaten Saudi Arabia. On the other hand, any new development (such as vastly increased government income from oil) that might tend to make North Yemen less dependent and more able to follow policy options and orientations that are at least potentially detrimental to the interests of Saudi Arabia will probably alter both the aims and the mechanisms by which Saudi Arabia seeks to maintain at least a minimum level of influence. Such a change could have serious consequences for what is, after all, still a very fragile economy and political system.

The situation is made considerably more volatile by the fact that relations with Saudi Arabia have not always been friendly, nor even correct. The interests of the Saudis are relatively clear if one bears in mind the politico-economic orientation and the policies of the People's Democratic Republic of Yemen: to minimize the influence of the PDRY, to keep North Yemen as a buffer between it and the PDRY, and most important, to prevent North Yemen from falling into the orbit of South Yemen (not to mention unity between the two). As a result, the major concern of North Yemen was to avoid becoming simply a puppet state of Saudi Arabia or a proxy for that country's conflict with the PDRY. In effect, the North Yemenis had to adjust to the notion (until 1989–1990) that their country was a buffer between Saudi Arabia and the PDRY— an adjustment that was considerably complicated by the fact that much of Yemeni popular opinion is pronouncedly anti-Saudi in orientation.

North Yemen's relationship with the PDRY was more complex and depended more upon the policies and initiatives of the latter than on its own goals and policies. Although it has been more than 250 years since the two Yemens were part of the same political entity, the indigenous leadership of both states rarely missed an opportunity to decry the "artificial division" of historic Yemen as a result of the policies of the Ottomans and British. (When the Ottoman authorities abandoned Yemen in 1630 to the Zaydi imams, these held dominion over nearly all of what is today the territory of North and South Yemen; in 1728, however, a number of the tribal rulers in the region around Aden declared their independence of the Zaydi imams, and this date is generally accepted as the end of a unified state of Yemen.)

The division between the two that stemmed from nineteenth-century Ottoman and British policies, on the other hand, produced significant differences in economic and social policies, not to mention political orientation. With the independence of the South in 1967, the adoption of a Marxist domestic policy, and a foreign policy oriented toward the Soviet Union and its goals, the gulf between the two Yemens appeared unbridgeable. Nevertheless, it was clear to observers that all the old patterns, orientations, priorities, loyalties, and alliances could not be, and were not, obliterated by the radicals associated with the ruling party (the Yemeni Socialist Party, an amalgamation of a number of leftist parties). In fact, the party and the government experienced a number of disruptive internal coups; the bloody paroxysm of early 1986, however, eliminated some of the most intransigent elements and brought to power more moderate elements.

The most important changes took place in the late 1980s: First, there was the discovery of major deposits of oil and natural gas in both states and a major field in the area where no definitive border had ever been demarcated. If these resources were not to be wasted or unexploited as a result of conflict between North and South, especially at a time when remittance income was declining, some measure of accommodation and cooperation was essential. And, no less important, the major changes in Soviet foreign policy inaugurated by Mikhail Gorbachev—the decision of the USSR to scale back its foreign policy commitments—hit the South Yemenis extremely hard; in fact, it made the continued independent existence of the state doubtful. Seeking to make the best of a deteriorating domestic situation and a seriously weakened regional status, the South Yemenis opted for union with the North in 1990.

The unification of North and South Yemen may achieve an important result for the Yemenis; much to their dismay, Yemen has been on the periphery of the consciousness of the major powers (the United States and the USSR). It is the fervent hope of the Yemenis that their high-quality oil, their larger size and population (due to unification), and the deteriorating position of traditional elites in the other peninsula states will once again give their country a status more in keeping with their own perceptions of its importance and role, both on the peninsula and in the Middle Eastern region as a whole.

The Economy

One of North Yemen's most important problems in the 1970s was the lack of any real source of foreign exchange earnings.[7] Although the country is the ancestral home of such rare and/or desirable commodities as myrrh and coffee, international production and trade of these (and some other potential Yemeni exports) have either disappeared, moved away from North Yemen entirely, suffered from decreased demand, or been affected by significant problems in marketing or quality control. The result was that, until the discovery of oil, North Yemen's visible commodity exports were miniscule (minimal amounts of coffee, cotton, hides and skins), and the proceeds from the export trade did not begin to cover the import demand for consumer goods, food, and other things the Yemenis craved. It was precisely an eruption of this pent-up demand, which had been stymied by the imams and then the civil war, that created a buying explosion in the 1970s and resulted in impossibly large deficits in the balance of payments. Luckily, North Yemen simultaneously benefited from its most profitable export in centuries, its adult male population. During the 1970s, hundreds of thousands of Yemenis left to find work and sent back millions, even billions, of dollars to their families. These remittances funded the import binge, but the reader should remember that these funds did not pass through the government's financial institutions, which is why the government remained so dependent upon Saudi budgetary support.

With the drop in the price of oil in the early 1980s, there was an inevitable impact upon the number and size of the development programs in the Gulf states that employed Yemeni workers. Furthermore, the Saudis, who had formerly preferred Yemenis (fellow Muslims and neighbors) as laborers, decided after events such as the attack on the Grand Mosque in Mecca (in 1979), which had Yemenis among the participants, that it would be safer and probably even cheaper to hire foreign contract laborers (South Koreans, Filipinos, Thais, etc.) who would fulfill their contract and go home without any participation (read intervention) in the social and political life of the Saudi state. The first Yemeni laborers began to return home, and the rate of remittances began to drop—slowly at first, then rather more precipitously in the mid-1980s. This change led international donors and lending agencies to demand more stringent domestic economic policies from the North Yemen government and a significant scaling back of development plans and programs.

At this critical juncture, the U.S. Hunt Oil company discovered a significant deposit of oil in Ma'rib Province—enough that the company and its partners were willing to invest heavily in a refinery and the necessary ancillary facilities (including a pipeline) to get the oil to the Red Sea. It appeared that there might be a quick and profitable solution to North Yemen's economic problems.

The dependence of the government upon the financial subsidies provided by the Saudis (which were at first paid directly to the tribes and then to the government at al-Hamdi's insistence) had always made the Yemenis uncomfortable at best and resentful at worst. Although relations have nearly always been at least correct since the Compromise of 1970, frictions have developed as certain Yemeni leaders adopted policies that did not accord well with the Saudis' perception of their own interests— in the southwestern corner of the peninsula in general and in North Yemen in particular. Further, there is no denying the widespread Yemeni resentment of the Saudi takeover and incorporation of Najran and Asir. There is, of course, a widespread hope, indeed expectation, that vastly increased government revenues will make it possible for the Yemenis to adopt a far more independent foreign policy as well as fund a much more extensive set of development projects and programs.

In the late 1980s, the situation seemed to have stabilized. There were still remittances flowing in; some oil revenue was being realized (with a concomitant decline in the amount spent for imported oil and petroleum products—largely from Saudi Arabia); and there was a decline in the rate of demand for consumer items (owing in part to the fact that the first great rush of buying had abated somewhat and in part to the fact that the government adopted and implemented a series of import-limitation policies). Nevertheless, the statistics for income, government revenue/

expenditures, and other indicators show that complacency with respect to the economy was not appropriate, and the value of the Yemeni riyal continued to decline.

If, in fact, North Yemen begins to earn substantial amounts of foreign exchange because of its oil holdings, it may be that how, where, and when the country will use its new wealth will present North Yemen and its people with the greatest challenge they will have to face. I am inclined to think so, and I am concerned about the effect upon Yemeni culture and civilization, both of which are so often severely affected by great wealth.

The Search for Legitimacy

Clearly, the issue of legitimacy has not been resolved. Ali Abdullah Salih has made a number of concrete moves in the direction of greater public participation in decision making, but tentative steps toward greater participation in policymaking that do not clearly allocate powers and responsibility to elements of the population, which appear to them as being in accord with their perception of their rights and powers, would seem to stand a slim chance of universal acceptance. To state the problem another way, it is highly unlikely that North Yemen is ready for a political system that produces decisions on the basis of one-person one-vote. On the other hand, it may be possible for the regime to base its continued acceptance on instrumental values, i.e., on the fact that it is able to consistently provide the population with the goods and services that are desired.

It is likely, then, that there will be further tentative and exploratory steps and experiments in expanding the popular basis of support of the government, but one should not be too disappointed if they do not accord with Western values, institutions, and orientations. Perhaps a much expanded ability to provide services to a growing percentage of the population will do more than anything else, for the moment, to bring about a higher level of commitment and a broader base of support for the governments of Yemen in the near future.

NOTES

1. The literature on the tribes of Yemen has grown significantly in recent years; for relevant sources, see the works cited in Chapter 2 note 6 as well as Ettore Rossi, "Il diritto consuetudinario delle tribu arabe del Yemen," *Rivista degli studi Orientali* 23 (1948), pp. 1–36; K. al-Iryani, "Un temoignage sur le Yemen: l'organisation sociale de la tribu des Hashid," *Cahiers de l'Orient Contemporain* 25 (1968), pp. 5–8; and Walter Dostal, "Sozio-oekonomische Aspekte der Stammesdemokratie in Nordost-Jemen," *Soziologus* 24 (1974), pp. 1–15. See also Paul

Dresch, "The Several Peaces of the Yemeni Tribes," *Journal of the Anthropological Society of Oxford* 12 (1981), pp. 73–86, and "Tribal Relations and Political History in Upper Yemen," in B. R. Pridham, ed., *Contemporary Yemen: Politics and Historical Background* (London: Croom Helm, 1984), pp. 154–174. And see Paul Dresch, *Tribes, Government, and History in Yemen* (Oxford: Clarendon Press, 1989).

2. On the politics of the civil war and its aftermath, see Fred Halliday, *Arabia Without Sultans* (New York: Vintage, 1975), esp. Part 2 (pp. 93–162); John E. Peterson, *Yemen: The Search for a Modern State* (London: Croom Helm, 1982), esp. Chapters 3 through 5; Robert D. Burrowes, *The Yemen Arab Republic* (Boulder, CO: Westview Press, 1987), esp. Chapters 3 through 8; Mohammed Ahmad Zabarah, *Yemen* (New York: Praeger, 1982), esp. Chapters 5 through 7; Robert W. Stookey, *Yemen* (Boulder, CO: Westview Press, 1978); and Robin Bidwell, *The Two Yemens* (London: Longman; Boulder, CO: Westview Press, 1983), esp. Chapters 7 through 9.

3. See esp. Mohamed el-Azzazi, *Die Entwicklung der Arabischen Republik Jemen* (Tübingen and Basel: Horst Erdmann Verlag, 1978), esp. pp. 118–156, and Ahmed al-Abiadh, "Modernisation of Government Institutions 1962–1969 [and 1970–1982]," in Pridham, *Contemporary Yemen*, pp. 147–153.

4. See Burrowes, *The Yemen Arab Republic*, esp. Chapter 9, and his essay, "Modernization and Political Development in the Yemen Arab Republic: The First Twenty-Five Years and Prospects for the Future," forthcoming in the *International Journal for Middle East Studies*.

5. See Isam Ghanem, *Yemen* (London: Arthur Probsthain, 1981), and the works cited in Chapter 2 note 8.

6. On North Yemen's relations with other powers see Stephen Page, *The USSR and Arabia* (London: Central Asian Research Centre, 1971), and *The Soviet Union and the Yemens* (New York: Praeger, 1985), esp. Part 3, pp. 157–201 and pp. 205–207; Mark N. Katz, *Russia and Arabia* (Baltimore, MD: Johns Hopkins Press, 1986), esp. Chapter 1; and M. S. el-Azhary, "Aspects of North Yemen's Relations with Saudi Arabia," in Pridham, *Contemporary Yemen*, pp. 195–207. Unfortunately, no full-length study of North Yemen's foreign policy is currently available; however, nearly all of the many works that have been cited in connection with various aspects of the economy and the political system at least mention some of the issues and problems. The most complete treatment of the foreign policy issue of most immediate interest in the late 1980s, YAR/PDRY unification, is F. Gregory Gause III, "Yemeni Unity: Past and Future," *Middle East Journal* 42:1 (1988), pp. 33–47. See also the relevant portions of Burrowes, *The Yemen Arab Republic*, esp. Chapters 6 through 8, and Bidwell, *The Two Yemens*, esp. Chapters 8 and 9, as well as Johannes Reissner, "Neue Schritte zur Jemenitischen Einheit," *Jemen-Report* 19:2 (1988), pp. 9–13.

7. An interesting and worthwhile overview of contemporary economic policies is V. A. Hauck, *Policy Choices in the Yemen Arab Republic* (Amsterdam: University of Amsterdam, 1987).

6

Conclusion

North Yemen is an Arab, a Muslim, and a Third World state, but to what extent do these terms tell us anything about the country's orientation, domestic and foreign policies, or its political system? Clearly the Yemenis, both the people and the state, consider themselves an integral part of the Arab world, insofar as that designation has any collective, policy-oriented meaning. This identification means, for example, that North Yemen is inclined to support "Arab" initiatives, policies, and goals. It does not mean, however, that the country will automatically adhere to policies and initiatives drafted by others, for it is influenced by local and regional concerns in such matters. For example, "anticolonialism" as an ideology or as a component of the Yemeni orientation/perception of the world is essentially irrelevant. Knowing, much less understanding, what the Yemeni position will be—on regional or even global issues—is not possible simply because one knows that the Yemenis are Arabs. It requires a more thorough understanding of, and sympathy for, the relevant factors in North Yemen's past as well as the present.

Just as clearly, Yemenis are overwhelmingly Muslims, whether they are Zaydis, Shafi'is, or Isma'ilis. Does that mean that the Yemenis are caught up in what is (especially in the West) perceived as the current wave of Muslim activism? In one respect, North Yemen provides an instructive counterexample to the contemporary perception that all of the Islamic world is consumed by an intense Islamic "revivalism" or wave of fundamentalism. Consider that the essential basis of the Zaydi conception of the state and the community is bound up in the theory of the imamate, which provided religious and political leadership for the community. Yet in 1970, the royalists and republicans reached a compromise on their differences and created a *secular* state that has no explicit or even implicit functions in the realm of religious affairs (though it continues to be considered Islamic). In other words, the country has a Muslim community that has lost its religious leadership and rationale and does not seem particularly disturbed by that fact.

In another respect, Yemen is also an instructive example for a better understanding of the Muslim Brotherhood. In the 1940s, the Brotherhood was a strong supporter of reform—of both the political and the economic systems of Yemen, less so of the social system. It is, therefore, still perceived by many Yemenis as an Islamic movement that is generally in tune with the Yemeni desire for progress, especially when such progress is phrased and understood in comparison with the situation as it existed under the imams. On the other hand, there is also the perception among some Yemenis that important aspects of their traditional way of life are being eroded by the current wave of consumerism, foreign participation in the economy, educational system, and development projects, as well as the secularization of many aspects of life that were formerly governed by Zaydi or tribal law. This view has produced a measure of support for an Islamic movement that expresses this resentment (including a strong dose of xenophobia).

Further, there is also an "Islamic Front," which tends to express differences over domestic policy (especially concerning such issues as decentralization, tribal relations, and many aspects of both economic and foreign policy) in Islamic terms. Some observers have suggested that the front and its use of Islam are merely a mechanism to divert or defuse potential opposition to the secularizing policies of the Salih government. On the other hand, it is clear that the primary opposition to the unification of North and South into one state is found among the religious groupings of the North, including different factions of the Muslim Brotherhood. The role of the various religious factions is likely to be of some concern to the newly unified state. It is, of course, possible that these elements will combine into a political party and seek to influence public policy through the new channels created as a result of the unity agreement.

Most contemporary responses to questions concerning the role of Islam ignore the idiosyncratic characteristics of Islam within different societies and states, since many people tend to assume that Islam is a monolithic entity. Yemeni customs and traditions, Yemeni experiences, and the particular features of the sects that constitute the Yemeni version(s) of Islam have all played a role in contemporary Yemeni Islam. At the same time, significant changes in the economy (e.g., the emigration of so much of the work force for employment abroad) have had their effects on gender roles, and these are often perceived to be a result of the mores of Islam. Visitors who were acquainted with North Yemen prior to the "decade of development" (the 1970s) have remarked on the increased use of the veil and the *sharshaf* (the Yemeni *chador*) in more recent years. Still others have remarked on the relative freedom of Yemeni women in many fields of activity, especially in comparison to their peninsular neighbors to the north. In other words, perceptions and conclusions are to a significant degree the result of one's baseline of comparison.

The point, of course, is that easy generalizations are not possible; indeed, they are probably not even desirable, since they imply that one has understood a situation and has somehow "solved" it in the sense that its origins, nature, and consequences have been explained. Contemporary North Yemen provides a multitude of conflicting signals and evidence, perhaps best understood as evidence that the society is undergoing a multitude of small, incremental changes in its culture, and its social system, as it adjusts to major changes in its economy and its political structures and mechanisms. It is, in other words, probably too soon for generalizations that can be adequately documented, especially concerning the role of Islam in the country. It is not, for example, inconceivable to think of a demand for the return of the imamate (albeit in some modified form) if the shocks to the economic, the social, and even the political systems, structures, and programs were massive enough to create a demand for radical change. The imamate would be the alternative that is most in accordance with the traditions and customs of the past. Yet, even if there were a return to that system of rule, it would be a serious misreading of the Yemenis to suggest that the changes which have been wrought since the revolution would be either eliminated or renounced. Unfortunately, the Western states would probably view such a change as another example of Islamic reaction to the presumed benefits and characteristics of Western civilization and culture.

In terms of income levels, disposable income, GNP/GDP, or whatever statistical data are in vogue, North Yemen ranks among the lowest of the states in the Third World (or even Fourth World) category. The standard conclusion then would be, the Yemenis are characterized by grinding poverty and gross malnutrition. In fact, of course, such is not the case. For many years the Yemeni government has been unwilling and/or unable to impose effective measures to route the remittances of its emigrant labor force through the central government's banking and financial system. The money has, as a result, gone directly to the families of the emigrants and not appeared on the government's records or, more important, in its budgets as a result of effective taxation. Furthermore, now—as in the past—it is likely that a substantial number of exchanges in the rural areas are not made on a cash basis. In other words, Western mechanisms for dealing with countries like North Yemen, and their unique problems, are often not adequate and wind up seriously misrepresenting reality.

The reality in North Yemen today is that while there are serious examples of under- and malnutrition, these are increasingly caused by poor knowledge of nutrition or the deleterious effects of significant changes in the diet and upbringing of children rather than by overall conditions of starvation and poverty. The average visitor to North Yemen is more likely to be astounded to find the most modern commodities in even the most remote mountain villages, and by the incredible amount of garbage produced by the consumption of a vast array of foods in plastic and metal containers—this in a country where foreign goods were utterly unknown only a few years ago, and where *everything* was either recycled or bio-degradable.

It is very difficult to put into words one's feelings for a country, its civilization and culture, and its people without sounding maudlin. Perhaps brevity is the easiest way to avoid that sin, as well as the accusation of having lost one's credibility as a social scientist. This book has been an effort to paint, in broad strokes, a picture of nearly all the aspects of a land that has captivated me ever since I first began to learn something of its history and then discovered its scenery, its architecture, and the various other elements that make up a culture and a civilization—and last but not least, its people. I can only hope that in this book I have both communicated an inkling of the characteristics that have captivated me and contributed in some small way to the ability of the Yemenis themselves to retain those same attributes of their civilization and culture at a time when they are facing perhaps the most serious threat in more than a millennium.

Selected Bibliography

The literature on North Yemen has grown astronomically in recent years, and it is simply not possible to list all of the works that deal with the various subjects which have been, albeit sometimes very briefly, covered in this book. What follows is a highly selective list that has been prepared primarily for the reader wishing more detailed treatment of these subjects. Some limitations have been arbitrarily imposed. First, although there are many works in Arabic and other languages that are essential for any complete treatment of contemporary North Yemen, only English-language ones have been listed. Second, with only a few exceptions, no works earlier than 1965 have been included, though many of the earlier titles are also invaluable for an understanding of various aspects of the country. Third, some of the volumes listed suffer from various deficiencies, but they have nevertheless been included because they can provide the reader with a relevant bibliography and a starting point for additional research. Fourth, with only rare exceptions, the bibliography concentrates on books rather than articles. In all cases, the primary consideration has been to provide the reader with some important works that can simplify the search for more data, information, and literature.

BIBLIOGRAPHIES

Labaune, Patrick. *Bibliographie de la Péninsule Arabique*. Vol. 2, *La République Arabe du Yémen*. Paris: C.N.R.S., 1985.

Macro, Eric. *Bibliography on Yemen and Notes on Mocha*. Miami, FL: University of Miami, 1960.

Mondesir, Simoné. *A Select Bibliography of Yemen Arab Republic and Peoples' Democratic Republic of Yemen*. Durham, Eng.: University of Durham Centre for Middle Eastern and Islamic Studies, 1977.

Nagy, Sultan. *Selected and Annotated Bibliography on Yemen*. Kuwait: Kuwait Universities Library Department, 1973.

Sayyid, Ayman Fu'ad. *Sources de l'histoire du Yémen a l'epoque Musulmane*. Cairo: Institut Français d'Archéologie Orientale du Cairo, 1974.

Books with Valuable Bibliographies

Chelhod, Joseph, et al. *L'Arabie du Sud: Histoire et civilisation.* 3 vols. Paris: Maisonneuve and Larose, 1984–1985.

el-Azzazi, Mohamed. *Die Entwicklung der Arabischen Republik Jemen.* Tübingen and Basel: Horst Erdmann Verlag, 1978.

Kopp, Horst. *Agrargeographie der Arabischen Republic Jemen.* Erlangen: Palm and Enke, 1981.

Serjeant, R. B., and Ronald Lewcock, eds. *Sana'a, An Arabian Islamic City.* London: World of Islam Festival Trust, 1983.

Stookey, Robert W. *Yemen: The Politics of the Yemen Arab Republic.* Boulder, CO: Westview Press, 1978.

Wenner, Manfred. *Modern Yemen 1918–1966.* Baltimore, MD: Johns Hopkins Press, 1967.

Periodicals with Bibliographies

AIYS Newsletter. Chicago, DeKalb, and Portland: American Institute for Yemeni Studies.

Jemen-Report. Freiburg im Breisgau: Deutsch-Jemenitische Gesellschaft.

Middle East Journal. Washington, DC: Middle East Institute.

TRAVEL BOOKS AND TOURIST GUIDES

Hämäläinen, Pertti. *Yemen: A Travel Survival Kit.* South Yarra, Australia: Lonely Planet, 1988.

Jenner, Michael. *Yemen Rediscovered.* London: Longman/Yemen Tourist Company, 1983.

Maréchaux, Pascal. *Arabia Felix.* Woodbury, NY: Barron's Educational Services, 1980.

Maréchaux, Pascal, and Maria Maréchaux. *Arabian Moons.* London: Concept Media Pte., 1987.

Rose, Lynda, and Rosalie Rakow. *Sana'a: City of Contrast.* Burke, VA: Tandem Publishers, 1981.

Tourist Guide of Yemen Arab Republic. Sana'a: General Tourism Corporation, 1983.

Varanda, Fernando. *Art of Building in Yemen.* Cambridge, MA: MIT Press, 1982.

Wenner, Manfred, and Lealan Swanson. *An Introduction to Yemen.* Rev. ed. DeKalb, IL: American Institute for Yemeni Studies, 1984.

SPECIFIC TOPICS

The Land and Its People

Bartelinck, Alexander, ed. *Yemen Agricultural Handbook.* Eschborn: German Agency for Technical Cooperation, 1978.

Becker, Hans, and Horst Kopp. *Resultate aktueller Jemenforschung.* Bamberg: Bamberg University Press, 1978.

Bonnenfant, Paul, ed. *La Péninsule Arabique d'Aujourd'hui.* 2 vols. Paris: C.N.R.S., 1982.

Bornstein, Annika. *Food and Society in the Yemen Arab Republic.* Rome: Food and Agricultural Organization, 1974.

Chelhod, Joseph. *L'Arabie du Sud: Histoire et civilisation.* 3 vols. Paris: Maisonneuve et Larose, 1984–1985.

Costa, Paolo. *Yemen: Land of Builders.* London: Academy Press, 1977.

Daum, Werner, ed. *Yemen.* Innsbruck: Pinguin; Frankfurt: Umschau [1988].

Dorsky, Susan. *Women of 'Amran.* Salt Lake City: University of Utah Press, 1986.

Dostal, Walter. "Sozio-ökonomische aspekte der stammesdemokratie in Nordost Yemen." *Sociologus* (Berlin) 24 (1974), pp. 1–15.

Dresch, Paul. "The Several Peaces of the Yemeni Tribes." *Journal of the Anthropological Society of Oxford* 12 (1981), pp. 73–86.

———. "Tribal Relations and Political History in Upper Yemen." In B. R. Pridham, ed. *Contemporary Yemen: Politics and Historical Background,* pp. 154–174. London: Croom Helm, 1984.

———. *Tribes, Governments, and History in Yemen.* Oxford: Clarendon Press, 1989.

Evin, Ahmet, ed. *Development and Urban Metamorphosis.* 2 vols. Geneva: Agha Khan Award for Architecture, 1983–1984.

Fleurentin, Jacques, and Jean-Marie Pelt. "Repertory of Drugs and Medicinal Plants of Yemen." *Journal of Ethnopharmacology* 6 (1982), pp. 85–108.

Friedlander, Jonathan, ed. *Sojourners and Settlers: The Yemeni Immigrant Experience.* Salt Lake City: University of Utah Press, 1988.

Gerholm, Tomas. *Market, Mosque, and Mafraj.* Stockholm: University of Stockholm, 1977.

Geukens, F. *Geology of the Arabian Peninsula: Yemen.* Washington, DC: U.S. Geological Survey, 1966.

Great Britain. Admiralty. Naval Intelligence Division. *Western Arabia and the Red Sea.* Oxford: Oxford University Press, 1946.

al-Haddad, Abdul Rahman. *Cultural Policy in the Yemen Arab Republic.* Paris: UNESCO, 1982.

Hermann, Jens. *Ambition and Reality: Planning for Health and Basic Services in the Yemen Arab Republic.* Frankfurt am Main: Peter Lang Verlag, 1979.

Kennedy, John G. *The Flower of Paradise.* Boston and Dordrecht, Netherlands: D. Reidel Publishing Company, 1987.

Khalidi, Tarif, ed. *Land Tenure and Social Transformation in the Middle East.* Beirut: American University of Beirut, 1984. See especially Gerd Puin, "The Yemeni Hijrah Concept of Tribal Protection," pp. 483–494, and Wilferd Madelung, "Land Ownership and Land Tax in Northern Yemen and Najran," pp. 189–207.

Kopp, Horst. *Agrargeographie der Arabischen Republik Jemen.* Erlangen: Palm and Enke, 1981.

Makhlouf, Carla. *Changing Veils.* London: Croom Helm, 1979.

Meissner, Jeffrey. "Tribes at the Core: Legitimacy, Structure and Power in Zaydi Yemen." Ph.D. dissertation, Columbia University, 1987.

Melrose, Dianna. *The Great Health Robbery: Baby Milk and Medicines in Yemen.* Oxford: Oxfam Public Affairs Unit, 1981.

Myntti, Cynthia. *Women and Development in Yemen Arab Republic*. Eschborn: German Agency for Technical Cooperation, 1979.

Nyrop, Richard F., et al. *The Yemens*. Washington, DC: Government Printing Office, 1986.

Pridham, B. R., ed. *Economy, Society, and Culture in Contemporary Yemen*. London: Croom Helm, 1985.

Schopen, Armin. *Das Qat*. Wiesbaden: Franz Steiner, 1978.

————. *Traditionelle Heilmittel in Jemen*. Wiesbaden: Franz Steiner, 1983.

Scott, Hugh. *In the High Yemen*. 2d ed. London: John Murray, 1947.

Serjeant, R. B., and Ronald Lewcock, eds. *Sana'a, An Arabian Islamic City*. London: World of Islam Festival Trust, 1983.

Steffen, Hans, et al. *Final Report of the Airphoto Interpretation Project*. Zurich: Swiss Technical Co-operation Service, 1978.

Stevenson, Thomas. *Social Change in a Yemeni Highlands Town*. Salt Lake City: University of Utah Press, 1985.

Swagman, Charles F. *Development and Change in Highland Yemen*. Salt Lake City: University of Utah Press, 1988.

University of Arizona. Arid Lands Information Center. *Environmental Profile of Yemen*. Tucson: University of Arizona, 1982.

Weir, Shelagh. *Qat in Yemen*. London: British Museum, 1985.

The Economy

el-Attar, M. Said. *Le Sous-Developpement economique et sociale du Yémen*. Algiers: Editions Tier-Monde, 1964.

Cohen, John, and David Lewis. *Traditional Organizations and Development: Yemen's Local Development Associations*. Ithaca, NY: Cornell University Center for International Studies, 1980.

Dequin, Horst. *Arabische Republik Jemen: Wirtschaftsgeographie eines Entwicklungslandes*. Riyadh: 1976.

Economist (London). *Quarterly Economic Review* of Bahrain, Qatar, Oman, and the Yemens. London: Economist Intelligence Unit, 1975–1988.

Hauck, V. A. *Policy Choices in the Yemen Arab Republic*. Amsterdam: University of Amsterdam, 1987.

Kopp, Horst, and Günther Schweizer, eds. *Entwicklungsprozesse in der Arabischen Republik Jemen*. Wiesbaden: Ludwig Reichert Verlag, 1984.

el-Mallakh, Ragaei. *The Economic Development of the Yemen Arab Republic*. London: Croom Helm, 1986.

Meyer, Günter. *Arbeitsemigration, Binnenwanderung, und Wirtschaftsentwicklung in der Arabischen Republik Jemen*. Wiesbaden: Ludwig Reichert Verlag, 1986.

Saqqaf, Abdulaziz Y. *The Middle East City*. New York: Paragon House, 1987.

Swanson, Jon. *Emigration and Economic Development*. Boulder, CO: Westview Press, 1979.

Tutwiler, Richard, and Sheila Carapico. *Yemeni Agriculture and Economic Change*. Milwaukee, WI: American Institute for Yemeni Studies, 1981.

World Bank. *Yemen Arab Republic: Development of a Traditional Economy*. Washington, DC: World Bank, 1979.

Yemen Arab Republic. Prime Minister's Office. Central Planning Organization. *Statistical Year Book* 1971-1972 through 1986. Sana'a: Central Planning Organization, 1972–1987.

———. *Summary of the First Five-Year Plan of the Yemen Arab Republic.* Beirut: Central Planning Organization, 1977.

———. *The Second Five-Year Plan, 1982–1986.* Sana'a: Central Planning Organization [printed in Washington, DC: Translation and Production/ArAme Corp.], n.d.

History and Politics

Abir, Mordechai. *Oil, Power and Politics.* London: Frank Cass, 1974.

Aliboni, Roberto. *The Red Sea Region.* Syracuse, NY: Syracuse University Press, 1985.

el-Azzazi, Mohamed. *Die Entwicklung der Arabischen Republik Jemen.* Tübingen and Basel: Horst Erdmann Verlag, 1978.

Bidwell, Robin. *The Two Yemens.* London: Longman; Boulder, CO: Westview Press, 1983.

Braun, Ursula. *Nord- und Südjemen in Spannungsfeld interner, regionaler und globaler Gegensätze.* Bonn: Deutsche Gesellschaft für Auswärtige Politik, 1981.

Burrowes, Robert D. *The Yemen Arab Republic.* Boulder, CO: Westview Press, 1987.

Daum, Werner, ed. *Yemen.* Innsbruck: Pinguin; Frankfurt: Umschau [1988].

Doe, Brian. *Southern Arabia.* London: Thames and Hudson, 1971.

Douglas, J. Leigh. *The Free Yemeni Movement 1935–1962.* Beirut: American University of Beirut, 1987.

Farid, Abdel Majid, ed. *The Red Sea: Prospects for Stability.* London: Croom Helm, 1984.

Gabriel, Erhard F. "Öl im Nordjemen." *Jemen-Report* 20:1 (1989), pp. 15–19.

Gause, F. Gregory, III. "The Idea of Yemeni Unity." *Journal of Arab Affairs* 6:1 (1987), pp. 55–81.

———. "Yemeni Unity: Past and Future." *Middle East Journal* 42:1 (1988), pp. 33–47.

———. *Saudi-Yemeni Relations.* New York: Columbia University Press, 1990.

Ghanem, Isam. *Yemen: Political History, Social Structure and Legal System.* London: Arthur Probsthain, 1981.

Groom, Nigel. *Frankincense and Myrrh.* London: Longman, 1981.

Halliday, Fred. *Arabia Without Sultans.* New York: Vintage, 1975.

Katz, Mark N. *Russia and Arabia.* Baltimore, MD: Johns Hopkins Press, 1986.

McClintock, David. *The Constitution of the Yemen Arab Republic.* New York: Oceana Publications, Constitutions of the World, 1971.

Macro, Eric. *Yemen and the Western World Since 1571.* New York: Praeger Publishers, 1968.

Nyrop, Richard F., et al. *The Yemens.* Washington, DC: Government Printing Office, 1985.

O'Ballance, Edgar. *The War in the Yemen.* Hamden, CT: Archon Books, 1971.

Page, Stephen. *The USSR and Arabia.* London: Central Asian Research Centre, 1971.

_____ . *The Soviet Union and the Yemens*. New York: Praeger Publishers, 1985.

Peterson, John E. *Conflict in the Yemens and Superpower Involvement*. Washington, DC: Georgetown University, 1981.

_____ . *Yemen: The Search for a Modern State*. London: Croom Helm, 1982.

Pridham, B. R., ed. *Contemporary Yemen: Politics and Historical Background*. London: Croom Helm, 1984.

Reissner, Johannes. "Neue Schritte zur Jemitischen Einheit." *Jemen-Report* 19:2 (1988), pp. 9–13.

Schmidt, Dana Adams. *Yemen: The Unknown War*. London: Bodley Head, 1968.

Stookey, Robert W. *Yemen: The Politics of the Yemen Arab Republic*. Boulder, CO: Westview Press, 1978.

Wenner, Manfred W. *Modern Yemen 1918–1966*. Baltimore, MD: Johns Hopkins Press, 1967.

Zabarah, Mohammed Ahmad. *Yemen: Tradition Vs. Modernity*. New York: Praeger Publishers, 1982.

A Brief Chronology

3d mil. BC	Earliest water conservation and control measures in the area around Ma'rib
10th c. BC	Traditional date for the Queen of Sheba
10th c. BC– 6th c. AD	Era of the great pre-Islamic empires: the Sabaean, Minaean, Qataban, Hadhramawt, Himyar
6th c. BC	Great dam at Ma'rib built
6th c. BC– 2d c. AD	Highpoint of Yemeni power: control of trade in frankincense, myrrh, and other commodities desired by Mediterranean states
24 BC	Roman legions under Aelius Gallus attempt to conquer Yemen
1st c. AD	*Periplus of the Erythraean Sea* published; first Jewish immigrants to Yemen; St. Bartholomew allegedly visits Yemen
2d c. AD	First Christians in Yemen (?)
356 AD	Constantine II sends mission to Himyarites; Christian churches established at Zafar, Aden; cathedral built in Sana'a
523	Massacre of Christians at Najran by the Jewish king, Dhu Nuwas
525	Ethiopian Christians invade to avenge the massacre; death of Dhu Nuwas
575	Great dam at Ma'rib ruptures; Persian Empire conquers Yemen
622	Muhammad's *hijra*; year one of the Muslim calendar
628	Last Persian governor of Yemen, Badhan, converts to Islam
8th c.	Widespread unrest: Muslims, Christians, Jews, and others battle for control of Yemen
897	al-Hadi ila al-Haqq Yahya ibn al-Husayn becomes first Zaydi imam of Yemen, with seat at Sa'dah; start of the Zaydi imamate
9–12th c.	Various dynasties in the Tihama and highlands: Ziyadids, Yu'firids, Sulayhids, etc.
1173–1228	Ayyubids control Yemen
1228–1454	Rassulids control Yemen

1454–1517	Tahirids control Yemen
Early 14th–15th c.	Traditional date for discovery of coffee as a beverage by the Shadhili Sufis of southern Arabia; spread of coffee drinking
1504	First Portuguese ships in the Red Sea
1517	Qansuh al-Ghawri, last Mamluk sultan, takes Yemen
1538	Ottoman Empire enters Red Sea; takes Yemeni Tihama
1597–1620	Reign of Qasim the Great who leads major revolt against Ottomans
17th c.	Yemen, esp. city of al-Mocha, becomes world's major source of coffee; English, Dutch, French, and other ships regularly call
1636	Ottomans leave Yemen (to Qasim the Great's son)
1803	First American ships arrive at Mocha to obtain coffee
Early 19th c.	Yemen conquered by the Wahhabis and then the Egyptians
1839	British take Aden
1848/1849	Ottoman Empire reconquers the Yemeni Tihama
1869	Suez Canal opens
1872	Ottomans conquer the Yemeni highlands (incl. Sana'a)
1890s	Yemenis under Imam Muhammad revolt against Ottoman rule
1904	Imam Muhammad's son Yahya becomes imam; revolt continues
1914–1918	World War I: Yemen only Arab state to side with Ottoman Empire
1918	Ottoman forces leave; de facto independence of North Yemen under Imam Yahya ibn Muhammad
1934	Yemen loses Asir Province to Saudi Arabia after brief war
1939–1945	World War II: North Yemen declares neutrality
1946	Yemen joins Arab League and the United Nations
1948	Imam Yahya assassinated; son Ahmad becomes imam and king
1949–1950	Majority of North Yemen's Jews leave for new state of Israel
1951	First archaeological investigations around Ma'rib
1962, Sept. 19	Imam Ahmad dies; his son Muhammad al-Badr becomes imam and king
1962, Sept. 26	Deposition of the imam; declaration of a republic
1962–1970	Civil war: "republicans" vs. "royalists" (supporters of the imamate); intervention by Egypt, Saudi Arabia, and others
1967	Independence of southern Arabia from Great Britain
1970	South Yemen becomes People's Democratic Republic of Yemen (PDRY); in North Yemen compromise ends civil war and creates a government of both republicans and royalists
1972	Border conflict with the PDRY
1974	Corrective movement of Ibrahim al-Hamdi
1976	Founding of the National Democratic Front (NDF), the major opposition movement
1977	Assassination of President Ibrahim al-Hamdi

1978	Assassination of President Ahmad al-Ghashmi, al-Hamdi's successor; Ali Abdullah Salih becomes president
1979	Border conflict with the PDRY
1982	NDF defeated by government forces in major confrontation
1985	Discovery of oil in the Ma'rib region
1986	Dedication of the new great dam at Ma'rib
1987, Sept. 26	Celebrations marking the twenty-fifth anniversary of the revolution
1987, Dec.	First oil flows through new pipeline
1988	Elections to national legislative assembly
1990, May 22	North Yemen and PDRY unite in the Republic of Yemen

About the Book and Author

The Yemen Arab Republic is a land of dramatic physical contrasts—from sea coast to craggy mountain ridges, barren deserts, and fertile agricultural regions—and a rich mosaic of life-styles and cultures. In this book, Manfred W. Wenner offers a detailed portrait of one of the world's least-known countries.

Early chapters discuss geographical and demographic features, uniquely Yemeni social institutions such as the *qat*-chew, architectural styles originating in Yemen, and village and community life. The author then presents a finely drawn overview of Yemen's complex and varied history. In ancient times Yemen controlled the world trade in frankincense and myrrh; in the fifteenth century, following the discovery of coffee, Yemen became a major international trading center; and over the centuries the country fell to various conquerors, most notably the Ottoman Turks. Dr. Wenner gives special attention to the revolution of 1962, which ended the rule of a religio-political elite that had kept Yemen closed to the outside world. Its economy, as a result, was among the most underdeveloped in the world. Since the revolution the traditional economy has been significantly altered in terms of production and consumption patterns, and education and health care have been given high priority. Finally, the author discusses such events following the revolution as the long civil war, the discovery of oil, and, most recently, reunification with South Yemen.

Manfred W. Wenner is professor of political science at Northern Illinois University, DeKalb. He is author of *Modern Yemen, 1918–1966* as well as numerous other works on Yemen and the Arabian Peninsula.

Index